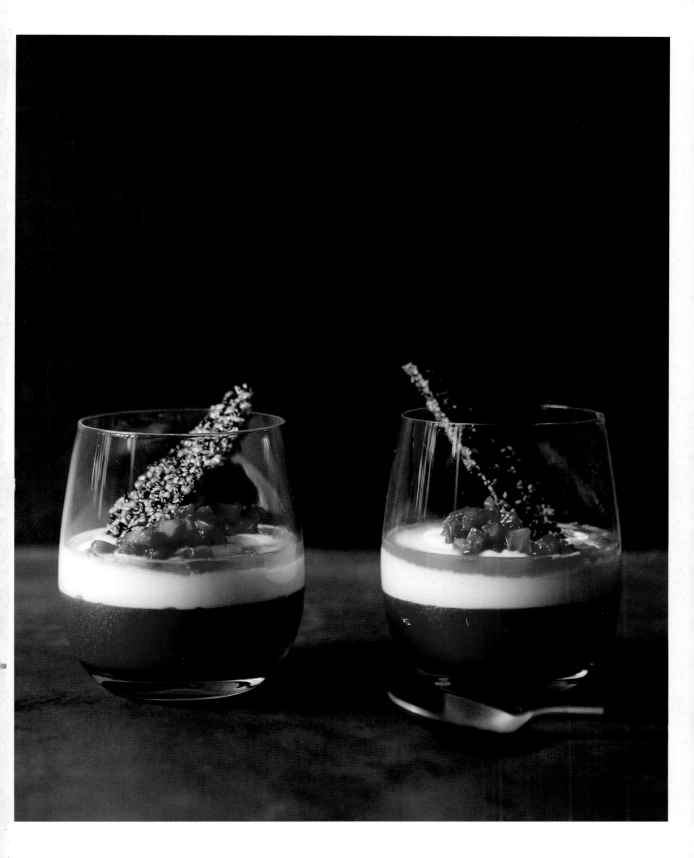

DANIEL
GALMICHE

REVOLUTIONARY
French Cooking

dbp

DUNCAN BAIRD PUBLISHERS

LONDON

REVOLUTIONARY FRENCH COOKING
Daniel Galmiche

First published in the United Kingdom and Ireland in 2014 by
Duncan Baird Publishers, an imprint of
Watkins Publishing Limited
PO Box 883
Oxford, OX1 9PL

A member of Osprey Group

enquiries@dbp.co.uk

Publisher: Grace Cheetham
Editors: Nicola Graimes and Wendy Hobson
Art Direction and Design: Manisha Patel
Cover Design: Georgina Hewitt
Commissioned Photography: Yuki Sugiura
Food Stylists: Daniel Galmiche with Aya Nishimura
Prop Stylist: Wei Tang
Production: Uzma Taj

Typeset in Eurostile
Colour reproduction by PDQ, UK
Printed in China

A CIP record for this book is available from the
British Library

ISBN: 978-1-84899-067-8

10 9 8 7 6 5 4 3 2 1

Publisher's note
While every care has been taken in compiling the recipes for
this book, Watkins Publishing Limited, or any other persons who
have been involved in working on this publication, cannot accept
responsibility for any errors or omissions, inadvertent or not, that
may be found in the recipes or text, nor for any problems that
may arise as a result of preparing one of these recipes. If you are
pregnant or breastfeeding or have any special dietary requirements
or medical conditions, it is advisable to consult a medical
professional before following any of the recipes contained in this
book. Ill or elderly people, babies, young children and women who
are pregnant or breastfeeding should avoid recipes containing raw
meat or fish or uncooked eggs.

Notes on the recipes
Unless otherwise stated:
• Use free-range eggs and poultry
• Use medium eggs, fruit and vegetables
• Use fresh ingredients, including herbs and chillies
• Do not mix metric and imperial measurements
• 1 tsp = 5ml   1 tbsp = 15ml   1 cup = 250ml

Watkins Publishing is supporting the Woodland Trust, the UK's
leading woodland conservation charity, by funding tree-planting
initiatives and woodland maintenance.

www.dbp.co.uk

Contents

24 LIBERTÉ

**Classic dishes released from
the constraints of traditional
French cookery**

82 EGALITÉ

**Democratic recipes that
elevate humble ingredients
to starring roles**

150 FRATERNITÉ

**Dishes that bring innovation and
style to classic combinations of
ingredients**

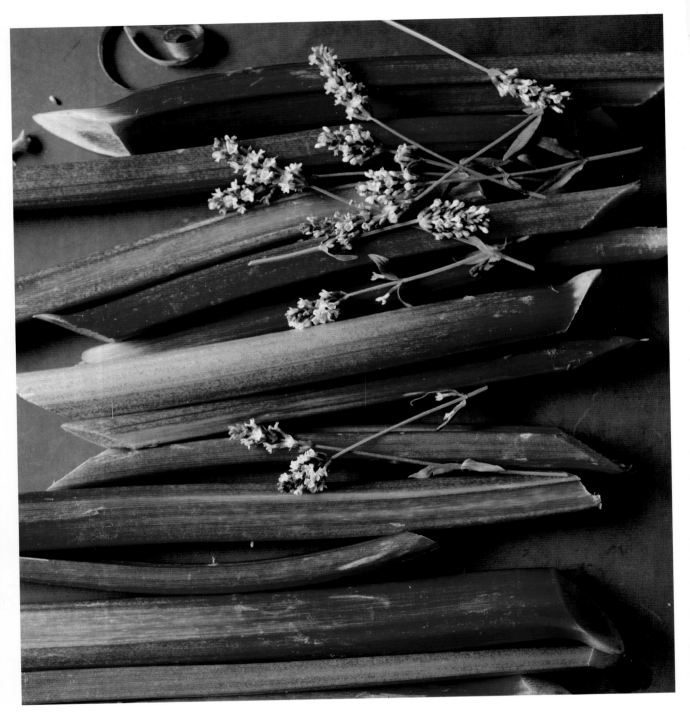

Dedication

This book is dedicated to two very special and important people – my wife, Claire, and my son, Antoine. Without them in my life, and their tremendous support, I would not be able to do what I do. They both love food, they have endless patience and they are fun to be with. They also understand what I do for living, which makes it so much easier for me when I am so often at work. So this cookbook is for you guys, with all my love – always.

Foreword

Daniel's new cookbook is well named as we're in the midst of a cooking revolution, especially in Britain. A few years ago some colleagues and I published a statement describing this revolution under the headings 'excellence', 'openness' and 'integrity'. Daniel, naturally, has categorized it under '*liberté*', '*égalité*' and '*fraternité*', but he identifies many of the same characteristics as typical of modern cuisine: respect for both tradition and innovation; enthusiasm and curiosity about the whole gamut of ingredients; and a determination to pursue excellence but also to demystify cooking.

Such sentiments are typical of Daniel. His cooking style is different from mine, but when I first met him I immediately recognized a kindred spirit — warm, energetic and completely caught up in the romance of cooking and the pleasures of the table. So when he became head chef at Cliveden, which is just a short drive from the Fat Duck, we would meet up regularly for a coffee and a chat about every aspect of cuisine.

Sadly, the ever-increasing pressures on our time mean we aren't able to do this any more. But in the pages that follow you'll get a taste of what it's like to hang out with Daniel and experience his brilliant cooking and infectious enthusiasm for anything to do with food.

Vive la révolution!

Heston Blumenthal

Introduction

I could almost have started this book with a story:

Once upon a time in Franche-Comté, a young boy was walking through the kitchen at his great aunt's house. Suddenly he stopped in his stride, looked up and shouted,
'When I grow up, I want to be a cuisinier.'
He was five years old. At that time, nobody thought anything about it and life went on as usual. But, some time later …

… that young boy did, indeed, become a chef. And I am sure you know who I am talking about!

I have always enjoyed my profession and, after many years, I still love it. It's challenging, exciting and fun. It gives me the chance to work with some fabulous people – dedicated, knowledgeable and hard-working – some with considerable experience and others young and eager to learn and experiment, always keen to try new techniques, new produce, new ideas.

Back to my roots
But that is moving ahead. From as long ago as I can remember, I was surrounded by gourmands. Food was very important in our house and I learnt all the time from my mum – for I watched her constantly. Mum was passionate about food, always testing, asking me what I thought, or calling Dad to make him try this sauce or that new dish. She went to so much trouble to cook for all of us and was always totally focused. She hated it when something wasn't right, even to the point of starting again from scratch if it was for the Christmas dinner, or another special day, and she was not happy with the dish.

The style of cooking reflected the classic cuisine of France, but even more it followed the traditional style of Franche-Comté. All the time, we followed the seasons and enjoyed the freshest produce at its best. Dad used to hunt, so Mum cooked whatever was in season, with fresh vegetables from our garden and fruit from the orchard. To this day, my favourite dish is *gibelotte de lapin*, farm rabbit casserole – always a delight.

When I was 15, I went to catering college for a year, and after that I began a three-year apprenticeship to learn the skills of my craft. That was really hard work – with the long hours, strict discipline and so much to learn. You had to stay focused every moment, which was very tiring at times. But that is something that never changes in a good kitchen. Dedication, focus, discipline and passion are vital if you want to be a good chef, and if you want to be successful.

Once I qualified, I clearly remember the first day I started work. It was in the Luxeuil-les-Bains Hotel, Beausite. The chef just put three large boxes of spinach leaves in front of me, showed me how he wanted it prepared and off I went. And I've never looked back. I loved cooking from the start, even though it was tough – like cleaning the stove, and replacing the coal early in the morning, in winter, when you were punished for not coming up to scratch. Luckily for me, though, that was the last winter before the coal-fired stove was replaced with a modern version.

When I finally emerged into the culinary world of France, I was imbued with the classic principles of French cuisine and I applied them rigorously. I strove for perfection in everything and honed my skills and experience in restaurants in France, Britain, Singapore and Portugal – among other places. Having settled in Britain in 1986, I gained a Michelin star in four different restaurants, and then was finally appointed executive head chef at The Vineyard in 2009.

French brasserie cooking

If I felt very fortunate to have advanced my career to such a level, I felt even more so in 2010 when I was offered the opportunity to publish my first book. As soon as we set to work on my *French Brasserie Cookbook*, I knew exactly what I wanted the concept to be and what I wanted the recipes to look like. This book would represent my childhood memories of cooking: using the seasons, featuring local specialities, the grandma way. I wanted it to be totally French, very regional and to paint a picture of the way we cooked in my home in Franche-Comté.

Setting the idea in a broader context, I had always believed that brasserie cooking had developed from that very same style of home cooking but that the link hadn't been made completely, and when I researched the idea I found that to be true. So the project not only allowed me to revisit so many of the recipes from my childhood, but also gave me the chance to learn so much more about where brasserie food originally came from, when it was created and why it has become so popular.

It is difficult to describe the emotions when you actually hold your first book in your hands. And what I love in particular is all the positive feedback. It pleases me enormously that you are out there cooking my recipes and enjoying them, so please do continue to cook – and to tell me all about your successes.

Looking back ... looking forward

When I came to think about a new book, I decided a complete change of perspective was needed. *French Brasserie Cookbook* was a book focused on my roots in French cooking – looking back to recapture the past traditions of my childhood (with some modern twists along the way, of course). But things have changed in cooking in France, as it has in countries all round the world, and I wanted to reflect those changes. This book, I decided, would have its gaze fixed firmly on the future.

It used to be the case that classic French cuisine was *the* cuisine – everything else was just cooking. French food stood alone as establishing the principles of how to cook: the ingredients, the methods, the presentation. Absolute rules were laid down on how you would make each recipe and chefs never strayed from those rules – there was one way to make a particular dish and that was the only way to do it. French style and technique set the benchmark for all cooking; it did not just consider itself superior, it was in a class of its own and, while some may have begrudged its eminence, most people agreed.

The rumblings of discontent

Slowly and surely, however, things began to change in the world of food and cooking. People began to travel further afield and try new ingredients and new flavours that they wanted to reproduce when they got home. As restaurants became more varied and accessible, an increasing number of people took advantage of the opportunity to dine out, and to experiment with new flavours and styles. The culinary public was becoming more knowledgeable and more sophisticated.

At that time, many ingredients that are now so easy to find in any supermarket were only available to the privileged few in London and major cities. It seems strange now that it was not so long ago that sun-dried tomatoes, balsamic vinegar, pistachio nuts and even crème fraîche – to name just a few – were hard to come by! So the supermarket chains began to change, too, broadening their scope and offering some of these new, 'exotic' ingredients.

Man the barricades

And so the real revolution began. Quietly at first but gaining increasing momentum, both chefs in restaurants and cooks at home began to experiment. They started to wonder if they could make dishes they enjoyed on holiday – even if they adapted them to suit the ingredients available –

and it worked. Cooks tried different international cuisines and learnt from them, mixing European with Asian, or African with Caribbean. They took full advantage of the exciting options in supermarkets and cooking became a playground for freedom and experimentation. And didn't we love it!

Many home cooks were spending more money on excellent-quality food, taking more time in the kitchen, especially at weekends, cooking for themselves or entertaining friends. Looking to expand their knowledge and broaden their skills, they absorbed recipes, techniques and ideas as fast as they could from the new food magazines and the flood of cookery programmes on television. Their kitchen shelves displayed a selection of excellent cookery books in which chefs shared their recipes, complete with beautiful photographs to illustrate the final results.

Blowing with these winds of change was another gust of fresh air: the move towards lighter, healthier foods with lower fat and less sugar.

The winner emerges

Emerging from this revolution came the less prescriptive, more eclectic style that is how we cook today. French cuisine first lost its unique status, then fell out of favour and began to fade into the background. Did we really need all that cream and those heavy sauces? Why should there be just one right way to make a dish when it could be delicious made in different, often simpler, ways? Why did cooking have to be so time-consuming if quicker techniques gave the same results? Why should cooks feel under pressure to do everything 'right' by the book, when cooking was meant to be fun? French cuisine was dismissed as outmoded – we had moved on.

The foundations remain

Meanwhile, I was enjoying this new way of cooking for a more modern, knowledgeable, relaxed audience but I never abandoned my roots in classic French cooking. At The Vineyard, we were introducing innovative ideas all the time, making our food lighter and more modern, trying to improve our offering and chime in with this modern zeitgeist. Our simpler techniques made cooking more fun and more accessible. Guests loved trying our taster menus and giving us their feedback on particular successes.

But just because something needs to change, it does not mean that it should be abandoned entirely. While we all need to break away from our parents and make our own way, the values and standards we have learnt from them remain vitally important. We may have shaken loose from the constraints of classic French style, but the foundations remained intact: quality ingredients treated with care and respect to create a range of delicious dishes.

And that is what this book sets out to do: show you just how wonderful French food can be when used as a sound and secure foundation on which to build. I have taken the best of French style and given it new twists and innovative touches that rejuvenate and energize this fabulous cuisine.

Liberté, égalité, fraternité

So what are we trying to achieve here? Having established the concept for this new book, it seemed only logical to use the motto of the French Revolution to define its heart: *liberté, égalité, fraternité*. The three main sections of the book bring a unique slant to modern French cooking. Each original recipe uses an unusual marriage of flavours with unexpected twists and surprises, plus I even let you in on some professional secrets.

Liberté showcases recipes that have been released from the shackles of traditional French cooking, replacing complex traditional French techniques with simpler ones and bringing fresh new ideas to the table. One I particularly like is a beautiful pork shoulder steak, a dish that seems so simple but is made sublime with the innovation of fresh cabbage, still crunchy and full of flavour, cooked with fresh chilli and ginger to give it strength, and drizzled with honey to lift the dish (see page 50).

Egalité brings democracy to the recipes by elevating humble ingredients to take the starring roles. Ingredients like the common Jerusalem artichoke become the basis for an imaginative recipe rather than being a scarcely noticed side dish – witness my Jerusalem Artichoke Velouté with Truffle Oil and Chive Cream (see page 97).

Fraternité celebrates traditional brotherhoods by creating dishes that bring innovation and style to classic combinations of ingredients. My Chocolate, Chilli and Lemongrass Tart (see page 208) beautifully illustrates this section of the book.

In each of these chapters, I have used ideas that we have been developing in our restaurant to make sure they are right up to date. That did raise the issue of whether they were too complicated for home cooks, or perhaps needed professional equipment that home cooks did not have, so I also thought about how easy the food would be to make at home. Recipes that are too daunting to attempt would have no place in my book! So I adapted the techniques to ensure that a competent cook would be able to recreate them without any problems. You won't need expensive, professional equipment; you will need a reasonably well-equipped kitchen, including a few small tools like a thermometer, a timer, a good blender, a steamer and a wok (we are going to use that for your smoking ingredients – how exciting is that?) but nothing out of the ordinary. Mind you, I do not promise that all the recipes are simple because some are not, but they are all achievable – and they all have a very interesting twist. Just follow the methods carefully and enjoy both cooking and eating the food.

Beyond the barricades

Hopefully you will agree that we have thrown open the door to a whole new range of interesting opportunities for home cooks to expand their repertoire and test their culinary skills.

I think you are going to really enjoy cooking the recipes in this book; they are different, entertaining and fun. I know every chef says the same but I am confident I am right! And the fact that my friend Heston Blumenthal has written the foreword for this book (as he did for my first book) is, for me, very flattering and humbling, and makes me think that he, too, likes the way I have presented these recipes for you. Because, trust me, Heston is no stranger to this type of cooking, as he has proved so many times.

Holding my *French Brasserie Cookbook* was a dream come true for me. Now another dream has come true because, if you are reading this, you are holding my second book in your hands. Enjoy!

BASIC RECIPES

In this chapter, you will find a few basic recipes that are essentials in many of my dishes, like a home-made stock and a salad dressing. Plus, I've selected some recipes that are perfect to serve with the main courses in this book. Complex dishes are complemented most effectively by the simplest accompaniments, and if they are carefully created using the best ingredients, then you really cannot go wrong.

Chicken Stock

MAKES 2l/70fl oz/8 cups
PREPARATION TIME 10 minutes, plus at
  least 1 hour cooling
COOKING TIME 2–2½ hours

2kg/4lb 8oz chicken wings or bones,
  or 2 chicken carcasses
1 thyme sprig
2 carrots, peeled and halved
  lengthways
1 small handful of parsley stems
1 small onion, unpeeled and halved
6 black peppercorns

1 Put all the ingredients in a large, heavy-based saucepan over a high heat. Add 4l/140fl oz/16 cups of cold water, bring to the boil, then skim off any foam that rises to the surface. Turn the heat down to low and leave to simmer, uncovered, for 2–2½ hours until the liquid has reduced by half.

2 Remove from the heat and pass through a sieve, using a ladle to help you, then leave to cool for at least 1 hour.

3 If you want to freeze the stock, divide the cooled stock into small plastic tubs with lids, leaving some space for it to expand, and pop the containers in the freezer for up to 4 weeks.

Beef or Veal Stock

MAKES 2l/70fl oz/8 cups
PREPARATION TIME 15 minutes, plus at
  least 1 hour cooling
COOKING TIME 3 hours 40 minutes

1.25kg/2lb 12oz beef bones from
  roast beef or veal bones
2 tbsp olive oil
1 thyme sprig
2 parsley sprigs
2 carrots, peeled and halved
  lengthways
2 onions, peeled and quartered
1 celery stick, chopped
1 garlic bulb, unpeeled and halved
  crossways
6 black peppercorns
2 bay leaves

1 Preheat the oven to 200°C/400°F/gas 6. Put the bones in a baking tray and roast for 20 minutes, stirring occasionally, until golden brown. Transfer the bones to a large, heavy-based saucepan, add all the remaining ingredients and cook over a medium heat for 10 minutes.

2 Add 4l/140fl oz/16 cups of cold water and bring to the boil over a high heat. Skim off any foam that rises to the surface, then turn the heat down to low and simmer, uncovered, for 1 hour.

3 Top up the water to the previous level, then return to the boil and simmer for a further 2 hours until the liquid has reduced by half. Remove from the heat and pass through a sieve, using a ladle to help you, then leave to cool for at least 1 hour.

4 If you want to freeze the stock, divide the cooled stock into small plastic tubs with lids, leaving some space for it to expand, and pop the containers in the freezer for up to 4 weeks.

NOTE AND VARIATION
Using Beef Stock: Most chefs use veal jus rather than beef stock as it can be too strong. Use the bones from your Sunday roast to make a good stock, or substitute a shop-bought veal jus.
For Lamb Stock: Use lamb instead of beef bones. Leave to cool, then chill. Lift off the layer of fat from the surface, then use or freeze as above.

Fish Stock

MAKES 2l/70fl oz/8 cups
PREPARATION TIME 10 minutes, plus
30 minutes soaking and at least
1 hour cooling
COOKING TIME 2¼–2¾ hours

1.25kg/2lb 12oz fresh fish bones,
flesh removed
1 small handful of parsley stems
1 onion, unpeeled and quartered
1 thyme sprig
1 celery stick, halved
6 black peppercorns

1 Put the fish bones in a large bowl, cover with cold water and leave to soak for 10 minutes, then rinse thoroughly using a sieve. Repeat 3 times.

2 Put the bones in a large, heavy-based saucepan with all the remaining ingredients and cover with 4l/140fl oz/16 cups of cold water. Bring to the boil over a high heat, then skim off any foam that rises to the surface. Turn the heat down to low and leave to simmer, uncovered, for 2–2½ hours until the liquid has reduced by half.

3 Remove from the heat and pass through a sieve, using a ladle to help you, then leave to cool for at least 1 hour.

4 If you want to freeze the stock, divide the cooled stock into small plastic tubs with lids, leaving some space for it to expand, and pop the containers in the freezer for up to 4 weeks.

Vegetable Stock

MAKES 1.5l/52fl oz/6 cups
PREPARATION TIME 15 minutes, plus at
least 1 hour cooling
COOKING TIME 2¼ hours

2 tbsp olive oil
1 celery stick, chopped
1 thyme sprig
1 spring onion, chopped
1 handful of parsley stems, chopped
1 garlic clove
2 carrots, peeled and halved
lengthways
2 new potatoes, halved
6 black peppercorns
2 button mushrooms, halved

1 Warm the oil in a large, heavy-based saucepan over a medium heat. Add all the remaining ingredients, partially cover, and cook for 10 minutes. Add about 3l/105fl oz/12 cups of cold water and bring to the boil over a high heat, then turn the heat down to low and leave to simmer, uncovered, for 2 hours until the liquid has reduced by half.

2 Remove from the heat and pass through a sieve, using a ladle to help you, then leave to cool for at least 1 hour.

3 If you want to freeze the stock, divide the cooled stock into small plastic tubs with lids, leaving some space for it to expand, and pop the containers in the freezer for up to 4 weeks.

Mayonnaise
with **Variations**

MAKES 200ml/7fl oz/scant 1 cup
PREPARATION TIME 10 minutes

2 egg yolks
1 tbsp French mustard
a squeeze of lemon juice
150ml/5fl oz/scant ⅔ cup sunflower
  oil or grapeseed oil
sea salt and freshly ground black
  pepper

1 Beat together the egg yolks and mustard in a bowl. Add a few drops of lemon juice and season with salt and pepper. Gradually drizzle in the oil, a little at a time, whisking continuously until the mayonnaise thickens.

2 For the variations, stir the additional ingredients into the mayonnaise, then whisk in 2 tablespoons of hot water to help bind the ingredients.

VARIATIONS (pictured on page 14) (optional)
For Chilli Mayonnaise: Add 1 long red chilli, deseeded and finely chopped
For Tarragon Mayonnaise: Add 1 tbsp tarragon vinegar, 1 tsp chopped tarragon leaves
For Garlic Mayonnaise: Add 2 garlic cloves, finely chopped

French Dressing

MAKES about 150ml/5fl oz/scant
  ⅔ cup
PREPARATION TIME 5 minutes

2 tsp Dijon mustard
2 tbsp white balsamic vinegar
60ml/2fl oz/¼ cup olive oil or
  sunflower oil
60ml/2fl oz/¼ cup extra virgin olive
  oil or sunflower oil
sea salt and freshly ground black
  pepper

1 Whisk together the mustard, vinegar and 2 tablespoons of water in a small bowl, then whisk in the olive oil and extra virgin olive oil until you have quite a thick, glossy liquid.

2 Season with salt and pepper to taste before drizzling over salad.

Croûtons

SERVES 4
PREPARATION TIME 5 minutes
COOKING TIME 5 minutes

25g/1oz unsalted butter
2 tbsp olive oil
2 small slices of sourdough bread,
  crusts removed and cut into
  1cm/½in cubes
sea salt and freshly ground black
  pepper

You can cut the bread into whatever size or shape croûtons you fancy, just make sure that you cook them until golden brown on each side, without allowing them to burn.

1 Heat a large frying pan over a medium heat. Add the butter and oil and when the butter is foaming, add the cubes of bread and fry for 45–60 seconds on each side until golden brown.

2 Drain on kitchen paper and season with salt and pepper.

Reduced Balsamic Vinegar

MAKES about 4 tbsp
COOKING TIME 12 minutes

125ml/4fl oz/½ cup balsamic
  vinegar

1 Pour the vinegar into a small sauté or frying pan, put over a medium heat and bring to a gentle simmer.

2 Turn the heat down to low heat and cook for 10 minutes until the liquid has reduced by half and is thickened and syrupy.

Chicory and Radish Salad

SERVES 4
PREPARATION TIME 10 minutes

2 large heads of chicory, halved
  lengthways and leaves separated
12 English radishes, thinly sliced
3 tbsp chopped parsley leaves
1 tbsp Chardonnay vinegar
3 tbsp extra virgin olive oil
sea salt and freshly ground black
  pepper

1 Toss the chicory leaves, radishes and parsley together in a bowl.

2 Whisk together the Chardonnay vinegar and oil in a small bowl and season with salt and pepper. Drizzle the dressing over the leaves and toss together to combine.

Tomato and Deep-Fried Caper Salad

SERVES 4
PREPARATION TIME 10 minutes
COOKING TIME 1 minute

4 large beef tomatoes, thinly sliced
1 red onion, very thinly sliced
100g/3½oz jar baby capers
about 170ml/5½fl oz/⅔ cup
  vegetable oil
135ml/4½fl oz/generous ½ cup
  extra virgin olive oil
1 tbsp good-quality sherry vinegar
1 small handful of basil leaves, torn
sea salt and freshly ground black
  pepper

1 Put the tomatoes and red onion on a serving plate and season with salt and pepper. Open the jar of capers, strain off 2 tablespoons of the liquid and leave to one side. Take out half the capers and pat them dry very carefully on kitchen paper.

2 Put the vegetable oil in a small saucepan over a medium heat until just shimmering. Be careful not to overheat the oil, it must not be smoking but needs to be hot enough to fry the capers. Carefully add the capers to the hot oil and fry for 30 seconds until nice and crisp – again, make sure you don't leave them frying for too long as they just need to be crisp. Drain on kitchen paper.

3 To make the dressing, whisk together the reserved caper liquid, the extra virgin olive oil and sherry vinegar, then pour over the tomatoes. Scatter the deep-fried capers over the top, then finish with freshly torn basil leaves.

Creamed Mashed Potatoes

SERVES 4
PREPARATION TIME 30 minutes
COOKING TIME 55 minutes

1kg/2lb 4oz floury potatoes, such as
 Desiree, unpeeled
100ml/3½fl oz/scant ½ cup full-fat
 milk
100ml/3½fl oz/scant ½ cup double
 cream
2 garlic cloves, sliced
2.5cm/1in piece of horseradish,
 peeled, or 2 tsp wasabi paste
sea salt and freshly ground black
 pepper

1 Put the potatoes in a large saucepan, cover with cold water and add a pinch of salt. Bring to the boil over a high heat, then turn the heat down to low, partially cover with a lid and simmer for 30–40 minutes, or until completely cooked through.

2 Meanwhile, preheat the oven to 200°C/400°F/gas 6. Drain the potatoes, then put them on a baking sheet and bake for 10 minutes. Remove from the oven and as soon as they are cool enough to handle, peel the potatoes, then pass them through a sieve, using a ladle to help you, or through a mouli. Cover with a lid and leave to one side but do not let them go cold or the mash will be gluey.

3 Put the milk, cream and garlic in a saucepan over a medium heat and bring to the boil. Pour half the mixture into the potatoes, mix well, then gradually add the remaining liquid, stirring all the time. Season with salt and pepper to taste, then grate 2 teaspoons of the horseradish directly over the mash so you get all the juices. Alternatively, sprinkle with the wasabi paste. Serve hot.

Swede Boulangère

SERVES 4
PREPARATION TIME 15 minutes, plus
 making the stock
COOKING TIME 55 minutes

a little butter, for greasing
2 large swede, about 500–600g/
 1lb 2oz–1lb 5oz each, peeled and
 cut into 5mm/¼in slices
2 large white onions, sliced
2 garlic cloves, finely chopped
2 thyme sprigs, leaves picked
500ml/17fl oz/2 cups Chicken Stock
 (see page 16)
sea salt and freshly ground black
 pepper

1 Preheat the oven to 200°C/400°F/gas 6 and lightly butter a shallow baking dish large enough to hold about 1.5l/52fl oz/6 cups. Bring a large saucepan of salted water to the boil over a high heat, add the swede and boil for 4–5 minutes, then drain and spread out on a clean tea towel to dry. Leave to cool slightly before building your *boulangère*.

2 Spread a layer of swede in the bottom of the prepared dish, followed by a layer of the onions and a sprinkling of garlic and thyme leaves. Season with a little salt and pepper. Repeat with as many layers as will fit in the dish, but finish with a layer of swede. Press down lightly.

3 Put the stock in a saucepan over a medium heat and warm slightly, then pour it over the *boulangère*. The stock should not cover the last layer of swede as the swede will sink down slightly as the dish cooks.

4 Bake for 45–50 minutes, then check to see that the swede is tender when pierced with the tip of a knife. If not, return it to the oven for a further 5 minutes and check again until the knife slides easily into the vegetables. Serve hot.

Thai-Style Pilau Rice

SERVES 4
PREPARATION TIME 10 minutes, plus
  making the stock
COOKING TIME 25 minutes

4 tbsp olive oil
1 large onion, diced
4cm/1½in piece of root ginger,
  peeled and diced
1 long red chilli, deseeded and finely
  diced
1 lemongrass stalk, split lengthways
200g/7oz/1 cup basmati rice
400ml/14fl oz/scant 1⅔ cups
  Vegetable Stock (see page 16)
40g/1½oz unsalted butter, chopped
grated zest and juice of 1 lime
sea salt and freshly ground black
  pepper

1 Preheat the oven to 150°C/300°F/gas 2. Heat an ovenproof frying pan over a medium heat, add the oil and onion and fry for 3 minutes until just softened, then add the ginger, chilli and lemongrass and fry for a further 3 minutes until softened but not coloured.

2 Turn the heat down to low and add the rice. Fold in gently, then sweat for 3–4 minutes. Add the stock, turn the heat up to high and bring to a simmer. Season with salt and pepper, dot the butter over the top of the rice, then cover with a *cartouche* (see page 218) or partially cover with a lid and transfer to the oven for 12–14 minutes.

3 Check to see if the rice is tender and the liquid has all been absorbed. If the rice is not quite tender, return it to the oven for a further 5 minutes, then check once more. Remove the *cartouche*, discard the lemongrass, then season the rice with the grated lime zest and juice, and salt and pepper to taste. Serve hot.

Tomato Coulis

MAKES 800ml/28fl oz/scant 3½ cups
PREPARATION TIME 20 minutes
COOKING TIME 40 minutes

12 ripe tomatoes
2 tbsp olive oil
1 red chilli, deseeded and chopped
290g/10¼oz jar roasted peppers,
  drained and finely chopped
1 small shallot, finely chopped
50g/1¾oz/⅓ cup strawberries,
  hulled
4 garlic cloves, crushed
a pinch of caster sugar
a pinch of smoked paprika
4 tbsp white balsamic vinegar
2 large basil leaves
sea salt and freshly ground black
  pepper

1 With a sharp knife, cut a small cross on the bottom of each tomato, then put them in a heatproof bowl and cover with boiling water. Leave for 30 seconds, then lift them out with a slotted spoon and put in a bowl of iced water. Lift the tomatoes out, then peel off and discard the skins. Cut the tomatoes into quarters, remove and discard the seeds, then roughly chop the flesh.

2 Heat a sauté pan over a high heat and add the tomatoes, oil, chilli, peppers, shallot, strawberries and garlic. Turn the heat down to low and sweat for 4–5 minutes until softened.

3 Add the sugar and paprika, then stir in the vinegar and deglaze the pan by stirring to remove any caramelized bits stuck to the bottom. Cover with a *cartouche* (see page 218) and cook over a low heat for 30–35 minutes, or until you have a very soft purée.

4 Transfer to a blender, add the basil and blitz to a fine purée, or use a hand-blender. Pass through a fine sieve, using a ladle to help you, and season with salt and pepper to taste.

Savoury Short Pastry

MAKES enough for a 28cm/11¼in tin
PREPARATION TIME 15 minutes, plus
 2 hours chilling

125g/4½oz unsalted butter,
 softened to room temperature and
 roughly diced
250g/9oz/2 cups plain flour, plus
 extra for dusting
a pinch of salt
1 egg yolk
3 tbsp milk or water

1 Put the butter, flour and salt in a mixing bowl and rub together with your fingertips until you have a crumbly, powdery texture. Add the egg yolk and milk and continue working the pastry until the ingredients are combined and the texture is smooth. Turn out the pastry onto a lightly floured work surface and knead for 1–2 minutes until silky smooth.

2 When the pastry is ready, either wrap it in a clean tea towel or put it on a plate, cover with a clean tea towel and leave in the fridge for 2 hours before using – this will relax the dough and make it easier to use.

Sweet Short Pastry

MAKES enough for a 20cm/8in tin
PREPARATION TIME 10 minutes, plus
 20 minutes chilling

grated zest of ½ blood orange
90g/3¼oz unsalted butter, softened
a pinch of salt
65g/2¼oz/heaped ½ cup icing sugar
25g/1oz/¼ cup ground almonds
1 egg
175g/6oz/heaped 1⅓ cups plain
 flour

1 Beat together the orange zest, butter, salt, sugar, ground almonds and egg in a bowl until light and fluffy, then sift in the flour and fold through. As soon as the dough is formed, stop! You don't want to work this pastry at all.

2 Wrap the pastry in cling film and put in the fridge for 20 minutes, then bake as directed in the recipe.

Beurre Noisette

MAKES 125ml/4fl oz/½ cup
COOKING TIME 5 minutes

125g/4½oz unsalted butter
2 tsp lemon juice
sea salt and freshly ground black
 pepper

1 Heat a frying pan over a medium-high heat, add the butter and cook for a few minutes until it turns a nutty golden brown.

2 Add the lemon juice, swirl to combine, then remove from the heat immediately. Season with salt and pepper.

Chilli Crème Anglaise

MAKES 1.4l/48fl oz/5½ cups
PREPARATION TIME 20 minutes, plus 30 minutes infusing and at least 1 hour chilling
COOKING TIME 15 minutes

1l/35fl oz/4 cups full-fat milk
1 long red chilli, halved lengthways and deseeded
1 vanilla pod, halved lengthways and seeds scraped out
8 egg yolks
200g/7oz/heaped ¾ cup caster sugar

1 Put the milk in a saucepan over a low heat. Add the chilli and vanilla seeds. Whisk, then throw in the vanilla pod as well. Bring to the boil, then remove from the heat, cover with cling film and leave to infuse at room temperature for 30 minutes.

2 Meanwhile, whisk together the egg yolks and sugar in a large bowl. Strain the chilli milk through a fine sieve into the egg yolk mixture and mix well, then pour it back into the saucepan. Put over a medium heat and cook for 5–8 minutes, stirring continuously (otherwise you will get scrambled eggs!) until it starts to thicken. You will be able to tell when the crème anglaise is ready if, when you run two fingers down the back of the spoon, the two lines don't immediately join. If the custard does start to scramble, don't panic – you can rescue it by pouring the mixture into a food processor and blitzing it until it regains a smooth, thick texture.

3 Strain once more into a clean bowl and mix for a few minutes to cool the custard down, then put it in the fridge to chill for at least 1 hour before using. It will keep in the fridge for about a week.

Real Vanilla Ice Cream

SERVES 4
PREPARATION TIME 10 minutes, plus 20 minutes infusing and at least 3 hours freezing
COOKING TIME 10 minutes

115ml/3¾fl oz/scant ½ cup full-fat milk
1 vanilla pod, split and seeds scraped out
3 egg yolks
200ml/7fl oz/scant 1 cup double cream

1 First make a sabayon (see page 218). Put the milk, vanilla pod and vanilla seeds in a saucepan over a low heat and bring just to a simmer. Remove from the heat, cover with a lid and leave to infuse for 20 minutes. Remove the vanilla pod, wash and pat dry with kitchen paper. (You can add the pod to a jar of sugar to make your own vanilla sugar.)

2 Whisk together the egg yolks and warm milk in a heatproof bowl set over a saucepan of gently simmering water, making sure the bottom of the bowl does not touch the water. Heat for 5–8 minutes, stirring continuously, until thickened. Remove from the heat and whisk continuously until the mixture cools completely.

3 Whip the cream until it forms soft peaks, fold it into the sauce, then pour into a 500ml/17fl oz/2 cup freezerproof container. Cover with cling film and put in the freezer for at least 3 hours until firm.

LIBERTÉ

Classic dishes released from the constraints of traditional French cookery

It is not easy to describe what we mean by '*liberté*' in cooking, especially for me as I have been classically trained and there are boundaries I have been taught not to cross. But I have found myself trying more and more new ideas and techniques that improve the taste, the flavour, the texture and the lightness of dishes.

And it is those dishes, generally very traditional French recipes, that I have released from the shackles of classical techniques and modernized to share with you in this chapter, for example Beef Carpaccio with Beef Tartare and Wasabi Cream (see page 30). But despite any changes, it is always important to retain the essence of the dish, whatever you combine with it. The best dishes need spontaneity, flexibility and that liberty of expression on the plate.

Chicken and Lemongrass Broth

My mother never let anything go to waste. She always made use of everything, so if we had a roast chicken she would keep the carcass and use it as the base of a beautiful clear soup, then add extras such as vegetables, herbs and lentils. I have always enjoyed making broths at home, and here I've added a new twist with fragrant lemongrass and lime zest. To make a more substantial soup, you could add a handful of cooked rice or lentils to the broth and heat through thoroughly before ladling it over the chicken.

SERVES 4
PREPARATION TIME 30 minutes
COOKING TIME 2 hours

FOR THE BROTH BASE

1 tbsp olive oil
1 small chicken, about 1kg/2lb 4oz
   total weight
2 carrots, peeled and roughly
   chopped
1 lemongrass stalk, bruised
3 thyme sprigs
1 small bunch of coriander, leaves
   picked and stalks reserved

FOR THE CHICKEN AND LEMONGRASS BROTH

2 large carrots, peeled and
   quartered lengthways
3 lemongrass stalks, 2 bruised,
   1 peeled
2 thyme sprigs
finely grated zest of 1 lime
2 tbsp extra virgin olive oil
sea salt and freshly ground
   black pepper

1 To make the broth base, heat a large, flameproof casserole dish or frying pan over a medium heat. Add the olive oil and chicken and seal for 3–4 minutes on each side until just starting to turn light golden brown. Add the chopped carrots, lemongrass stalk, thyme and half the coriander stalks and cook for a further 5 minutes until the chicken is browned all over and the vegetables just coloured.

2 Transfer the browned chicken and vegetables to a large, deep saucepan, cover with about 2l/70fl oz/8 cups of cold water and bring to the boil over a high heat, skimming off any foam that rises to the surface, as this helps to keep the soup clear. Add the quartered carrots, the bruised lemongrass, the thyme and the remaining coriander stalks. Return to a simmer, then turn the heat down to very low, cover with a lid and simmer for 1¼–1½ hours until the chicken is very tender and starts to fall apart.

3 Carefully remove the chicken from the pan and leave to one side to cool slightly. Strain the vegetable broth into a clean pan, reserving the solids, and return the broth to a low heat. Simmer for about 10–15 minutes, uncovered, until the broth has reduced by one-third and is full of flavour.

4 Meanwhile, carefully lift the quartered carrots out of the strainer, discarding the rest of the solids. Finely chop the carrots and put in deep soup bowls. When the chicken is cool enough to handle, remove and discard the skin, then pull the chicken meat off the bones and tear it into small pieces. Add the chicken and a pinch of salt and pepper to the soup bowls, then scatter over the coriander leaves. Sprinkle the lime zest over and drizzle with the extra virgin olive oil.

5 Remove the tough outer leaves, top and root from the remaining lemongrass stalk, then slice very thinly and add to the bowls. By now, the broth should be ready, so simply add a couple of ladlefuls to each bowl before serving.

Coriander and Star Anise Pork Rillettes

In my first book, the *French Brasserie Cookbook*, I included a recipe for a classic duck rillettes, but in this book I wanted to bring a different and more modern character to this popular dish by replacing the herbs with spices such as star anise. It brings an exotic yet delicate scent that goes perfectly with the pork. Use the whole spice rather than ground as the latter just doesn't have the same depth of flavour.

SERVES 4
PREPARATION TIME 10 minutes,
  plus 6–12 hours marinating
  and at least 24 hours chilling
COOKING TIME 4 hours

1.2kg/2lb10oz pork shoulder, diced
60g/2¼oz/¼ cup sea salt
2 tsp coriander seeds
2 star anise
1.5kg/3lb 5oz goose fat
leaves from 2 coriander sprigs
freshly ground black pepper
toast or warm crusty bread,
  to serve

1 Put the pork, salt, half the coriander seeds and 1 star anise in a large bowl and season with pepper. Turn everything until combined, then cover with cling film and leave to marinate in the fridge for 6–12 hours. The longer you leave the pork to marinate, the better the flavour will be.

2 After the pork has marinated, preheat the oven to 140°C/275°F/gas 1. Rinse the marinade off the pork, reserving the star anise, and pat dry with kitchen paper.

3 Melt the goose fat in a large, flameproof casserole dish over a low heat. Add the pork and turn until well coated, then transfer the casserole dish to the oven and cook, uncovered, for 4 hours until the meat falls apart when prodded with a fork. Strain the pork through a fine sieve, reserving the fat, and put in a bowl. Shred the pork using two forks, then add about 125ml/4fl oz/½ cup of the cooking fat to moisten.

4 Transfer the shredded pork to a sealable jar or small earthenware dish and press down lightly. Pour enough of the cooking fat over the top to cover the pork and seal it, then add the reserved star anise and scatter with the remaining coriander seeds and coriander leaves. (If there is any remaining goose fat, it can be put in a jar and kept for other uses, such as roasting potatoes.) Cover with a lid or baking paper and chill for at least 24 hours before serving to allow the flavours to mingle. Serve with warm crusty bread.

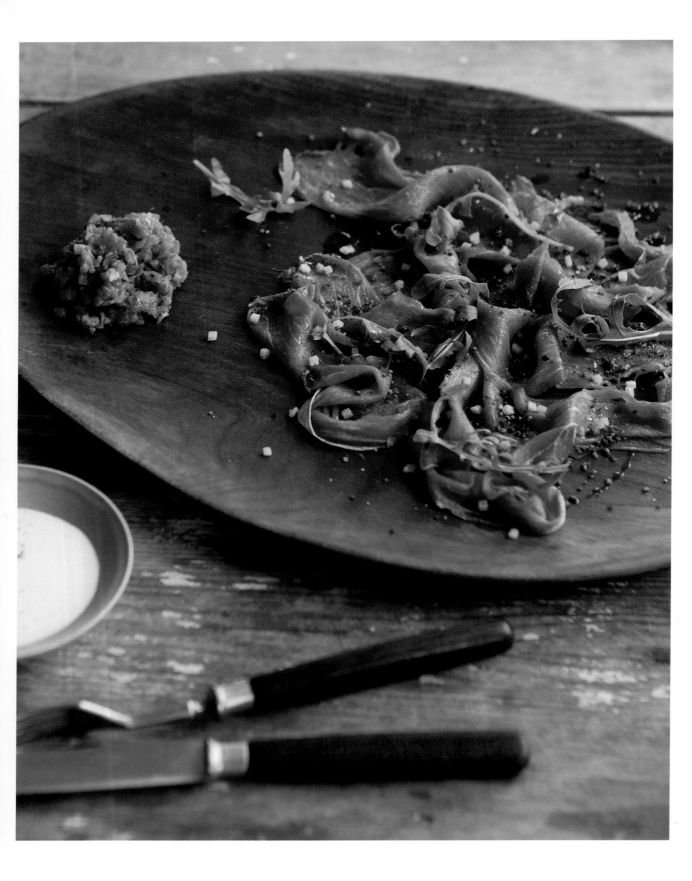

Beef Carpaccio
with **Beef Tartare** and **Wasabi Cream**

The dish carpaccio was first created in 1950 by Giuseppe Cipriani for the Comtesse Amalia Mocenigo, who had been advised by her doctor that she should eat her meat raw. At the same time, works by the famous 15th-century painter, Vittore Carpaccio, were being exhibited. His paintings almost always contained large areas of red in varying tones, and this reminded Cipriani of meat, and so he gave his dish the name carpaccio. Although other meats and fish, particularly tuna, can be used for carpaccio, this dish is made with tender beef fillet. I have given it a modern twist by serving it with a piquant wasabi cream accompanied by beef tartare seasoned with capers and shallot, and some tiny, delicate croûtons, fresh chives and rocket.

SERVES 4

PREPARATION TIME 25 minutes, plus 2–3 hours freezing and making the croûtons

350g/12oz beef fillet, trimmed
3 tbsp olive oil
100ml/3½fl oz/scant ½ cup whipping cream
1 tsp wasabi paste
3 tbsp finely chopped chives
40g/1½oz very small Croûtons (see page 18)
sea salt and freshly ground black pepper
1 handful of rocket leaves, to serve

FOR THE TARTARE
2 tsp finely diced shallot
1 tsp chopped parsley leaves
1 tsp tomato ketchup
1 tsp chopped capers
1½ tsp olive oil
150g/5½oz beef fillet, trimmed and very finely chopped

1 To make the carpaccio, lay two pieces of cling film, about 30 x 20cm/ 12 x 8in in size, on top of each other to form one sheet of cling film. Put the beef fillet in the centre, then drizzle with 1 tablespoon of the oil and wrap in the cling film to form a tight cylinder. Put in the freezer for 2–3 hours, or until firm but with a slight softness when pressed.

2 Meanwhile, prepare the tartare. Mix the shallot, parsley, tomato ketchup and capers in a bowl. Season with salt and pepper, then drizzle in the remaining oil, stirring continuously. Finally, stir in the chopped beef and season with salt and pepper to taste. Cover with cling film and chill until ready to serve.

3 Just before serving, gently whisk together the cream and wasabi paste in a bowl until soft peaks form. Cover with cling film and leave at room temperature.

4 Take the beef out of the freezer and remove the cling film. Using a very sharp knife, cut it into very thin slices and lay over serving plates, spreading the slices out. Work quickly, as the beef will soon defrost and it is much easier to work with them when still slightly frozen.

5 Season with salt and pepper to taste, sprinkle with the chives, croûtons and a drizzle of oil, and serve with the tartare, wasabi cream and some fresh rocket leaves.

Scallops with Cauliflower Purée and Hazelnut Dressing

This noble shellfish is delicate and sweet, and simply needs sealing briefly in butter and olive oil before serving. Try to find scallops in the shell, but if you can't, you can use prepared or frozen scallops. The apple lends a fresh crispness to the dish and offers a wonderful contrast to the softness of the scallops and the cauliflower purée. Enjoy with a glass of Condrieu or Viognier.

SERVES 4
PREPARATION TIME 20 minutes
COOKING TIME 45 minutes

1 cauliflower, leaves and stem
   removed, cut into large florets
110g/3¾oz unsalted butter
2 tbsp olive oil
12 scallops, rinsed
5mm/¼in slice of crisp green eating
   apple, such as Granny Smith,
   unpeeled, cut into thin strips
sea salt and freshly ground black
   pepper

FOR THE HAZELNUT DRESSING
1 tsp hazelnut oil
2 tsp extra virgin olive oil
1 tsp white balsamic vinegar
½ tsp finely chopped celery leaves

1 Cut 2 of the large cauliflower florets into 12 mini florets, about 1cm/½in each, and leave to one side. Bring a large saucepan of salted water to the boil over a high heat, add the large cauliflower florets and cook for 7–8 minutes until very soft when pierced with a knife. Drain and pat dry with kitchen paper.

2 Heat a large sauté pan over a medium-low heat. Add 75g/2½oz of the butter, half the olive oil and the cooked cauliflower, then fry for 30 minutes, stirring occasionally, until the cauliflower is very soft (actually overcooked) and golden brown. Keep the heat medium-low and take care not to burn the butter or the cauliflower.

3 Meanwhile, make the hazelnut dressing. Whisk together the hazelnut oil, extra virgin olive oil and white balsamic vinegar in a bowl until just emulsified. Bring a small saucepan of salted water to the boil, add the small cauliflower florets and boil for 2 minutes until just tender. Drain and refresh under cold running water, then pat dry and add to the dressing.

4 Put the sautéed cauliflower in a blender with 2 tablespoons of hot water and blitz to a fine, smooth purée. Add a little extra hot water if the purée is coarse or very thick. Season with salt and pepper to taste, then pass the purée through a fine sieve, using a ladle to help you, into a small, clean saucepan. Cover with a lid and keep warm.

5 Remove the roes from the scallops, trim off any tough flesh and remove any veins, then season with salt and pepper. Heat half the remaining butter and oil in a non-stick frying pan over a medium heat. When the butter is a hazelnut colour, add half the scallops and cook for 1½–2 minutes, depending on their size, until light golden. Turn the scallops over and cook for a further 1 minute, then remove from the pan, put on kitchen paper and keep warm. Repeat with the remaining oil and butter to cook the remaining scallops.

6 Add the celery leaves to the dressing. Top the cauliflower purée with the the scallops, then drizzle with the dressing. Scatter the florets over the top and finish with the apple strips to serve.

Poached Oysters with **Cucumber Fricassée**

In France, oysters are massively popular. Here, I've served them with lightly cooked cucumber, which although is best known as a salad vegetable, is delicious prepared this way – its fresh taste and crisp texture complements the oysters perfectly and tastes superb with slices of brown bread.

SERVES 4
PREPARATION TIME 35 minutes
COOKING TIME 15 minutes

16 oysters in the shell
Fish Stock (see page 17) (optional)
1 tbsp gin
25g/1oz unsalted butter
1 small cucumber, peeled, deseeded, cut into 5cm/2in lengths and thinly sliced lengthways into julienne strips
4 tbsp Greek yogurt or crème fraîche
leaves from 4 watercress sprigs, roughly chopped
finely grated zest of 1 lime
sea salt and freshly ground black pepper

1 To open the oysters put them flat-side up, one at a time, on a clean folded tea towel. Holding the rounded side of the shell in your hand, insert the tip of an oyster knife into the top edge and wiggle it slightly from side to side, at the same time as pressing it in a little further. As you twist the knife, the top half of the shell should pop open. Lift off the top shell carefully and discard it, keeping the oyster, juices and bottom half of the shell. Strain the juices into a bowl, adding enough fish stock to make it up to 250ml/9fl oz/1 cup. Push the knife under the oysters to separate them from the shells, then leave the oysters to one side. Bring a large saucepan of water to the boil over a high heat, add the bottom shells and return to the boil, then remove from the heat, drain and put the shells outer-side up on a clean tea towel to dry. Leave to one side until ready to use.

2 Divide the juices/stock between two small saucepans – ideally one shallow and the other slightly deeper. Bring the liquid in the shallow pan to the boil over a high heat, then turn the heat down to low and simmer for a few minutes until the liquid has reduced by three-quarters and is syrupy. Add the gin, return to a simmer and cook for 5–7 minutes until syrupy again. Remove from the heat, cover with a lid and leave to one side.

3 Meanwhile, heat a frying pan over a medium heat. Add the butter and when foaming, add the cucumber and fry for 1–2 minutes until just light golden but still crisp. Season with salt and pepper to taste, then tip onto kitchen paper to drain. Spoon into the cleaned oyster shells.

4 Bring the second pan of juices/stock to the boil over a medium heat, add the oysters, then turn the heat down to low, cover with a lid and simmer for 2–3 minutes until just cooked. Check they are ready by pressing very lightly with your finger – there should be a little resistance but you don't want them to be firm. Discard the cooking liquid, then spoon the oysters on top of the cucumber.

5 If the reduced liquid has become cold, gently warm it up again. Whisk in the yogurt, taking care not to overheat or it will separate. Add the watercress, then remove the pan from the heat and stir through. Season the sauce with pepper to taste, then spoon over the oysters and sprinkle with the lime zest before serving.

Provençale Salad with **Courgette Flower Tempura**

SERVES 4
PREPARATION TIME 25 minutes, plus 30 minutes marinating and 5 minutes chilling
COOKING TIME 25 minutes

1 courgette, cut lengthways into long, thin strips
2 tbsp olive oil
a pinch of fresh edible lavender flowers or rosemary flowers
1 tbsp white balsamic vinegar
2 tbsp extra virgin olive oil
juice of ½ lemon
6 purple baby artichokes or bottled artichokes in oil, drained
2 thick slices of pancetta, about 40g/1½oz total weight, cut into lardons
1 small handful of rocket leaves
1 small handful of baby red chard leaves
½ white onion, finely sliced
6 yellow cherry tomatoes, halved crossways or quartered
2 tbsp black olives, pitted and roughly chopped
sea salt and freshly ground black pepper

FOR THE COURGETTE FLOWER TEMPURA
sunflower oil, for deep-frying
2 eggs
250ml/9fl oz/1 cup cold sparkling or still water
2 tbsp cornflour
160g/5¾oz/heaped 1¼ cups plain flour
a pinch of salt
1 tsp lemon juice
8 courgette flowers with the small courgettes attached

1 Mix the courgette with ½ teaspoon of the olive oil and half the lavender flowers, then season with salt and pepper. Cover with cling film and leave to marinate in the fridge for about 30 minutes. Whisk together the balsamic vinegar and extra virgin olive oil in a bowl until just combined, then season with a little salt and pepper. Leave to one side.

2 While the courgettes are marinating, prepare the artichokes. Fill a large bowl with water and stir in the lemon juice. Remove and discard the outer leaves from the first artichoke and cut off the top. Trim and peel the stalk, then cut the artichoke into quarters lengthways. Cut out and discard the choke (the 'furry' centre) and put the artichoke in the lemon water to stop it discolouring. Repeat with the other artichokes, then drain and pat dry.

3 Heat a large frying pan over a medium heat. Add 1 tablespoon of the olive oil and the artichokes and cook for about 8–10 minutes, turning occasionally, until just tender. Transfer to a plate and leave to one side. Add the remaining olive oil and the lardons to the frying pan and fry for 3 minutes until golden brown and crisp. Drain on kitchen paper and leave to one side. Bottled artichokes don't need cooking.

4 Heat a ridged griddle pan over a high heat until very hot. Add the courgette slices and griddle for 10 seconds on each side until just coloured in places. Transfer to a plate and leave to one side.

5 To make the tempura, pour in enough sunflower oil to fill a deep-fat fryer or deep, wide saucepan by two-thirds. Heat to 170°C/325°F, or until a cube of bread browns in 40 seconds. While the oil is heating, prepare the batter. Beat together the eggs and water in a large bowl until foaming. Sift the cornflour and flour over the top and gently mix with a pair of chopsticks until just combined. It doesn't matter if the batter is slightly lumpy as it's important not to over-whisk it. Stir in the salt, lemon juice and a handful of ice cubes, cover with cling film and leave to rest in the fridge for 5 minutes. Dip the courgette flowers and courgettes, one at a time, into the batter, then lower them straight into the hot oil. Deep-fry for 2 minutes, then flip over and fry for a further 2 minutes until the batter is crisp but not coloured. Drain on kitchen paper and season with a pinch of salt.

6 Top the rocket and chard with the artichokes, courgettes, onion, tomatoes and olives. Drizzle the dressing over the salad and add the lardons. Toss to combine, then put the courgette flowers on top and serve immediately while the batter is still crisp.

Tomato Confit, Chilli and Lemon Thyme Tarts

This classic tart represents, for me, all that I love about the Mediterranean, such as the climate, the colours, the heat, the scents and the goodness of the fresh local and seasonal ingredients. My new additions of tomato confit, chilli and lemon thyme give a freshness and great depth of flavour. You could also top the tarts with a few peppery rocket leaves.

SERVES 4
PREPARATION TIME 20 minutes
COOKING TIME 2 hours 20 minutes

8 large vine-ripened plum tomatoes, cut into 1cm/½in round slices, ends discarded
4 tbsp olive oil
leaves from 6 lemon thyme sprigs
375g/13oz ready-rolled puff pastry
6 vine-ripened tomatoes
1 garlic clove, unpeeled, lightly crushed
1 white onion, finely diced
2 long red chillies, deseeded and finely diced
3 tbsp extra virgin olive oil, plus extra for drizzling
sea salt and freshly ground black pepper
Chicory and Radish Salad (see page 19), to serve

1 Preheat the oven to 150°C/300°F/gas 2 and line a baking tray with baking paper. Put the sliced plum tomatoes on the prepared tray, drizzle with half the olive oil, scatter over one-third of the lemon thyme and season with salt. Bake for 2 hours, turning once, until dried and wrinkly. If they don't look quite ready, return the tomatoes to the oven for a further 30 minutes, then check once more. Leave to one side on the baking tray.

2 Turn the oven up to 180°C/350°F/gas 4. Cut the pastry into 4 discs, each about 10cm/4in in diameter, then prick all over with a fork. Put the pastry discs on a flat baking sheet and put a second baking sheet on top. Put the pastry, sandwiched between the baking sheets, in the oven for 10–12 minutes, or until golden brown and cooked through. Carefully lift off the top baking sheet and leave the pastry to cool.

3 Meanwhile, with a sharp knife, cut a small cross on the bottom of each of the remaining tomatoes, then put in a heatproof bowl and cover with boiling water. Leave for 30 seconds, then lift them out with a slotted spoon and put in a bowl of iced water. Lift the tomatoes out, then peel off and discard the skins. Cut the tomatoes into quarters, remove and discard the seeds, then roughly chop the flesh.

4 Heat a sauté pan over a medium heat. Add the remaining olive oil and the chopped tomatoes and cook for a few minutes to release the tomato juices. Add the garlic, onion and chillies, turn the heat down to medium-low and cook for 20–30 minutes until thickened and very soft. Stir once in a while to make sure that the tomato mixture doesn't catch or stick to the bottom of the pan. Season with salt and pepper to taste, then add another one-third of the lemon thyme and the extra virgin olive oil

5 To assemble the tarts, divide the chopped tomato mixture between the pastry discs and spread it over the tops with the back of a spoon. Lay the slices of tomato confit on top, overlapping them slightly. Drizzle with a little extra virgin olive oil and scatter over the remaining lemon thyme. Return to the oven for a further 5–8 minutes to warm through. Serve the tarts warm with a chicory and radish salad.

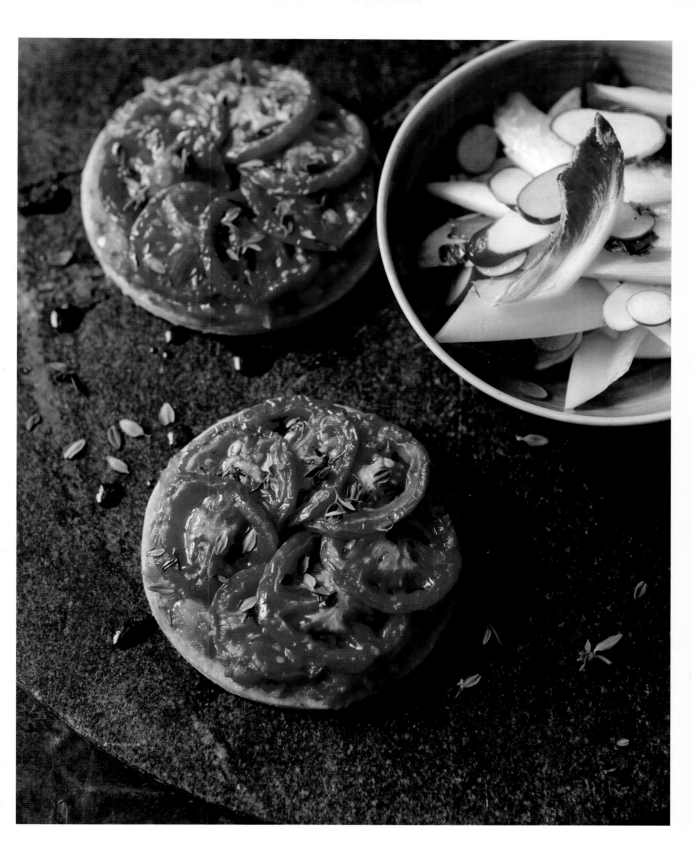

Semolina Gnocchi with **Almond Crumb**

Gnocchi is a kind of dumpling made with potato or semolina, and the name comes from the Italian word *nocchio* meaning 'knot in the wood', which I find very charming. You will see I've changed the shape slightly to make the gnocchi easier to roll and I also deep-fry them to give a crisp, golden outside. The carrot juice dressing is great and so is the crunchy almond topping.

SERVES 4
PREPARATION TIME 20 minutes,
  plus 10 minutes cooling
COOKING TIME 30 minutes

500ml/17fl oz/2 cups almond milk
175g/6oz/scant 1⅓ cups extra fine
  semolina, plus extra for dusting
50g/1¾oz unsalted butter, softened
40g/1½oz Parmesan cheese, finely
  grated
1 tsp sunflower oil, plus extra for
  deep-frying
100g/3½oz/⅔ cup blanched
  almonds
40g/1½oz stale sourdough bread,
  torn into small pieces
1 garlic clove, finely chopped
1 tbsp roughly chopped chervil, or
  dill or chives, plus extra to serve
570ml/20fl oz/scant 2⅓ cups
  carrot juice
sea salt and freshly ground black
  pepper

1 Pour the almond milk into a large saucepan and bring to a simmer over a high heat, then slowly pour in the semolina. Cook for about 5 minutes, stirring continuously with a spatula, until you have a thick, stiff paste. Remove from the heat, season with salt and pepper, then stir in half the butter and all of the Parmesan.

2 Generously dust a work surface with semolina. Take a small ball of the mixture about 2.5cm/1in in diameter. Roll on the work surface with the palm of your hand into a cylinder about 1.5cm/⅝in in diameter, gently pressing one end, while still rolling, to form a point. Roll again in the semolina to fully coat, then leave to one side. Repeat to make the remaining gnocchi.

3 Heat a large frying pan over a medium heat. Add the oil and the almonds and cook for 1–2 minutes, shaking the pan occasionally, until slightly browned. Drain off any excess oil, then add the remaining butter, the bread and garlic and toss to combine. After another 1–2 minutes, when the butter is foaming, toss once more, then drain in a sieve. Tip the contents of the sieve onto a double layer of kitchen paper and leave to cool and turn crunchy. Roughly chop to a crumble consistency, season with a little salt and pepper, then stir in the chervil and leave to one side.

4 Pour the carrot juice into a saucepan and cook over a medium heat for about 10 minutes, stirring occasionally, until reduced by half and slightly syrupy. Season with salt and pepper to taste.

5 Meanwhile, pour enough sunflower oil to deep-fry the gnocchi into a deep-fat fryer or deep, wide saucepan and heat to 170°C/325°F, or until a cube of bread browns in 40 seconds. Add the gnocchi, a few at a time, to the hot oil and deep-fry for 3–4 minutes, turning occasionally, until cooked all the way through and crisp and golden on the outside. Drain on kitchen paper and keep warm while you fry the remaining gnocchi. (You can reheat the fried gnocchi just before serving by briefly returning them to the hot oil, then draining again on kitchen paper.) Serve the gnocchi hot, sprinkled with the almond crumb and finished with a generous drizzle of carrot juice and a sprinkling of chervil.

Eggs en Cocotte with **Dried Mushrooms** and **Rosemary Croûtes**

I've used duck's eggs to give a rich and interesting flavour to the *cocottes*, but do watch the timing so the yolks remain soft and runny. The dried mushrooms add an intense burst of flavour to the finished dish. They can be prepared up to a week in advance and kept in an airtight container.

SERVES 4
PREPARATION TIME 30 minutes,
 plus 1 hour infusing
COOKING TIME 25 minutes,
 plus 2½ hours drying

FOR THE DRIED MUSHROOMS
200g/7oz button mushrooms,
 thinly sliced
2 egg whites, lightly beaten
1 tsp crushed sea salt, plus
 extra to season

FOR THE ROSMARY CROÛTES
3 tbsp olive oil
leaves from 1 rosemary sprig
8 slices of day-old baguette,
 about 3mm/⅛in thick each

FOR THE EGGS
200g/7oz mixed wild mushrooms,
 roughly chopped
1 tsp olive oil
½ small shallot, finely diced
½ garlic clove, finely diced
5 thyme sprigs, leaves picked from
 1 sprig
40g/1½oz unsalted butter, softened
4 duck's eggs or large hen's eggs
300ml/10½fl oz/scant 1¼ cups
 chilled whipping cream (it must
 be straight from the fridge)
freshly ground black pepper

1 To dry the mushrooms, preheat the oven to 70°C/150°F/gas ¼, not on a fan setting, and line a large baking tray with baking paper. Put the mushrooms on the prepared tray in a single layer, brush lightly with the egg whites, sprinkle with the salt and bake for 2½ hours until dry and crisp. Remove from the oven and leave to cool. Blitz 2 small handfuls to a powder in a mini food processor, then leave to one side. (You can store the remaining mushrooms in a sealed container for up to a week.)

2 Meanwhile, to make the rosemary croûtes, put the oil and rosemary leaves in a saucepan and warm through. Remove from the heat and leave to infuse for 1 hour. Strain through a fine sieve and discard the rosemary.

3 Turn the oven up to 140°C/275°F/gas 1 and line a baking tray with baking paper. Put the bread slices on the prepared tray and brush both sides with the rosemary oil until just coated. Cover with a second sheet of baking paper and a slightly smaller baking tray, which fits inside the large one. This will help the bread stay flat and cook evenly. Bake for 8–10 minutes until light golden, then leave to cool between the trays.

4 Meanwhile, bring a saucepan of water to the boil, add the chopped wild mushrooms and return to the boil. Drain well, then tip the mushrooms onto kitchen paper and pat dry. Heat a large frying pan over a medium heat. Add the oil, shallot and garlic and cook for 2 minutes until softened but not coloured. Turn the heat up to high, add the mushrooms and sauté for a further 2 minutes until just softened. Season with salt and pepper to taste, then add the thyme leaves, cover with a lid and leave to one side.

5 When the croûtes are ready, turn the oven up to 180°C/350°F/gas 4 and brush the insides of four 150ml/5fl oz/scant ⅔ cup ramekins with the softened butter. Spoon the mushrooms into the ramekins and crack an egg into each one. Pour the cream over to just cover, season with salt and pepper and top each one with a thyme sprig. Put the ramekins in the roasting tray, pour in enough hot water to come halfway up the sides and bake for 10–12 minutes until the tops are just set. Turn off the heat and leave in the oven for a further 2–3 minutes but make sure the yolks remain runny. Sprinkle with the dried mushrooms and serve with the rosemary croûtes for dipping into the egg.

DEHYDRATING FOOD

Intensity of flavour has to be the number one reason for dehydrating foods. Although, of course, it originated in ancient times as a simple but effective means of preserving foods through the lean winter months, now it's more about the fact that taking out the water not only means bacteria can't grow, it also produces some radical transformations, concentrating both taste, texture and goodness. Plus, it still means you don't have to waste any seasonal gluts but can instead easily transform all kinds of foods into handy storecupboard items, from fruit strips that make a great lunch-box snack to dried mushrooms to sprinkle into a risotto to intensify the flavour.

Of course, drying food will never replace freezing, as that does a better job of retaining the taste, appearance and goodness of fresh food. But dehydrating is easy, costs virtually nothing, needs no special equipment — and still gives you a huge range of flavoursome and densely textured treats to enjoy.

Sun-dried produce
Not surprisingly, the original dehydrator was the sun! And you'll still see fruit, vegetables or herbs spread out on cloths or wooden trays in a sunny courtyard or barn roof when you are on holiday in hotter climes. In Portugal, Spain or even Madagascar, you might come upon rows of flattened fish laid out to dry, a traditional practice as popular as salting or smoking.

Drying food in hot countries is virtually effortless. In cooler, more humid areas, it can be more challenging. If you are not careful, food can go mouldy on the drying tray, so techniques have to be different. Reindeer meat in Scandinavia, for example, is pickled in salt water before being dried in the spring sunshine when the air temperature is below zero, while in Iceland, shark meat is also dried in sub-zero temperatures.

But commercial dehydrators don't need sunlight. They push hot air around the food to dry it quickly and conveniently whatever the weather.

At The Vineyard
In The Vineyard kitchen, as in many professional kitchens, we often use dehydrators. A subtle, sweet celery leaf sprinkled with sugar can become as transparent and fragile as glass to finish a terrine. Slices of pancetta, gently oven-crisped, then finished in the dehydrator, are perfect crumbled over a pea velouté, roasted poultry, risotto or even roast pork. A few blanched, dried mushrooms can be blitzed to a dust to flavour soup or an *oeuf en cocotte*.

Dehydrating at home
But you don't need a commercial dehydrator, and you don't need to live in the land of eternal sunshine either — though wouldn't that be nice! In our house back in France, drying ingredients was a seasonal affair. Every autumn, wooden boxes lined with newspaper would appear in the boiler room, perched on the top of the boiler, and gradually be filled with our harvest of mushrooms. The boiler room was always the warmest part of the house. Not surprisingly, our dogs soon realized this and selected it as their winter bedroom — sensible creatures! That memory makes me smile as it is so fresh in my mind.

Newspapers, by the way, are ideal for absorbing moisture from drying foods and I still use them today. I dry foods in my glass greenhouse — the sun's heat on the enclosed space dries foods such as tomatoes perfectly. I also dry herbs, especially basil and tarragon, and use them to flavour oils, but I do that in the microwave. Just spread out the separate leaves on a sheet of kitchen paper, lay another sheet on top, then microwave on High for three or four 30-second bursts, watching carefully.

Mostly, however, I dry foods in my ordinary oven on a very low setting. I usually make use of the time control, then I can just leave it alone to do its own thing for long periods without interruption. It's quicker to dry food in an oven than by sun-drying or even using a dehydrator, and you only need a couple of oven trays and a thermometer. It's true you can only make small quantities in an oven, but I think that can be an advantage. It means you can experiment with plenty of different foods and there's no risk of making the effort to dry a large quantity of something you later decide you don't like!

You can dry most foods, apart from those with a high water content, such as cucumbers, as they are likely to spoil before the process is finished. Fruits tend to go crisp more quickly than vegetables, but you can dry most things in 8–12 hours. Good vegetables to start with are onions, garlic and peppers. For fruits, try apples, peaches, apricots or pears.

How to dehydrate food in your oven
- Make sure equipment, surfaces and hands are clean.
- Only fresh, good-quality food will give the best results. Wash it, then pat dry with kitchen paper.
- Prepare the food as though you were cooking it, so you might peel and core an apple, remove the stone from a plum, trim the fat off meat. Then leave them whole, or cut into thin slices or strips.
- For foods like apple that tend to go brown, add ½ tablespoon of vinegar or lemon juice to 250ml/ 9fl oz/1 cup of water, then dip the slices as you cut.
- Blanch hard fruits or vegetables in a saucepan of boiling water for a few seconds, then refresh in iced water and pat dry.
- Fruits like apples, peaches and rhubarb will keep their flavour if you poach them first in a light syrup.
- You could marinate meats in olive oil and vinegar, then toss with seasonings before dehydrating.

- Put food in a single layer, not overlapping, on a lined baking sheet or a wire rack in the oven (or the racks in your hydrator). Put a drip tray under meat. Items with similar drying times can be mixed on a rack.
- Switch on the oven to 45–70°C/115–150°F/gas ¼ or less, depending on the recipe. If your oven doesn't go below 70°C/150°F/gas ¼, don't worry. Set it to its lowest temperature but leave the oven door slightly open, enough for the air to circulate and keep a constant temperature.
- Turn the tray every 30 minutes or so if you can until the food is completely dry. That will be about 4–5 hours for beetroot, onions and peppers; 6–8 hours for garlic; 8–10 hours for apples, mushrooms and pears; 10–12 hours for apricots, peaches and potatoes.

Most dried foods will last well, so keep them in sterilized airtight jars in a cool, dark, dry place – then you can enjoy intriguing your friends at your next dinner party.

Dehydrated Pumpkin Crisp
This makes an easy introduction to drying so do have a go at making this delicious sprinkle for your next risotto.

Start by preheating the oven to 70°C/150°F/gas ¼ and lining a large baking sheet with baking paper. Then, simply grate the flesh of 100g/3½oz of peeled butternut squash or pumpkin into long spaghetti-like strips straight over the baking sheet. Bake for 4½ hours, turning halfway through. The strands will stick together in a net-like shape and go dry and crisp. Simply break them over the dish to serve. They'll keep in an airtight container for up to a month.

Follow the same recipe using strips of grated carrot or parsnip for delicious versions of the crisp. Or why not try making a batch of each and breaking a colourful selection to finish off your dish.

Lime-Leaf Poached Chicken

I love the fragrance of kaffir lime leaves as much as I like the smell of lime blossom, or even lemon or orange. When I lived in Portugal in the Algarve, the scent of citrus blossom was all around us from morning to night, invading our apartment and, when mixed with the breeze and the heat, was such a great fragrance. Here, the lime leaves gently lift the bouillon by adding a delicate scent and a refreshing flavour that goes so well with the chicken.

SERVES 4
PREPARATION TIME 10 minutes, plus making the stock
COOKING TIME 30 minutes

4 chicken breasts, skin on, about 175g/6oz each
1 tbsp olive oil
1 thick slice of fresh horseradish
6 kaffir lime leaves
1.2l/40fl oz/4¾ cups Chicken Stock (see page 16)
300g/10½oz potatoes, peeled and cut into 1cm/½in dice
400g/14oz pointed or sweetheart cabbage, finely sliced
1 small handful of coriander leaves, roughly chopped
sea salt

1 Put the chicken breasts in a large saucepan and just cover with lukewarm water. Put over a medium-low heat for about 5 minutes and gently bring to a simmer. Lift the chicken out of the water and drain on kitchen paper then, when cool enough to handle, carefully remove the skin from each breast and reserve. Cover the chicken breasts with cling film and leave to one side. Discard the poaching water.

2 Preheat the oven to 190°C/375°F/gas 5 and line a baking tray with baking paper. Put the skin, flesh-side down, on the prepared tray and brush with the oil. Cover with a second sheet of baking paper and a slightly smaller baking tray, which fits inside the large tray. This will help to keep the skin flat and let it cook evenly. Roast for 10–12 minutes until golden brown and nearly crisp. If it's not ready, return it to the oven for a further 5 minutes, then check again. Leave the skin to cool between the baking trays so that it crisps up further.

3 Meanwhile, to make the bouillon, put the horseradish, kaffir lime leaves and stock in the sauté pan and bring almost to the boil over a high heat. Turn the heat down to medium and simmer for 10–12 minutes until reduced by one-third, skimming off any foam that rises to the surface.

4 Add the poached chicken breasts and potato to the simmering bouillon and cook for 8 minutes, then add the cabbage and simmer for a further 2 minutes until the chicken is cooked through and the cabbage just wilted. Season with salt to taste, then scatter over the coriander leaves.

5 Remove the chicken, lime leaves and horseradish from the bouillon. Leave the chicken to one side and discard the flavourings. Ladle the broth and vegetables into shallow soup bowls. Slice the chicken breasts and put them on top, then break the crisp chicken skin into pieces and scatter over before serving.

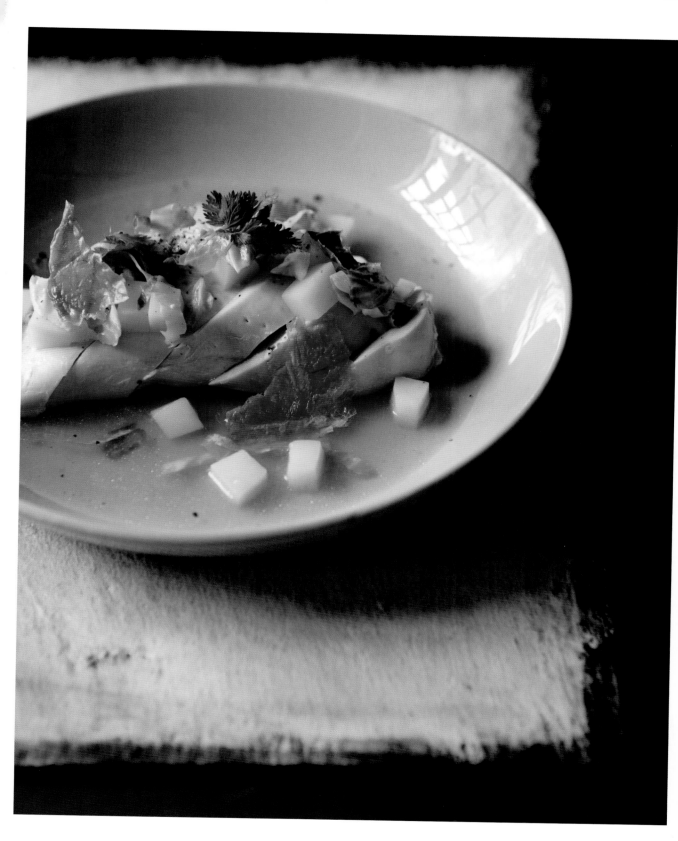

Pot-Roasted Cider and Paprika Chicken

I have always enjoyed the delicate flavour of smoked sweet paprika, which is milder than smoked hot paprika but should still be used carefully. Often found in Eastern European and Spanish cooking, sweet paprika brings an original twist to this French-style chicken pot-roasted in cider.

SERVES 4
PREPARATION TIME 10 minutes, plus making the stock
COOKING TIME 1 hour

1 tbsp olive oil
4 chicken legs
350ml/12fl oz/1½ cups good-quality dry cider
500ml/17fl oz/2 cups Chicken Stock (see page 16)
1 tsp smoked sweet (mild) paprika
12 small turnips, quartered
sea salt and freshly ground black pepper
Thai-Style Pilau Rice, to serve (see page 21)

1 Heat a flameproof casserole dish over a high heat. Add the oil and the chicken legs, skin-side down, and seal for 5–6 minutes, turning once, until browned all over. (You may need to do this in batches.) Spoon off any excess oil, then add the cider and deglaze the casserole dish by stirring to remove any caramelized bits stuck to the bottom. Cook for a few minutes until the cider has reduced by half, stirring occasionally.

2 Add the stock and paprika and bring to a simmer over a medium heat, then turn the heat down to low, partially cover with a lid and simmer for about 15 minutes. Add the turnips, partially cover again and simmer for a further 15 minutes until the chicken is cooked through and the turnips are tender.

3 Remove the chicken and turnips from the casserole dish and put on separate plates. Season the chicken with salt and pepper.

4 Return the casserole dish to a medium heat and cook for 6–8 minutes until the sauce has reduced to a glaze and you have about 500ml/17fl oz/ 2 cups. Return the chicken and turnips to the casserole and heat through, spooning the sauce over the chicken and turnips. Serve with pilau rice.

Warm Soy-Glazed Quail Salad

Szechuan peppercorns have a big, bold flavour, yet they are seldom used outside Chinese cooking. This fragrant spice works well with quail – which for me is a much under-used meat – but make sure you toast it well first.

SERVES 4
PREPARATION TIME 30 minutes,
plus making the croûtons
COOKING TIME 40 minutes

4 quails, about 140g/5oz each,
gutted and cleaned
250g/9oz duck or goose fat
4 quail's eggs
12 baby courgettes, sliced into thin
ribbons using a vegetable peeler
leaves from 1 thyme sprig
2 tbsp olive oil
1 tbsp clear honey
2 tbsp rice wine vinegar
1 tbsp soy sauce
½ tsp Szechuan peppercorns,
toasted and crushed (see page 68)
2 small or 1 large head of chicory,
sliced crossways
1 handful of Croûtons (see page 18)
1 handful of flat-leaf parsley leaves,
chopped
sea salt and freshly ground black
pepper

1 Prepare the quails by removing the legs and breasts from each one (or ask your butcher to do this for you). Wrap each leg tightly in cling film and then kitchen foil. (Leave the breasts to one side, covered.) Spoon the duck fat into a saucepan over a low heat until melted and starting to shimmer. Add the foil-wrapped legs and return the fat to a shimmer. Cook for 20–25 minutes until cooked through and tender. Remove from the heat and leave to one side in the fat.

2 Meanwhile, bring a small saucepan of water to the boil, add the quail's eggs and cook for 2 minutes, then drain and refresh in iced water – the yolks should still be slightly runny. Peel the eggs and leave to one side.

3 Put the courgette ribbons in a bowl with the thyme and oil, season with salt and turn until coated. Heat a ridged griddle pan over a high heat until very hot, then griddle the courgettes in batches for 1–2 minutes, turning once, until charred in places. Transfer to a plate, cover and keep warm.

4 Unwrap the quail legs and brush with half the honey. Heat a large frying pan over a high heat. Add 1–2 tablespoons of the duck fat from the pan, then add the quail legs, skin-side down, and cook for 2–3 minutes until the skin is crisp and golden brown. Transfer to a plate, cover with foil and leave to rest while you cook the breasts.

5 Season the quail breasts with salt and pepper. Put them in the frying pan, skin-side down, and cook over a high heat for 2–3 minutes until the skin starts to crisp. Turn the breasts over and cook for about a further 2 minutes until cooked through but still nicely moist. Transfer to the plate with the legs. Pour the rice wine vinegar and soy sauce into the pan and deglaze by stirring to remove any caramelized bits stuck to the bottom. Stir in the Szechuan peppercorns and remaining honey and heat briefly. Before the honey starts to colour, add the quail legs and turn to coat them in the honey glaze, then remove and add the breasts to the pan, skin-side down only, and glaze until they are a lovely golden colour.

6 Cut the quail breasts in half diagonally, then put on top of the chicory and the courgette ribbons with the legs. Halve the quail's eggs and put on top, then sprinkle with the croûtons and parsley. Drizzle with any glaze left in the pan and serve immediately.

Medallions of Pork
with **Coriander** and **Garlic**

I often make this dish for myself at home, partly because it's so quick but also as I love the mix of flavours, and I always use good-quality pork to make sure the results are really tender. The garlic, sautéed in its skin until soft, perfectly complements the nuttiness of the crushed coriander seeds, then both combine with the buttery pork juices and fresh coriander. And all this served with succulent slices of pork tenderloin. Fantastic!

SERVES 4
PREPARATION TIME 5 minutes, plus at least 1 hour marinating and making the stock
COOKING TIME 15 minutes

2 pork tenderloin fillets, about 300g/10½oz each, trimmed and cut into 2.5cm/1in slices
1 tbsp olive oil
½ tsp coriander seeds, crushed
8 garlic cloves, unpeeled, lightly crushed
1 tbsp vegetable oil
100g/3½oz unsalted butter
100ml/3½fl oz/scant ½ cup Chicken Stock (see page 16)
1 small handful of coriander leaves, roughly chopped
sea salt and freshly ground white pepper
boiled, mashed carrot, to serve

1 Put the pork in a large dish, pour over the olive oil and sprinkle with the crushed coriander seeds. Cover with cling film and leave to marinate in the fridge for at least an hour, or until ready to use.

2 Bring a small saucepan of water to the boil over a high heat, add the garlic, then turn the heat down to low and simmer for 5 minutes until softened (taking care to simmer and not boil, so the skins stay attached to the garlic). Lift out with a slotted spoon and drain on kitchen paper.

3 Heat a large sauté pan over a medium-high heat. Add the vegetable oil and 20g/¾oz of the butter, then add the pork and when it has just started to brown, add the garlic. Cook the pork and garlic for 2–3 minutes on each side until both are golden brown, taking care not to burn the garlic. Remove the pork and garlic from the pan and leave to one side on a plate, covered with foil to keep warm.

4 Discard the fat in the pan, then return it to a medium heat, making sure the pan does not get too hot. Pour in the stock and deglaze the pan by stirring to remove any caramelized bits stuck to the bottom. Add the remaining butter to the pan, a little at a time, whisking to incorporate it into the sauce. When all the butter has been added, add the unpeeled garlic and the resting juices from the pork and heat through.

5 Just before serving, add the fresh coriander leaves to the sauce and season with salt and pepper to taste. Spoon the sauce over the pork and serve with mashed carrot.

Pork Shoulder with **Chilli-Ginger Cabbage**

Pork shoulder is a very tasty part of the pig and as it has a little fat it brings a lovely flavour to this dish. Although I think the secret to the success of this recipe lies in the cabbage! I have used a pointed cabbage, also called sweetheart, which is braised in a delicious combination of chilli, ginger and honey that gives it a wonderful balance of flavours.

SERVES 4
PREPARATION TIME 10 minutes
COOKING TIME 20 minutes

2 tbsp sunflower oil
4 pork shoulder steaks, about
    150g/5½oz each
90g/3¼oz unsalted butter
1 pointed or sweetheart cabbage,
    quartered lengthways, stem
    removed and shredded
2 long red chillies, deseeded and
    finely chopped
50g/1¾oz piece of root ginger,
    peeled and cut into julienne strips
2 tbsp clear honey
1 tbsp roughly chopped flat-leaf
    parsley leaves
2 tbsp extra virgin olive oil
sea salt and freshly ground black
    pepper

1 Preheat the oven to 140°C/275°F/gas 1. Heat a large frying pan over a medium heat. Add the sunflower oil and the pork and cook for 3–4 minutes until golden brown underneath, then add one-third of the butter, turn the pork and cook the other side until golden. Transfer the pork to a plate, cover with foil and keep warm in the oven. Leave the frying pan to one side.

2 Bring a saucepan of salted water to the boil, add the cabbage, cover with a lid and return to the boil, then drain immediately. Return the cabbage to the saucepan and add 1½ of the red chillies, the ginger, honey and half the remaining butter and season with salt and pepper. Cover the pan with a lid, put over a very low heat and braise gently for 2–3 minutes until just tender. Remove from the heat, cover with a lid and leave to one side while you finish making the sauce.

3 Return the frying pan to a high heat. When the juices are bubbling, add 100ml/3½fl oz/scant ½ cup of water and cook for 2 minutes until reduced by half. Reduce the heat to medium, add the remaining butter to the pan, a little at a time, whisking to incorporate it into the sauce. Add the remaining chilli and half the parsley and stir through. Check the seasoning, adding more salt and pepper to taste. Remove the pork from the oven and pour any resting juices into the sauce, stirring one last time.

4 Stir the remaining parsley into the cabbage. Scoop the cabbage out of the pan with a slotted spoon into a warm bowl, making sure that any residual liquid stays in the pan. Return the pan to a high heat and cook the liquid until reduced and slightly syrupy. Add the extra virgin olive oil, season with salt and pepper to taste, then spoon the sauce over the cabbage. Serve the pork with the buttery sauce spooned over the top and with the honey-coated cabbage.

Tomato Farci with Lamb and Lavender

In this book you'll come across a few *farci* (stuffed) dishes as it's a very typical style of cooking in France, and in this recipe I have given it a modern approach. I do like lavender with lamb so I decided that instead of simply sprinkling roast lamb with lavender flowers, I would use them to flavour minced lamb, then stuff the mixture into large beef tomatoes before roasting them. It's important to use lavender that hasn't been sprayed with chemicals so try to buy from an organic source. This makes a great family dish that only needs a mixed salad to go with it.

SERVES 4
PREPARATION TIME: 15 minutes
COOKING TIME 35 minutes

4 beef tomatoes
400g/14oz minced lamb
2 edible lavender sprigs, young
  leaves only from the tips
2–3 tbsp olive oil
sea salt and freshly ground black
  pepper
mixed salad, to serve

1 Preheat the oven to 170°C/325°F/gas 3 and line a baking dish large enough to hold the tomatoes with baking paper. Cut the top off each tomato, about one-quarter of the way down, and reserve to make 4 lids. Turn the tomatoes upside-down and press to squeeze out the seeds, then discard the seeds. Scoop the flesh out of the inside of each tomato, then season the insides with salt and pepper to taste.

2 Roughly chop the tomato flesh and mix it with the minced lamb. Add a pinch of the blue tips of the lavender, then season well with salt and pepper. Divide the lamb mixture into 4, then roughly roll each quarter into a ball and press into a tomato shell so that the filling comes a little above the top of the tomatoes. Put the reserved tomato lids on top, then put the stuffed tomatoes in the prepared baking dish.

3 Drizzle the tomatoes with the oil and bake for 35 minutes until the lamb is cooked through. To check the lamb is ready, insert a skewer into the centre and if it comes out clean, the meat is cooked. If not, return to the oven for a further 5 minutes and repeat. Serve with a mixed salad.

Roast Marinated Lamb with Liquorice

In France, as in Spain, we use liquorice root quite a lot. In fact, I remember as a young boy buying liquorice root and chewing it on my way to school, then keeping it in my bag during lessons and getting it out again to chew on my way back home – great memories! In this recipe, I use it to skewer the lamb rump to infuse the meat while cooking, without the flavour becoming overpowering. The lamb is also really good served with very thin strips or 'tagliatelle' of courgette sautéed in olive oil with a little garlic and chilli and finished with some chopped flat-leaf parsley.

SERVES 4
PREPARATION TIME 10 minutes, plus 1 hour soaking and overnight marinating
COOKING TIME 20 minutes

1 small stick of liquorice root, about 10cm/4in long x 1cm/½in thick
4 small lamb rumps, about 150g/5½oz each
125ml/4fl oz/½ cup olive oil
20g/¾oz unsalted butter
200ml/7fl oz/scant 1 cup Lamb Stock or Chicken Stock (see page 16)
sea salt and freshly ground black pepper
steamed Swiss chard, to serve

1 Put the liquorice in a small bowl of warm water and leave for about 1 hour until it is soft enough to bend easily. Working from the centre of the root towards the end, peel away the outer layer, reserving the peelings. Cut the root lengthways into quarters, leaving the long pieces to dry on a plate.

2 Put the lamb in a shallow bowl and pour over the oil, then add a generous pinch of pepper and the liquorice peelings. Stir to coat, then cover each rump tightly with cling film, pressing the cling film directly onto the lamb so that there is no air inside. Leave to marinate in the fridge overnight to help to tenderize the meat.

3 The next day, preheat the oven to 140°F/275°F/gas 1. Remove the lamb from the marinade and, using a skewer, make incisions through the centre of each piece of meat. Insert a liquorice root piece into each one, pressing them into the lamb.

4 Heat an ovenproof frying pan over a medium-high heat. Add the lamb and cook for about 3–4 minutes on all sides, adding the butter when cooking the final side. Transfer the lamb, still in the pan, to the oven and cook for 5–8 minutes, then turn the oven up to 180°C/350°F/gas 4 and cook for a further 4 minutes until cooked but still slightly pink in the centre. Transfer the lamb to a warm plate, cover with foil and leave to rest while you make the gravy.

5 Return the pan that you cooked the lamb in to a high heat and when the juices are bubbling, add the stock and deglaze the pan by stirring to remove any caramelized bits stuck to the bottom. Cook for 5 minutes until reduced by half, then add any resting juices from the lamb and season with salt and pepper to taste. Serve with steamed Swiss chard.

Venison Bourguignon with Dark Chocolate and Star Anise

Venison is a great alternative to beef in a bourguignon and it's a dish I like to put on the menu at The Vineyard restaurant when venison is in season, usually as my 'dish of the week'. This modern version of the French classic is finished with dark chocolate, providing a hint of tobacco and bark, which combines beautifully with the earthy flavour of the wild mushrooms and woody aroma of the star anise. To bring the dish together, you need to use a robust red wine, such as one from the southern Rhône region, which also has a hint of spice and chocolate. All in all, a magical combination. I like to serve it with roughly mashed buttered swede or turnip.

SERVES 4
PREPARATION TIME 20 minutes, plus making the stock and at least 3 hours marinating
COOKING TIME 2 hours 25 minutes

800g/1lb 12oz venison haunch, cut into large cubes
1l/35fl oz/4 cups red wine, such as French southern Rhône
2 thyme sprigs
3 garlic cloves, crushed with the blade of a knife
1 star anise
3 tbsp Cognac
100ml/3½fl oz/scant ½ cup olive oil
2 tbsp plain flour
600ml/21fl oz/scant 2½ cups Beef Stock (see page 16)
1 bouquet garni, made with 1 thyme sprig, 1 parsley sprig and 1 bay leaf, tied with kitchen string
2 carrots, peeled, halved lengthways and cut into chunks
12 silverskin onions or small shallots
30g/1oz dark organic chocolate, 70% cocoa solids, grated
100g/3½oz thick pancetta, diced
2 handfuls of mixed seasonal wild mushrooms, such as girolles, horn of plenty and chanterelles
1 handful of flat-leaf parsley leaves, roughly chopped
sea salt and freshly ground black pepper

1 Mix together the venison, wine, thyme, garlic, star anise and Cognac in a large bowl. Cover with cling film and leave to marinate in the fridge for at least 3 hours. Drain the venison through a colander into a bowl, reserving the flavoured marinade.

2 Heat 4 tablespoons of the oil in a large, flameproof casserole dish over a medium heat. Add the venison and cook for at least 20 minutes until very well coloured on all sides but not burnt. Season with salt and pepper, then sprinkle in the flour and cook, stirring, for a further 2–3 minutes until the meat is lightly coated. Add the stock and the reserved marinade and bring to the boil, skimming off any foam that rises to the surface. Add the bouquet garni, carrots and onions, turn the heat down to low, partially cover and simmer for 1 hour 50 minutes, stirring occasionally, until the meat is very tender and the sauce has become rich and silky.

3 Five minutes before the venison is ready, remove 2 ladles of the sauce into a bowl. Whisk in the chocolate until melted and combined. Return the chocolate-flavoured sauce to the casserole dish, stir together well, then cover with a lid and turn off the heat.

4 Heat the remaining oil in a frying pan over a medium heat. Add the pancetta and fry for 2–3 minutes until just coloured, then stir in the wild mushrooms and fry for a further 1–2 minutes until just tender. Add to the venison and stir through. Season with salt and pepper to taste, then stir in the parsley, taking care not to break up the venison, and serve.

Pan-Fried Skate Wings with Chilli-Lime Butter

Skate wings are classically served with a Beurre Noisette (see page 22) and capers, but I think they go just as well with this chilli and lime butter. It's the same basic idea but the chilli brings a touch of heat and sunshine to the dish, which skate has the depth of flavour to take. Add, too, a splash of fresh lime and a little garlic and you have a cracking meal.

SERVES 4
PREPARATION TIME 10 minutes
COOKING TIME 5 minutes

4 skate wings, about 150g/5½oz
  each, cleaned and prepared
15g/½oz unsalted butter
1 tbsp olive oil
1 tbsp chopped flat-leaf parsley
  leaves
boiled new potatoes, to serve

FOR THE CHILLI-LIME BUTTER
250g/9oz unsalted butter, softened
1 red chilli, deseeded and finely
  chopped
1 garlic clove, crushed
finely grated zest of 1 lime
juice of ½ lime
leaves from 2 flat-leaf parsley
  sprigs, chopped
sea salt and freshly ground black
  pepper

1 To make the chilli-lime butter, put the butter, chilli, garlic, lime zest, lime juice and parsley in a non-metallic bowl and season with salt and pepper. Mix together with a wooden spoon, then put 4 heaped teaspoons to one side. (The rest of the chilli-lime butter can be frozen for future use. Wrap half the remaining butter in cling film, roll it into a log shape and twist the ends. Repeat with the remaining butter. Wrap each log in a piece of foil and put in the freezer to firm up. You can then cut pieces off at your convenience for use on grilled, barbecued or pan-fried meats or fish.)

2 Briefly rinse the skate wings in ice-cold water, then pat dry with a clean tea towel (not paper as it will stick).

3 Heat a non-stick frying pan, large enough to hold the skate, over a medium heat. Add the unflavoured butter and the oil and heat until just melted. Add the skate wings and fry for 5 minutes, turning once, until just golden brown. As you turn the skate wings, add the reserved chilli-lime butter to the pan and spoon it over the fish. (Alternatively, cook the skate one or two at a time, using a little butter and oil for each one, and keep them warm in the oven at 140°F/275°F/gas 1 while you cook the remaining skate.)

4 Remove the skate wings from the pan and put on serving plates. Stir the parsley into the pan, then spoon the flavoured butter over the top of the skate wings. Serve with boiled new potatoes.

Mussel, Ginger and **Lemongrass Gratin**

Moules marinière is the classic way to cook mussels and a very good way at that, but mussels in a gratin with a creamy, aromatic sauce flavoured with lemongrass, ginger and fresh coriander is rather delicious, too. Mussels are very good value and easy to cook, just make sure that they are very fresh and throw away any with broken shells before cooking and those that don't open once cooked. Don't forget a fresh baguette or homemade chips to dip into the sauce – it wouldn't be the same without them!

SERVES 4
PREPARATION TIME 20 minutes, plus making the stock
COOKING TIME 20 minutes

3kg/6lb 8oz mussels, rinsed
40g/1½oz unsalted butter, softened
2 tbsp olive oil
1 large shallot, roughly chopped
2 lemongrass stalks, bruised
50g/1¾oz piece of root ginger, peeled and roughly chopped
250ml/9fl oz/1 cup not too acidic or dry white wine, perhaps an Alsace or Riesling
2 handfuls of coriander leaves, chopped
200ml/7fl oz/scant 1 cup Fish Stock (see page 17)
400ml/14fl oz/scant 1⅔ cups whipping cream
50g/1¾oz pecorino cheese, grated
sea salt and freshly ground black pepper

1 Thoroughly scrub the mussels under cold running water and rinse well. Remove the beards by pulling them towards the large part of the shell. If any of the mussels are open, tap them hard against a work surface and if they don't close, discard them.

2 Generously butter four flameproof 18cm/7in gratin dishes. Heat a large, deep saucepan over a medium heat. Add the oil, shallot, lemongrass and ginger and fry for 2–3 minutes until just softened but not coloured. Turn the heat up to high, add the wine and cook until reduced by one-third, allowing the alcohol to evaporate. Add the mussels and half the coriander leaves, cover with a lid and cook for about 5 minutes at the very most, shaking the pan occasionally, until the mussels have opened. Discard any that remain closed. Remove from the heat and scoop all the mussels into a colander using a slotted spoon. Leave to cool slightly before shelling them. Discard the shells.

3 Spoon the shelled mussels into the prepared gratin dishes and put on a grill tray. Strain the juices from the pan and bowl through a fine sieve into a measuring jug. Reserve 200ml/7fl oz/scant 1 cup of the liquid.

4 Preheat the grill to high. Pour the mussel liquid into a sauté pan and add the stock and cream. Put over a low heat and bring almost to the boil, then simmer for about 5 minutes until reduced by half and thickened enough to coat the back of a wooden spoon. Season with pepper to taste and a little salt, if necessary.

5 Ladle the cream sauce over the mussels in the gratin dishes. Sprinkle the remaining coriander on top, then finish with a sprinkling of cheese, making sure the cheese covers the coriander so that it doesn't discolour. Put under the hot grill for a minute or so until bubbling and golden brown. Serve hot.

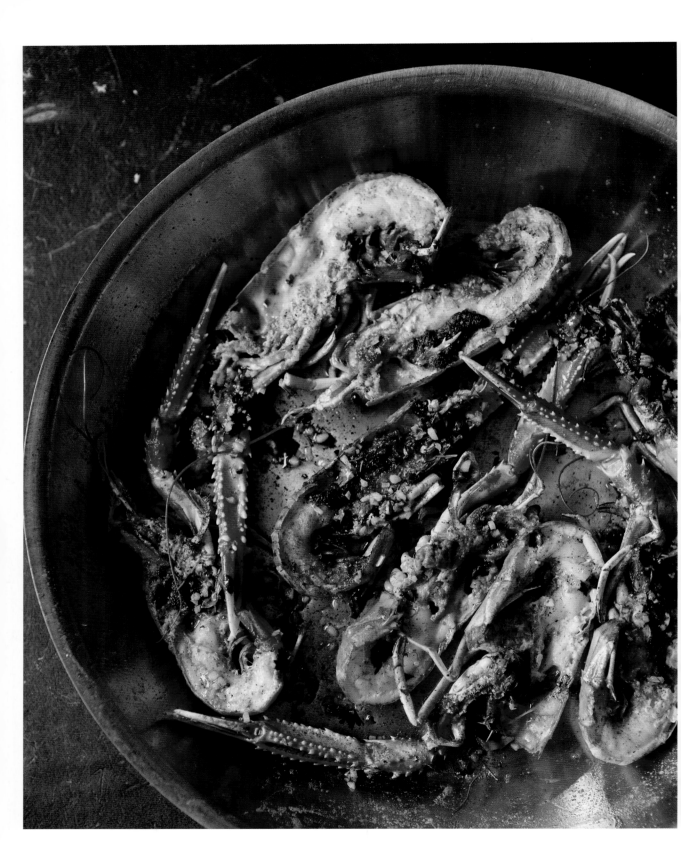

Pan-Roasted Langoustines with **Coriander**

What makes this dish is the quality and freshness of the langoustines – make sure they are absolutely fresh and you will have a super-simple yet very tasty dish. The shellfish come in a fragrant butter sauce, flavoured with aromatic coriander, garlic and fresh lime juice. This is great served with buttery pilau rice flavoured with fresh ginger or just a simple salad.

SERVES 4
PREPARATION TIME 10 minutes
COOKING TIME 8 minutes

16 whole langoustines, shell on
1 tsp olive oil
150g/5½oz unsalted butter
2 garlic cloves, finely chopped
1 handful of coriander leaves,
  roughly chopped
1 lime, cut into wedges
Thai-Style Pilau Rice (see page 21),
  to serve

1 Preheat the grill to high. To prepare the langoustines, cut them in half lengthways, then put cut-side down on kitchen paper to absorb any water. This is particularly important if the langoustines have been frozen.

2 Heat a large, non-stick frying pan over a high heat until searing hot. Add the oil and one-third of the butter and when the butter is foaming, put half the langoustines, flesh-side down, in the pan. Cook for about 2 minutes, then flip them over, transfer to a roasting tray and repeat with the remaining langoustines.

3 Melt the last of the butter in the frying pan until foaming. Stir in the garlic and coriander, then spoon straight away over the langoustines. Put under the grill for 2 minutes, then squeeze the lime juice over the top and serve with pilau rice.

Ragoût of Summer Vegetables with Vanilla Beurre Blanc

This is a perfect summer dish as it's colourful, light and fresh. The vegetables only need a minimal amount of cooking before they are coated in a light butter sauce, scented with fresh vanilla seeds and thyme. One small point – don't over do the vanilla or you will disturb the delicately balanced flavour of the dish. It's delicious served on its own or with roasted meats.

SERVES 4
PREPARATION TIME 20 minutes, plus making the stock
COOKING TIME 40 minutes

100g/3½oz podded broad beans, grey outer casing removed
200g/7oz peas, podded
100g/3½oz green beans, halved
100g/3½oz baby carrots, scrubbed
100g/3½oz baby leeks, trimmed and each cut into 3 pieces
100g/3½oz baby turnips, peeled and quartered
1 bunch of asparagus tips
1 baby cauliflower, cut into florets
leaves from 1 thyme sprig
sea salt and freshly ground black pepper

FOR THE VANILLA BEURRE BLANC
500ml/17fl oz/2 cups Vegetable Stock (see page 17)
200g/7oz unsalted butter, softened, cut into cubes
1 shallot, finely chopped
finely grated zest and juice of ½ lime
1 vanilla pod, split in half lengthways and seeds scraped out (you can keep the pod for vanilla sugar)

1 Pour the stock for the vanilla *beurre blanc* into a small sauté pan and cook over a medium-high heat for 15 minutes until reduced to 150ml/5fl oz/scant ⅔ cup. Leave to one side.

2 Meanwhile, bring a saucepan of salted water to the boil over a high heat and cook the vegetables, one type at a time, for 2–5 minutes each until just tender. Lift out with a slotted spoon, refresh in iced water, then drain once more, tip carefully into a bowl and leave to one side. Put a lid on the pan of water and reserve for reheating the vegetables just before serving.

3 To make the *beurre blanc*, melt 20g/¾oz of the butter in a small pan over a medium heat and fry the shallot for 2 minutes until just softened. Stir in the lime juice, then add the reduced stock and the vanilla seeds. Bring to a simmer and cook for 5–8 minutes until there is about 110ml/4fl oz/scant ½ cup of buttery stock.

4 Turn the heat down to very low and gradually whisk in the remaining softened butter, a few cubes at a time. Keep whisking until the butter has been incorporated before adding the next batch. This will stop the sauce splitting by keeping it at a constant temperature. As you are whisking, you should see a foam of tiny bubbles form on top of the mixture and when all the butter has been added, the sauce should be pale in colour and light in consistency, similar to a very thin custard, and should just coat the back of the spoon. This will take 10–12 minutes. At this point, season with salt and pepper to taste and add the lime zest. Cover with a lid and leave to one side in a warm place.

5 Return the saucepan of water to the boil over a high heat and add the vegetables. Cook for a minute or so until heated through, then drain on kitchen paper. Serve the vegetables with the vanilla *beurre blanc* spooned over the top and sprinkled with the thyme.

Butternut Squash and **Saffron Risotto**

This is the most popular risotto we serve at The Vineyard and I love it, too. The saffron-infused stock and mashed roasted squash seem to intensify the flavour of the risotto. If you are using Carnaroli rice, my grain of choice, follow the recipe closely and keep the heat low when you add it, otherwise the rice could break down and give a sticky risotto. You could finish it with a sprinkling of dehydrated crispy butternut squash along with the Parmesan. A small herb salad will also go down a treat with this.

SERVES 4
PREPARATION TIME 20 minutes, plus making the stock
COOKING TIME 55 minutes

1 small butternut squash, unpeeled, quartered lengthways and deseeded
875ml/30fl oz/3½ cups Vegetable Stock (see page 17)
2 pinches of saffron strands
150g/5½oz unsalted butter
1 onion, finely chopped
300g/10½oz/scant 1⅓ cups risotto rice, such as Carnaroli or Arborio
90g/3¼oz Parmesan cheese, grated
2 heaped tbsp Greek yogurt
1 tbsp chopped chives
sea salt and freshly ground black pepper
Dehydrated Pumpkin Crisp (see page 41), to serve (optional)

1 Preheat the oven to 160°C/315°F/gas 2½. Put the butternut squash in a roasting tray, cover with foil and roast for 45 minutes until very tender.

2 When the squash has been in the oven for about 30 minutes, start to make the risotto. Heat the stock and saffron in a saucepan and bring to a simmer, then turn the heat down to very low. Melt 75g/2½oz of the butter in a frying pan over a low heat. Add the onion and cook for 3–4 minutes, stirring occasionally, until softened. Add the rice and turn the heat down to very low. Mix with a wooden spoon until the rice is well coated in the butter and onion mixture.

3 Add the hot stock to the pan, little by little, stirring continuously until the liquid has been absorbed before adding more stock. Carry on adding the stock, stirring to stop it sticking, for about 20 minutes until the rice has a lovely creamy texture.

4 When the squash is cooked, and while the risotto is still cooking, remove the squash from the tray and leave until just cool enough to handle. Scoop the flesh away from the skin into a bowl and mash roughly with a fork. When the rice is almost cooked, fold in the mashed squash, the Parmesan, yogurt, chives and the remaining butter. If the risotto is a little thick, add a few more spoonfuls of stock to loosen it, then season well with salt and pepper and serve immediately with pumpkin crisp, if you like.

Grapefruit Gratin with **Honey-Saffron Sabayon** and **Nut Brittle**

I love all sorts of fruit — well perhaps with the exception of durian. I am using pink grapefruit here, which is one of my favourites. I find it so refreshing with its own mix of sweet and sour. The combination of honey and saffron in the sabayon makes it feel really exotic, too, as well as lovely and light and frothy on top of the sharp grapefruit. It does seem as if they were all meant for each other.

SERVES 4
PREPARATION TIME 20 minutes, plus cooling
COOKING TIME 30 minutes

FOR THE NUT BRITTLE
100g/3½oz/scant ½ cup caster sugar
50g/1¾oz/heaped ⅓ cup blanched or unblanched hazelnuts, very finely chopped

FOR THE GRAPEFRUIT AND SABAYON
a pinch of saffron strands, infused in 4 tbsp warm water
4 large pink grapefruits, scrubbed and patted dry
2 tbsp clear honey
3 egg yolks

1 To make the nut brittle, line a large baking tray with baking paper. Heat the sugar in a dry, non-stick frying pan over a medium heat until the sugar melts to a light brown caramel and reaches 160°C/320°F. Remove the pan from the heat, stir in the hazelnuts, then return to the heat until the caramel becomes liquid again, stirring to coat the nuts completely.

2 Pour immediately into the prepared baking tray. Cover with a second sheet of paper, then, using a rolling pin, roll into a thin, even layer about 5mm/¼in thick. Leave to cool and harden, then remove the paper and break into small pieces. Alternatively, put in a food processor and pulse to a coarse crumble consistency. Leave to one side.

3 To make the sabayon, heat the saffron water in a small pan over a low heat until reduced by one-third and dark orange in colour. Pass through a sieve into a large heatproof bowl. Leave to one side.

4 Finely grate the zest of one of the grapefruits, then peel all of them, removing the skin and white pith. Segment the grapefruits over a sieve suspended over a saucepan to catch the juices. Line a baking tray with a clean tea towel, then put the segments on the prepared tray and leave to dry slightly.

5 Add the honey to the grapefruit juices and bring to the boil over a medium heat, then turn the heat down to low and simmer for 6–8 minutes until reduced to a thick syrup. Add the syrup and egg yolks to the saffron water and mix together. Set the bowl over a saucepan of gently simmering water, making sure the bottom of the bowl does not touch the water. Whisk the mixture, using an electric whisk, for 8–10 minutes until it turns pale and thick.

6 Preheat the grill to high. Put the grapefruit segments in fan shapes on four flameproof plates. Spoon the sabayon over the top to cover the segments, then grill briefly until light golden brown. Sprinkle with the nut brittle and serve.

Cocoa-Infused Pain Perdu with Roasted Peaches

My mum often made *pain perdu* for me when I was growing up. It was seen as a sin to throw bread away so any leftover bread was sliced and dipped into egg and milk and fried in butter. In this new version, the cocoa transforms this classic dish to create a stylish, modern dessert with the added elegance of roasted peaches. You can also adapt this dish and serve it with pears, apricots or plums instead of peaches, if you like, or even make it with coconut milk instead of cow's milk.

SERVES 4
PREPARATION TIME 10 minutes
COOKING TIME 25 minutes

75g/2½oz unsalted butter
2 large, firm peaches, quartered
   and stones removed
3 tbsp maple syrup
20g/¾oz/scant ¼ cup good-quality
   dark cocoa powder
200ml/7fl oz/scant 1 cup full-fat
   milk, slightly warmed
2 eggs, lightly beaten
2 tbsp caster sugar
4 x 2.5cm/1in slices of *pain de
   campagne* or country-style bread
20g/¾oz/scant ¼ cup flaked
   almonds, toasted
3 tbsp crème fraîche
1 tsp chopped rosemary leaves

1 Preheat the oven to 180°C/350°F/gas 4. Heat an ovenproof sauté pan over a medium heat. Add half the butter and sauté the peaches for 2–3 minutes, turning once, until golden on both sides. Add 2 tablespoons of the maple syrup, turn to coat the peaches in the syrup, then transfer to the oven and roast for 5–8 minutes until just soft. Remove and leave to one side on a plate, but leave the oven on.

2 Mix half the cocoa powder with the warm milk, eggs and sugar in a wide, shallow bowl, stirring until the sugar dissolves. Leave to cool slightly, if necessary. Add 2 slices of the bread and soak both sides. Put the bread on a clean tea towel to drain slightly, then repeat with the remaining slices of bread.

3 Heat a large, non-stick frying pan over a medium heat. Add the remaining butter and maple syrup and, when melted, swirl the pan until combined. Put the egg-soaked bread in the pan and cook for 1–2 minutes on each side until just golden and slightly crisp, taking care they do not burn. You may need to do this in batches.

4 Put the *pain perdu* in a shallow baking tray and top with the roasted peaches, a sprinkling of toasted almonds and a dusting of the remaining cocoa powder. Heat through in the oven for 2–3 minutes.

5 Meanwhile, mix together the crème fraîche and rosemary. Serve the *pain perdu* and peaches with the rosemary crème fraîche.

Soft Pan-Fried Pears with Cardamom and Szechuan Pepper

Ever since I lived in South East Asia, I've enjoyed adding Asian spices to my cooking, not only for their flavour but for their fragrance, too. Pears can take lots of different spices, especially cardamom and Szechuan pepper, yet the right quantity is critical as too much would overwhelm the subtlety of this delicate fruit. You can use the same quantity of syrup and adjust the number of pears according to the size of the pears and your guests' appetites. This dessert goes really well with the Pistachio Madeleines (see page 75).

SERVES 4
PREPARATION TIME 10 minutes
COOKING TIME 35 minutes

1 tsp Szechuan peppercorns
200g/7oz/heaped ¾ cup caster
   sugar
1 tsp cardamom pods, lightly
   crushed
juice of ¼ lime
4 large or 8 small, firm pears, such
   as William, Rocha or Comice,
   peeled with the stalks left on
25g/1oz unsalted butter

1 Put the Szechuan peppercorns in a small, dry frying pan over a medium heat and toast for 1–2 minutes, shaking the pan occasionally, until just coloured and aromatic. Tip onto a plate and crush lightly with the flat blade of a knife.

2 Bring the sugar, half the cardamom, the lime juice and 800ml/28fl oz/ scant 3½ cups of water to the boil in a saucepan over a medium heat. Stir occasionally for about 5–8 minutes until the sugar dissolves and starts to turn syrupy.

3 Add the pears to the pan with the syrup. You need to cover the pears with a *cartouche* (see page 218). Turn the heat down to very low and simmer for 8 minutes, or until the pears have softened very slightly. To check the pears, insert the tip of a knife into the thickest part – there should still be a little resistance. Put the pears on a clean tea towel to drain. Return the pan to the heat and simmer for 8–10 minutes until the syrup has reduced by about three-quarters.

4 Meanwhile, melt the butter in a large, non-stick frying pan over a medium heat. When the butter is foaming, add the pears and the remaining cardamom and cook for 3–4 minutes, turning occasionally, until they are slightly golden all over.

5 Add 4 tablespoons of the reduced syrup to the pan and cook the pears for 4–5 minutes, basting them occasionally with the syrup, until tender but not mushy. Baste the pears again with the syrup and add the crushed Szechuan pepper. Serve the pears with the syrup poured over the top and any remaining syrup served separately.

Pineapple, Chilli and **Lemongrass Tarte Tatin**

One of the sweetest fruits – and a particular favourite of mine – is the pineapple. This exotic fruit tastes wonderful cooked in a tarte tatin in place of the traditional apples and, of course, it needs less added sugar. The confident aroma and lusciousness of the pineapple pairs remarkably well with stronger spices and flavourings, and in this recipe I have contrasted it with fragrant lemongrass and a hint of chilli. You may be surprised by how successfully these two spices marry with the fruit – and with the buttery flavour of the pastry – to make a truly superb dessert. If you like, you can serve it with a scoop of coconut ice cream or sorbet.

SERVES 4
PREPARATION TIME 20 minutes, plus 30 minutes chilling and at least 5 minutes resting
COOKING TIME 1 hour

220g/7¾oz ready-made puff pastry, defrosted if frozen
plain flour, for dusting
80g/2¾oz/⅓ cup caster sugar
1.2kg/2lb 10oz pineapple, peeled, cored and cut into large wedges
40g/1½oz unsalted butter
1 red chilli, deseeded and finely chopped, plus ½ red chilli in strips, to serve (optional)
½ lemongrass stalk, bruised and halved lengthways

1 Roll out the pastry on a lightly floured work surface, then cut out a circle slightly larger than a 20cm/8in tatin pan or flameproof baking dish. Roll the pastry over the rolling pin and transfer to a baking sheet, cover with cling film and chill in the fridge for 30 minutes to prevent the pastry shrinking during baking.

2 Preheat the oven to 190°C/375°F/gas 5. Melt the sugar gently in the tatin pan over a medium heat until golden brown. Add the pineapple and cook for 6–8 minutes, or until lightly golden. Remove the pan from the heat. Using a slotted spoon, transfer the pineapple to a plate and leave to rest for 5–8 minutes to release the juice.

3 Stir the butter into the sugar in the pan. Sprinkle one-third of the chopped chilli over the pan. Put the pineapple wedges tightly around the edge of the pan in a circle, then make smaller circles of tightly fitting pineapple within this circle until the base is covered and all the pineapple is used. Put the lemongrass on top of the pineapple, add the strips of chilli, if you like, and bake for 30 minutes.

4 Remove from the oven and sprinkle another one-third of the chilli over the pineapple. Put the pastry on top, pushing the edges into the pan. Return the pan to the oven and bake for a further 20 minutes, or until the pastry is golden brown and crisp.

5 Remove the tart from the oven and leave to cool for a few minutes. Put an upside-down plate, slightly larger than the pan, on top of the tart and, holding both the plate and pan, turn the pan over to transfer the tart to the plate. Sprinkle with the remaining chilli, if you like. Serve warm, removing the lemongrass and chilli strips before cutting into portions.

Pineapple Beignets with **Mango Carpaccio**

In my view, pineapple is made for a *beignet* or fritter, as its fresh, slightly sharp taste has just the right amount of acidity to cut through the rich batter coating. The thin slices of sweet mango go well with the acidity of the pineapple, too, while the piquancy of the pink peppercorns add that unusual finishing touch.

SERVES 4

PREPARATION TIME 20 minutes, plus 20 minutes cooling

COOKING 25 minutes

FOR THE MANGO CARPACCIO

1 large semi-ripe mango, peeled, pitted and thinly sliced

50g/1¾oz/scant ¼ cup caster sugar

2 pinches of dried pink peppercorns

FOR THE PINEAPPLE BEIGNETS

1 small pineapple, peeled, cored, quartered lengthways and cut into small chunks about 1.5cm/⅔in thick

125g/4½oz/1 cup plain flour

2 eggs, separated

a pinch of salt

125ml/4fl oz/½ cup beer, preferably bitter, or good dry cider

2 tbsp sunflower oil, plus extra for deep-frying

2 tbsp caster sugar, plus extra for dusting

1 To make the carpaccio, put the mango in a deep-sided roasting tin. Put the sugar and 150ml/5fl oz/scant ⅔ cup of water into a small saucepan and bring to the boil over a medium heat, swirling the pan occasionally, until the sugar dissolves. Pour it over the mango and scatter with the peppercorns. Cover with cling film and leave to infuse and cool.

2 Strain the mango over the small pan. Put the mango on serving plates and leave to one side. Return the peppercorns to the pan with the syrup and bring to the boil, then boil for 5 minutes until the syrup is thick enough to coat the back of a spoon. Remove from the heat and leave to cool once more.

3 To make the *beignets*, line a baking tray with a clean tea towel and spread the pineapple out on the tray in a single layer. Cover with another tea towel and press down firmly to remove any liquid. Leave to dry, covered, while you prepare the batter. Mix together the flour, egg yolks, salt, beer and oil to make a thick, smooth paste. Whisk together the egg whites and sugar in a separate bowl, using an electric whisk, until soft peaks form. Gently fold them into the beer batter.

4 Meanwhile, pour enough oil to deep-fry the *beignets* into a deep-fat fryer or a deep, wide saucepan and heat to 170°C/325°F, or until a cube of bread browns in 40 seconds.

5 Thread a piece of pineapple onto a long skewer and dip briefly into the batter until completely coated. Using a fork, carefully push the pineapple off the skewer into the hot oil. Repeat with the rest of the pineapple, frying about 6 pieces at a time. When the *beignets* start to float to the surface, carefully turn them over and continue to fry for about 4–5 minutes until golden and crisp. Remove with a slotted spoon, drain on kitchen paper, then dust immediately with sugar. Put the *beignets* on top of the mango carpaccio, then spoon over a little of the cooled syrup to serve.

Warm Chocolate Cookies with Coconut Ice Cream

When you are cooking with chocolate, the choice of chocolate is very important. Here I have chosen chocolate with 60% pure cocoa – not over-bitter, as a lot of people don't like that, but instead one that is a touch richer, with hint of tobacco leaf, bark and spices coming through to give a thoroughly modern twist. The warm cookies have a soft, cake-like texture.

SERVES 4
PREPARATION TIME 25 minutes,
 plus at least 3 hours freezing
COOKING TIME 15 minutes

FOR THE COCONUT ICE CREAM
3 egg yolks
115ml/3¾fl oz/scant ½ cup coconut
 milk
4 tbsp toasted desiccated coconut
200ml/7fl oz/scant 1 cup double
 cream

FOR THE CHOCOLATE COOKIES
100g/3½oz unsalted butter, plus
 extra for greasing
150g/5½oz dark chocolate, 60%
 cocoa solids, broken into pieces
2 eggs, separated
55g/2oz/¼ cup caster sugar
75g/2½oz/scant ⅔ cup plain flour
a pinch of salt

1 To make the ice cream, first make a sabayon. Whisk together the egg yolks and coconut milk in a heatproof bowl set over a saucepan of gently simmering water, making sure the bottom of the bowl does not touch the water. Whisk for 5–8 minutes until thickened. Remove from the heat, add the desiccated coconut and whisk continuously until the mixture cools completely.

2 Whip the cream, using an electric whisk, until soft peaks form, then fold it into the sabayon. Pour into a 500ml/17fl oz/2 cup freezerproof container. Cover with cling film and put in the freezer for at least 3 hours until firm.

3 To make the cookies, preheat the oven to 220°C/425°F/gas 7. Lightly grease two 12-hole mini tart tins. Melt the chocolate and butter in a small saucepan over a low heat, stirring occasionally.

4 Meanwhile whisk together the egg yolks and sugar in a large mixing bowl, using an electric whisk, for about 5 minutes until pale, thick and doubled in volume.

5 As soon as the chocolate has melted, fold in the flour with a wooden spoon or spatula until combined. You must be very careful when doing this and work quite quickly. Pour the chocolate mixture slowly into the egg mixture and fold together.

6 Whisk the egg whites with the salt in a large clean bowl until soft peaks form, then fold them into the chocolate mixture. Spoon the cake mixture into the prepared tart tins, half-filling each hole, to make 12–18 cookies. Bake for 5–6 minutes until risen and slightly firm to the touch. Remove from the oven and turn out onto a wire rack to cool until just lukewarm, then serve with the coconut ice cream.

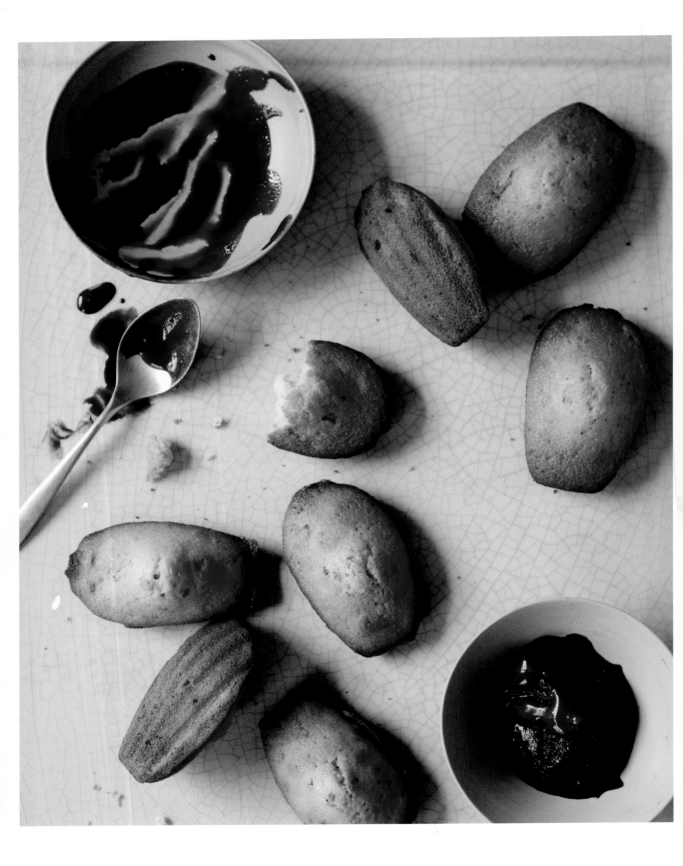

Pistachio Madeleines with Chocolate Sorbet

This makes for a perfect combination, but you may also like to serve the madeleines with a simple vanilla ice cream or even a dessert pear. They go well with the strawberries (see page 79) too instead of the lime shortbread. So many flavours seem to be made for madeleines – vanilla, cinnamon, star anise, hazelnut, orange, honey – but, for me, the one thing you certainly can't beat is when they are served warm straight out of the oven.

SERVES 4
PREPARATION TIME 30 minutes, plus overnight resting and making the *beurre noisette*
COOKING TIME 15 minutes

FOR THE CHOCOLATE SORBET
125g/4½oz/heaped ½ cup caster sugar
50g/1¾oz/scant ½ cup good-quality dark cocoa powder
125g/4½oz dark chocolate, 60% cocoa solids, broken into small pieces

FOR THE PISTACHIO MADELEINES
unsalted butter, for greasing
140g/5oz/heaped 1 cup plain flour
¾ tsp baking powder
2 eggs
90g/3¼oz/heaped ⅓ cup caster sugar
3 tbsp milk
25g/1oz light clear honey
145ml/4¾fl oz/scant ⅔ cup warm Beurre Noisette (see page 22)
25g/1oz/scant ¼ cup pistachio nuts, toasted and chopped

1 First, prepare the madeleines. Lightly grease a 12-hole madeleine tray. Sift the flour and baking powder into a mixing bowl and leave to one side. Whisk together the eggs and sugar in a large mixing bowl, using an electric whisk, for about 10 minutes until the mixture is pale, thick and doubled in volume.

2 Heat the milk and honey together in a small saucepan until just melted. Fold the flour mixture into the egg mixture, then pour in the milk and honey, stirring until combined. Add the warm *beurre noisette* and mix slowly until fully incorporated, then fold in the pistachios. Spoon the mixture into the prepared madeleine tray, half-filling each hole. Cover with cling film and leave to rest in the fridge overnight.

3 To make the sorbet, pour 300ml/10½fl oz/scant 1¼ cups of water into a small saucepan. Mix together the sugar and cocoa powder, then add to the water and bring to the boil, whisking continuously. It's very important not to let the cocoa powder sink to the bottom of the pan and burn.

4 Put the chocolate pieces in a heatproof bowl. When the cocoa mixture has reached a boil, pour the hot liquid onto the chocolate pieces and whisk until the chocolate has melted. Pass the mixture through a fine sieve into a 500ml/17fl oz/2 cup freezerproof container and freeze until hard.

5 When the sorbet is hard, cut the mixture into pieces and blitz in a food processor until smooth. Return to the freezer container and freeze for at least 3 hours until firm.

6 The next day, preheat the oven to 200°C/400°F/gas 6. Bake the madeleines for 5 minutes, then turn the tray around in the oven, front to back, even if you have a fan oven, and cook for a further 5 minutes until light golden and slightly firm to the touch. Insert a skewer into a madeleine and if it comes out clean, they are ready. If not, bake for a further 2 minutes and check again. Remove from the oven and leave to cool for 5 minutes until lukewarm before turning out and serving with the chocolate sorbet.

Orange and Tarragon Gâteau with **Candied Orange**

We rarely consider herbs in a dessert, and particularly in baking, but the mix of tarragon and orange works so well. I'd had an idea of using these together for a while but hadn't quite got the correct balance. So my chef and I tried and tried and finally got it right in this gâteau. It's all in the quantity – you can't be heavy-handed with the tarragon – but the end result is fantastic.

SERVES 4–6
PREPARATION TIME 30 minutes, plus 30 minutes cooling
COOKING TIME 30 minutes

50g/1¾oz unsalted butter, melted
90g/3¼oz/scant 1 cup ground almonds
40g/1½oz/⅓ cup plain flour
½ tsp baking powder
4 egg whites, about 100ml/3½fl oz/ scant ½ cup
40g/1½oz/scant ¼ cup caster sugar
finely grated zest and juice of 1 small orange
2 tbsp roughly chopped tarragon leaves, plus leaves from 1 tarragon sprig, to decorate

FOR THE CANDIED ORANGE
100g/3½oz/scant ½ cup caster sugar
1 large unwaxed orange, cut crossways into 5mm/¼in thick slices, discarding the end slices

1 Preheat the oven to 160°C/315°F/gas 2½. Lightly grease a loose-based 18cm/7in cake tin with about 1 tablespoon of the melted butter and line the base with baking paper. Sift the ground almonds, flour and baking powder into a bowl and leave to one side.

2 Whisk together the egg whites and sugar in a large bowl, using an electric whisk, until soft peaks form. Mix together the orange juice and remaining melted butter, then gently fold into the whisked egg whites. Gradually fold in the almond mixture, orange zest and chopped tarragon, a spoonful at a time, until incorporated.

3 Pour the mixture into the prepared cake tin and level the top, then bake for 18–20 minutes until risen and golden. Check the cake is cooked by inserting a skewer into the deepest part. If it comes out clean, then it is ready. If not, bake for a further 2–3 minutes and check again. Remove from the oven and leave to cool for 5 minutes before turning out onto a wire rack, bottom-side up, removing the paper and leaving to cool.

4 Meanwhile, make the candied orange. Line a baking tray with baking paper. Pour 150ml/5fl oz/scant ⅔ cup of water into a saucepan and stir in the sugar. Heat over a high heat until the sugar dissolves and the liquid becomes slightly syrupy. At the same time, put the orange slices in a small saucepan and just cover with water. Bring to the boil over a high heat, then discard the water. Repeat this again with fresh water. Drain the oranges again, add them to the pan containing the syrup and bring to a simmer. Cook for a further 5 minutes until the orange slices are tender but still hold their shape. Lift the orange slices out of the syrup and leave to cool on the prepared baking tray.

5 Return the syrup to a low heat and simmer for 8–10 minutes until thick enough to coat the back of a spoon. Leave to cool. When the oranges have cooled, cut each slice in half into a half-moon shape. Lay the orange slices, slightly overlapping, around the edge of the cake. Brush the warm syrup over the top of the oranges, then sprinkle the remaining tarragon over the top.

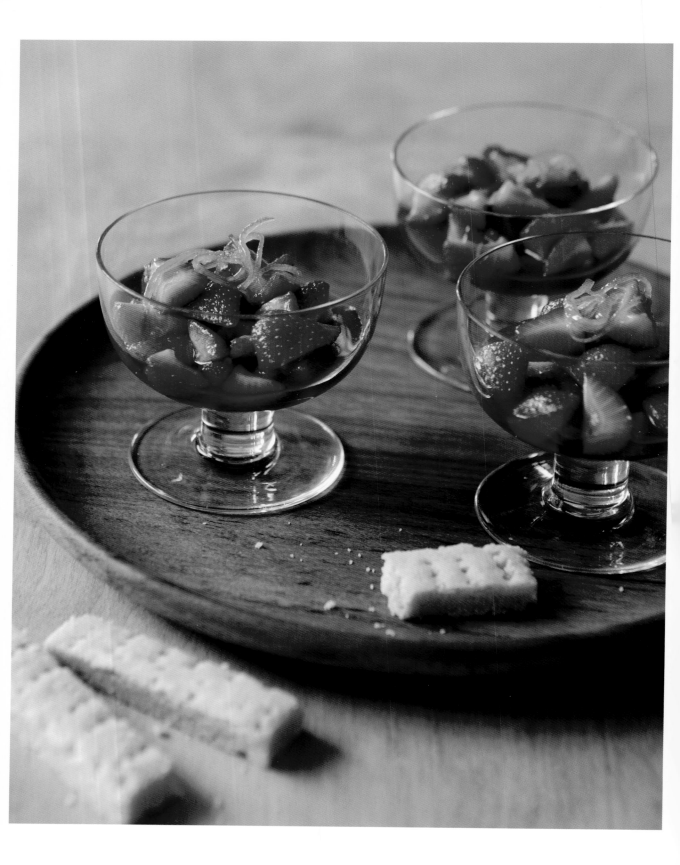

Orange-Blossom Strawberries with Lime Shortbread

When I was younger, we used to grow strawberries, and our favourite dessert was freshly picked ripe strawberries folded into whipping cream, just a touch, sprinkled with caster sugar and chilled for an hour or so. We would then crush them with a fork before eating them. When I go home in the summer, I still love to eat them like this. Another family favourite is this stylish strawberry dessert, which I often call Strawberry Soup, although it isn't really a soup. I just call it that because the strawberries are served with lots of wonderful fresh fruit juice, scented with orange blossom. You could use the orange zest to make candied orange (see page 77) and sprinkle it over the top of the soup before serving.

SERVES 4
PREPARATION TIME 25 minutes, plus 20 minutes macerating
COOKING TIME 20 minutes

500g/1lb 2oz/3⅓ cups strawberries, hulled and quartered
4 tsp sherry vinegar
100g/3½oz/scant ½ cup caster sugar
juice of 2 oranges
4 tsp orange blossom extract

FOR THE LIME SHORTBREAD
finely grated zest of 1 lime
175g/6oz unsalted butter, softened
75g/2½oz/scant ⅓ cup caster sugar, plus extra for sprinkling
200g/7oz/scant 1⅔ cups plain flour

1 Preheat the oven to 160°C/315°F/gas 2½. To make the lime shortbread, beat together the lime zest, butter and sugar in a large bowl, using an electric mixer, until light and fluffy, then fold in the flour to make a soft dough. Press out between two sheets of baking paper until about 1cm/½in thick. Transfer to a baking sheet and lift off the top sheet of paper. Mark a pattern on the top with a fork, if you like. Bake for 12–18 minutes until just light golden and slightly firm to the touch.

2 Cut the shortbread straight away into whatever shape you fancy and sprinkle with sugar. You must cut the shortbread as soon as it comes out of the oven, while still soft and pliable. Put the baking sheet on a wire rack and leave the shortbread to cool and crisp up.

3 While the shortbread is baking, put the strawberries into a bowl and add the sherry vinegar. Reserve 2 tablespoons of the sugar, then sprinkle the remainder over the strawberries. Toss them together, cover with cling film and put in the fridge to macerate for 15–20 minutes only.

4 Pour the orange juice into a bowl and add the orange blossom extract. Take the strawberries out of the fridge and turn them in the macerating liquid. Using a slotted spoon, divide the strawberries into four large *coupé* glasses, leaving the residual juice in the bowl. Add the orange juice to the strawberry juice, mix well, then spoon over the strawberries and serve with the lime shortbread.

Blood Orange and Star Anise Tart

SERVES 4–6
PREPARATION TIME 30 minutes, plus
  1 hour infusing and at least
  2 hours 50 minutes chilling
COOKING TIME 20 minutes

FOR THE SWEET ORANGE PASTRY
90g/3¼oz unsalted butter, softened,
  plus extra for greasing
finely grated zest of ½ blood orange
a pinch of salt
60g/2¼oz/½ cup icing sugar
25g/1oz/¼ cup ground almonds
1 egg
175g/6oz/heaped 1⅓ cups plain
  flour, sifted

FOR THE ORANGE AND STAR ANISE FILLING
1½ leaves of gelatine, about
  3g/¹⁄₁₆oz total weight
juice of 4 unwaxed blood oranges
2 star anise
3 eggs
90g/3¼oz/heaped ⅓ cup caster
  sugar
75g/2½oz unsalted butter, softened

FOR THE CANDIED ORANGE ZEST
finely pared zest of 3 unwaxed blood
  oranges
2 tbsp caster sugar

1 To make the pastry, lightly grease an 18 x 4cm/7 x 1½in deep loose-bottomed tart tin. Whisk together the butter, orange zest, salt, icing sugar, ground almonds and egg in a large bowl, using an electric whisk, until light and fluffy. Fold in the flour to form a dough. (Try not to overwork the pastry. It is ready as soon as it comes together.) Wrap it in cling film and chill for 20 minutes.

2 Roll out the pastry between two sheets of baking paper until 3mm/⅛in thick and use to line the base and the sides of the prepared tart tin, pressing it into the edges without overstretching the dough. Trim off any excess pastry, prick the base with a fork and chill for 30 minutes to prevent the pastry shrinking during baking.

3 Preheat the oven to 180°C/350°F/gas 4. Line the pastry with baking paper and baking beans. Bake for 6 minutes, then turn the oven down to 160°C/315°F/gas 2½. Remove the beans and baking paper, then return the pastry to the oven and bake for a further 3–4 minutes until cooked through and light golden brown. Leave to cool on a wire rack.

4 To make the filling, soak the gelatine leaves in a bowl of cold water for about 5 minutes until softened, then squeeze out the water. Pour the orange juice into a saucepan and bring to the boil over a high heat. Remove from the heat and whisk in the softened gelatine, then add the star anise. Cover with cling film and leave to infuse for 1 hour in a warm place. You don't want the gelatine to set.

5 After 50 minutes, whisk the eggs with the caster sugar, using an electric whisk, for 3–4 minutes until pale and thickened. Beat in the butter, a little at a time, then remove the star anise and whisk in the orange juice mixture. (Blitz in a blender if you prefer a smooth filling.) Pour into the cooked pastry case and chill for at least 2 hours to set.

6 Meanwhile, make the candied orange zest. Line a baking tray with baking paper. Put the orange zest in a small saucepan, cover with cold water and bring to the boil over a medium heat, then remove from the heat, drain and refresh the zest in cold water. Drain again and repeat the entire process once more. Return the zest to the pan and add the caster sugar and 3 tablespoons of water, then bring to the boil, stirring until the sugar dissolves. Boil for 4–5 minutes until the zest becomes transparent, then remove from the heat and leave the zest to cool. Strain the zest, discarding the syrup, then spread it out on the prepared baking tray. Remove the tart from the tart tin and decorate with the candied zest.

Lemon and Chilli Cake with Chilli Glaze

I'm not a pastry chef but when I have the time, I love to work with my head pastry chef, Anthony, in the restaurant. We have tried all sorts of desserts but I wanted to do a cake with chilli, lemon, flecks of fresh chilli and a chilli glaze that I just knew would work. So, here it is... lemon is a classic flavouring for cake but the chilli is the icing on the cake, so to speak! Make sure that you soak the cake while it's still warm so it absorbs the syrup. It makes a fabulous dessert, but you can also enjoy a slice with a cup of tea.

SERVES 6–8
PREPARATION TIME 25 minutes, plus 5 minutes infusing and 30 minutes cooling
COOKING TIME 40 minutes

110g/3¾oz/scant 1 cup plain or superfine cake flour
½ tsp baking powder
finely grated zest and juice of 2 small lemons
200g/7oz/heaped ¾ cup caster sugar
4 eggs
60g/2¼oz/¼ cup crème fraîche
3 red chillies, deseeded and finely chopped

1 Preheat the oven to 160°C/315°F/gas 2½. Line the base and sides of a 1kg/2lb 4oz loaf tin, preferably non-stick, with baking paper. Sift together the flour and baking powder into a bowl.

2 Whisk together half the lemon juice, 125g/4½oz/heaped ½ cup of the sugar and the eggs in a large bowl, using an electric whisk, for about 10 minutes until pale, thick and doubled in volume. Whisk in the crème fraîche, then gently fold in the sifted flour mixture. Fold in 2½ of the chillies and all the lemon zest until combined.

3 Pour into the prepared loaf tin, smooth the top and bake for 15 minutes, then open the oven door. Carefully pull the shelf out slightly with the loaf tin on it and mark the cake with a knife lengthways down the centre. (This will help the cake open up and give it a light texture.) Slide it back into the oven and bake for a further 20 minutes.

4 While the cake finishes baking, make the syrup. Put the remaining lemon juice, 2 tablespoons of the sugar and 2 tablespoons of water in a saucepan and heat over a high heat for 2 minutes until the sugar dissolves and the liquid turns slightly syrupy. There should be about 3–4 tablespoons of liquid. Remove from the heat and leave to one side.

5 Check to see if the cake is cooked by inserting a skewer into the deepest part and if it comes out clean, then it is ready. If not, return the cake to the oven, bake for a further 5 minutes and check again. Leave the cake to cool for 5 minutes, then turn out onto a wire rack placed over a baking tray. Peel away the baking paper and put the cake top-side up. Immediately spoon the lemon syrup evenly over the top of the cake, then leave on the rack to cool completely.

6 Put the remaining sugar in a saucepan with 3½ tablespoons of water and heat over a medium heat for 5 minutes, or until it forms a thick, shiny syrup. Remove from the heat and add the remaining chilli, then leave to infuse for 5 minutes. When the cake is completely cool, brush the top with the chilli syrup to give a nice, shiny coating.

EGALITÉ

Democratic recipes that elevate humble ingredients to starring roles

'*Egalité*' is a lovely word, and it would be great to drift away into all sorts of discussions and explanations – but that's not for now. In this chapter, I will be talking about ingredients that were originally perceived as peasant fodder, but are now being rediscovered and enjoying new recognition. I'm sure you know what I mean by that – ingredients like rabbit, mushrooms, potatoes and simple herbs.

Underpin that with beautifully complementary ingredients. I've tried to create recipes in which the relationship between two, or sometimes more, ingredients, when combined with one another, make a perfectly balanced pairing – they are just great for each other. So you see, in that brief description, what we have captured in *égalité*.

So let me give you an example of some of the ingredients I have used in these recipes. There's a beautiful Rabbit Terrine with Onion Marmalade (see page 86), a lovely Pomme Farcie with Braised Pork Shoulder (see page 117), Plaice with Celeriac and Pancetta Galette (see page 130) and Lamb Sweetbread and Wild Mushroom Vol-au-Vent (see page 123). *Egalité* of both humble and sophisticated ingredients!

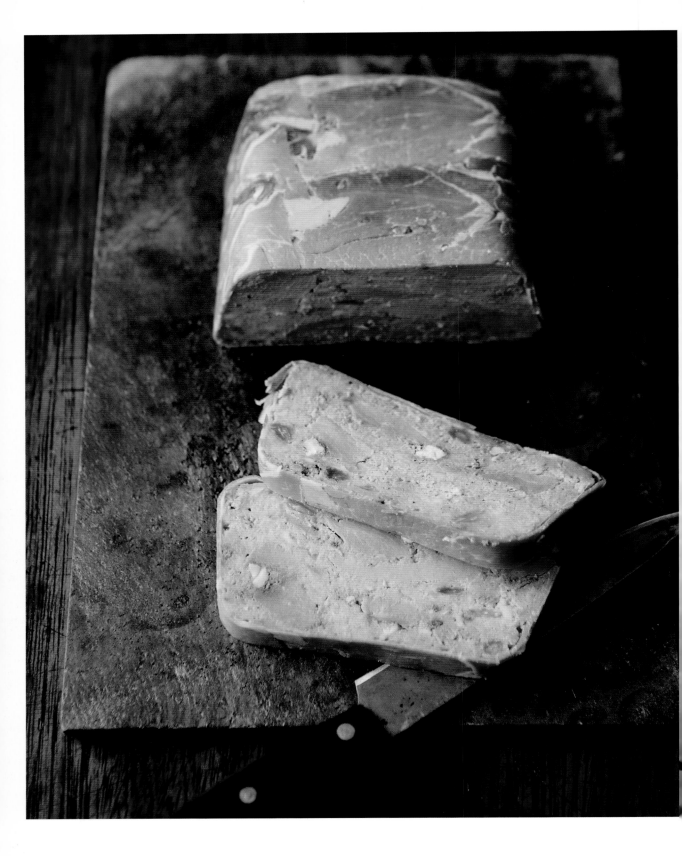

Game, Chestnut and **Sultana** Terrine

Game birds, such as pheasant and partridge, are a seasonal favourite of mine, and much under-used. I've combined these two in this terrine and, to add to the autumn theme, I've added chestnuts, with their lovely earthiness, as well as sultanas for a touch of sweetness. You can buy ready-cooked and peeled chestnuts in the supermarket, which are wonderfully easy to use. I find that Muscatel sultanas give the best flavour. Make sure you follow the timings as you don't want a dry terrine, which can easily happen if bird game is overcooked.

SERVES 6–8
PREPARATION TIME 45 minutes, plus
    3–4 hours marinating, cooling and
    2 days chilling
COOKING TIME 1 hour

35g/1¼oz/heaped ¼ cup sultanas,
    such as Muscatel
3 tbsp Madeira
2 pheasant breasts and legs, about
    200g/7oz total weight, skinned,
    boned and cut into large dice
4 partridge breasts and legs, about
    200g/7oz total weight, skinned,
    boned and cut into large dice
300g/10½oz pork fat from the belly,
    minced
80ml/2½fl oz/⅓ cup Manzanilla or
    other dry sherry
¾ tsp sea salt
½ tsp freshly ground black pepper
12 slices of smoked streaky bacon
2 eggs
100ml/3½fl oz/scant ½ cup double
    cream
½ tsp dried tarragon
35g/1¼oz cooked whole chestnuts,
    roughly chopped
chargrilled warm toast and mixed
    leaf salad, to serve

1 Put the sultanas in a bowl with the Madeira and leave to soak while you prepare the pheasant and partridges. Put the pheasant and partridge leg meat into a food processor and pulse to a coarse mince. Put the mince in a bowl with the diced pheasant and partridge breasts and minced pork fat, and mix well. Add the soaked sultanas and any Madeira left in the bowl, the sherry, salt and pepper and mix once more. Cover and leave to marinate in the fridge for 3–4 hours.

2 Preheat the oven to 140°C/275°F/gas 1. Line the base and sides of a 24 x 10cm/9½ x 4in and 8cm/3¼in deep terrine dish (preferably cast iron) with a double layer of cling film. Line with the bacon, allowing both ends to overhang the sides. Leave to one side.

3 Whisk together the eggs, cream and tarragon until combined. Using a spatula, gradually mix them into the meat, then stir in the chestnuts. Spoon the mixture into the prepared terrine and press down with the back of a spoon until even. Fold the overhanging bacon over the top to cover, then fold over the cling film and cover with the terrine lid.

4 Put the terrine in a deep roasting dish and pour in enough just-boiled water to come two-thirds of the way up the sides of the terrine. Bake for 1 hour, then check to see if it is cooked by inserting a thermometer into the centre. It should read about 68°C/154°F. If the terrine is not ready, carefully return it to the oven for a further 15 minutes. Alternatively, you can insert a knife into the terrine and it should come out hot and dry if the terrine is ready.

5 Remove the terrine from the roasting dish, take off the lid and top with a piece of baking paper and a heavy weight, about 1–2kg/2lb 4oz–4lb 8oz. Leave to cool completely at room temperature. Once cold, cover and leave in the fridge for a couple of days before serving to allow the flavours to develop. Serve in thick slices with chargrilled toast and a mixed leaf salad.

Rabbit Terrine with Onion Marmalade

SERVES 12–14
PREPARATION TIME 35 minutes, plus
   at least 10 hours chilling
COOKING TIME 10 hours overnight
   cooking, plus 2 hours

16 small rabbit legs, about 3kg/
   6lb 8oz total weight
2 tbsp olive oil, plus extra for
   brushing
4 thyme sprigs
12 silverskin baby onions, peeled
   and cut in half
8 spring onions
6 rabbit fillets, about 300g/10½oz
   total weight
1 tsp roughly chopped flat-leaf
   parsley leaves
sea salt and freshly ground black
   pepper

FOR THE ONION MARMALADE
2 tbsp olive oil
1kg/2lb 4oz large white onions,
   cut in half and thinly sliced
175g/6oz/heaped ¾ cup caster
   sugar
200ml/7fl oz/scant 1 cup cider
   vinegar
500ml/17fl oz/2 cups dry white wine
2 tbsp white balsamic vinegar
1 thyme sprig

1 Preheat the oven to 70°C/150°F/gas ¼. Put the rabbit legs on a baking tray, season with salt and pepper, drizzle with the oil, then scatter over the thyme and cover with baking paper. Cook in the oven overnight, or for at least 10 hours. The next day, remove the baking tray from the oven and leave to one side.

2 Turn the oven up to 160°C/315°F/gas 2½. Put the baby onions and spring onions on a baking tray, brush with oil and roast for 20 minutes. Remove the spring onions and leave to one side, then roast the baby onions for a further 25 minutes. Remove from the oven and leave to one side, then turn the oven down to 70°C/150°F/gas ¼.

3 Put the rabbit fillets on a baking tray, season with salt and bake for 12 minutes so they remain soft, then leave to one side. Take the leg meat off the bone and put in a large bowl. Strain the cooking juices through a fine sieve into a saucepan. Bring to the boil, then turn the heat down to medium and simmer for 10 minutes until reduced by two-thirds. Shred the leg meat using two forks, then stir in the parsley and reduced liquid.

4 To assemble the terrine, cover the base and sides of a 24 ×10cm/ 9½ × 4in and 8cm/3¼in deep terrine dish with cling film, letting it hang over the sides. Cover the base with some of the rabbit leg mixture, then lay the baby onions along the centre of the terrine at regular intervals. Cover with more of the rabbit leg mixture, then lay half of the fillets side by side along the centre. Put half the spring onions on either side of the fillets and cover with more rabbit leg mixture. Repeat with the remaining fillets and spring onions, then cover with the remaining rabbit leg mixture. Fold the cling film over the terrine to cover it completely, then put a 1–2kg/2lb 4oz–4lb 8oz weight, such as a bag of sugar, on top. Leave in the fridge to chill for at least 10 hours, or overnight.

5 To make the onion marmalade, put the oil in a saucepan over a medium-low heat, add the onions and cook gently for 15 minutes until softened but not coloured. Meanwhile, dissolve the sugar in the cider vinegar in a bowl. Add the vinegar solution to the pan with the wine, balsamic vinegar and thyme. Bring to the boil over a medium-high heat, then turn the heat down to medium and cook for a further 15 minutes, stirring occasionally, then turn the heat down to low and cook for about 10 minutes until the liquid becomes thick and syrupy. Leave to cool completely, discard the thyme, then pour into a sterilized jar and seal. Serve the terrine with the onion marmalade. The marmalade can be stored in the fridge for up to 2 months.

Lentil and Bacon Soup with Mushrooms and Thyme Cream

Where I'm from in the Haute-Saône region of France we use lentils a lot, particularly the slate-green-coloured Puy lentils. The first record of the famous *lentilles vert du Puy* dates back to 1643, and the Puy lentil was awarded Protected Designation of Origin status (PDO) in 2009. Known as the 'caviar of the poor', the earthy flavour of these lentils blends beautifully with the pancetta, mushrooms and thyme.

SERVES 4
PREPARATION TIME 25 minutes, plus making the stock
COOKING TIME 30 minutes

1 tbsp olive oil
100g/3½oz thick pancetta or streaky bacon, cut into small lardons
1 shallot, finely sliced
1 carrot, peeled and diced
1 bouquet garni, made with 1 thyme sprig and 1 parsley sprig, tied together with kitchen string
200g/7oz/1 cup Puy lentils, picked over and rinsed
1.2l/40fl oz/4¾ cups Vegetable Stock (see page 17)
150ml/5fl oz scant ⅔ cup whipping cream
leaves from 2 thyme sprigs
40g/1½oz unsalted butter
100g/3½oz Paris, chestnut or button mushrooms, thickly sliced
sea salt and freshly ground black pepper
crusty bread, to serve

1 Heat a saucepan over a medium heat. Add the oil and pancetta and fry for 3–4 minutes, stirring occasionally, until golden brown. Add the shallot and carrot and cook for 2–3 minutes until slightly softened, then add the lentils, bouquet garni and stock. Bring to the boil over a medium-high heat, then turn the heat down to low and simmer for 8 minutes. Pour in 100ml/3½fl oz/scant ½ cup of the cream, return to a simmer and cook for a further 7–8 minutes until the lentils are tender. Discard the bouquet garni.

2 Ladle the soup into a blender and blitz until smooth and creamy. Return the soup to a saucepan and add a little water or more stock to the pan if the soup is very thick. Season to taste with salt and pepper, cover with a lid and keep warm.

3 Whip the remaining cream until soft peaks form, then fold in two-thirds of the thyme and season with a touch of pepper.

4 Heat a frying pan over a high heat. Add the butter and when foaming, add the mushrooms and sauté for 3–4 minutes until golden brown. Season with salt and pepper to taste, then add the remaining thyme. Divide the mushrooms into four shallow soup bowls, piling them in the middle and put a spoonful of the thyme cream on top. Finally ladle the soup around the mushrooms and cream and serve with crusty bread.

Snail, Fennel and Almond Casserole in **Red Wine Sauce**

You will recall the classic dish of snails with garlic butter which, when made the right way, is delicious. Well, this recipe is different but no less tasty. It's a bit like a bourguignon but with snails, toasted almonds and fennel. You will have to buy some good-quality pre-cooked snails, and just make sure you rinse them properly before use. It's delicious served with Swede Boulangère (see page 20) or sautéed potatoes with pancetta.

SERVES 4
PREPARATION TIME 15 minutes,
  plus making the stock
COOKING TIME 35 minutes

500g/1lb 2oz tinned snails,
  shells discarded
25g/1oz unsalted butter
1 tbsp olive oil
1 shallot, finely chopped
2 tbsp good-quality dry sherry
  vinegar
5 tbsp good-quality Burgundy red
  wine
500ml/17fl oz/2 cups good-quality
  Beef Stock (see page 16)
2 fennel bulbs, outer leaves
  discarded and fronds reserved,
  finely sliced using a mandolin, if
  possible
1 handful of flaked almonds, toasted
sea salt and freshly ground black
  pepper
crusty bread, to serve

1 Rinse the snails in warm water, then tip onto kitchen paper, pat dry and leave to one side.

2 Heat the butter and half the oil in a non-stick frying pan over a low heat. Add the shallot and fry gently for 2 minutes until softened. Pour in the sherry vinegar, turn the heat up to high and deglaze the pan by stirring to remove any caramelized bits stuck to the bottom, then cook until the liquid has almost evaporated. Add the red wine and cook for a further 3–4 minutes until reduced by half. Add the stock and simmer for 10–15 minutes until reduced by two-thirds and the sauce becomes glossy and almost syrupy. Season with salt and pepper to taste. Cover, leave to one side and keep warm. Preheat the oven to 200°C/400°F/gas 6.

3 Meanwhile, bring a saucepan of salted water to the boil, add the sliced fennel and blanch for 2–3 minutes until softened slightly. Drain and refresh in iced water, then drain again and pat dry with kitchen paper.

4 Heat the remaining oil in a large, non-stick frying pan over a medium heat. Add the fennel and fry for 2–3 minutes, stirring, until just golden. Add the snails and the reserved fennel fronds and cook for 2–3 minutes until just heated through – you don't want to overcook the snails. Add the toasted flaked almonds and toss to combine. Finally, season with salt and pepper to taste.

5 Divide the snails into four small ovenproof dishes or wide ramekins. Spoon the red wine sauce over the top of the snails until just coated. Put the dishes on a baking tray and cook in the oven for 4–5 minutes until heated through and just bubbling. Serve hot with crusty bread.

Pickled Mackerel with **Warm Potato** and **Radish Salad**

This colourful salad reminds me of the time I spent in Sweden as it is fairly typical of something you would eat for breakfast there. I was staying in the Grand Hotel in Lund and remember so well the breakfast table laden with smoked, marinated and pickled fish. It was amazing! My version features warm potatoes and fresh coriander with a yogurt French dressing. You could use some of the pickling liquid instead of the French dressing, if you like.

SERVES 4
PREPARATION TIME 20 minutes, plus 30 minutes cooling and 6 hours marinating
COOKING TIME 25 minutes

2 large pinches of coriander seeds
120ml/4fl oz/½ cup white balsamic vinegar
120ml/4fl oz/½ cup Chardonnay vinegar or white wine vinegar
4 tbsp light soft brown sugar
4 whole mackerel, about 250g/9oz each, heads removed, filleted and skin lightly scored
1 tbsp sea salt
1 small red onion, finely sliced
2 coriander sprigs, plus 2 tbsp chopped coriander leaves
1 garlic clove
300g/10½oz small new potatoes, such as Charlotte or Pink Fir Apple, scrubbed
3 tbsp French Dressing (see page 18)
2 tbsp Mayonnaise (see page 18)
1 tbsp Greek yogurt
finely grated zest and juice of 1 lime
8 large radishes, very thinly sliced
1 spring onion, thinly sliced diagonally
sea salt and freshly ground black pepper

1 Heat a frying pan over a medium heat. Add the coriander seeds and lightly toast for 1 minute, shaking the pan occasionally, until they colour slightly and smell aromatic. Tip them onto a plate and lightly crush with the blade of a knife. Leave to one side.

2 Pour both types of vinegar into a small saucepan. Add the sugar and put over a medium heat to warm for 2–3 minutes, or just long enough for the sugar to dissolve, stirring occasionally. Remove from the heat, stir in the toasted coriander seeds and leave to cool.

3 Put the mackerel in a shallow, non-metallic dish, skin-side down, and sprinkle with the sea salt. Pour over the cold vinegar mixture and top with three-quarters of the red onion. Cover with cling film and leave to marinate in the fridge for about 6 hours until pickled, turning the fish over after 3 hours.

4 Just before the mackerel is ready, put a saucepan of water, one-third full, on to simmer with a steamer insert on top. Put the remaining red onion, the coriander sprigs and garlic in the water. Put the potatoes in the steamer, cover and cook for 12–18 minutes until just tender. Turn the heat off and continue to steam the potatoes in the residual heat for a further 5 minutes.

5 While the potatoes are cooking, whisk together the French dressing, mayonnaise and Greek yogurt in a bowl, then stir in the lime juice and zest. Season with salt and pepper to taste. When the potatoes are cool enough to handle, cut into 5mm/¼in slices and put in a large serving bowl. Add the radishes and chopped coriander, then drizzle the dressing over and toss gently without breaking up the potato slices. Scatter with the spring onion. Lift the mackerel out of the pickling liquor and put on serving plates. Scatter some of the red onion over the top and serve with the potato salad.

Heirloom Beetroot 'Tagliatelle' and Carpaccio

Heirloom beetroot comes in fantastic colours – from ruby red to vibrant yellow – and its earthy, nutty flavour goes really well with the freshness of the chervil. Try not to overcook the beetroot though, as it will break when you cut it into thin slices. It should be soft but with a slight crunch. You could scatter some small crispy lardons over the top instead of the goats' cheese, if you like, and serve with some crusty bread.

SERVES 4
PREPARATION TIME 25 minutes
COOKING TIME 1½ hours

4 heaped tbsp sea salt, plus extra
  to season
4 beetroot, different colours if
  possible
100ml/3½fl oz/scant ½ cup
  beetroot juice
1 tbsp good-quality balsamic vinegar
2 tbsp extra virgin olive oil
a few chives, cut into 5cm/2in
  pieces
½ tbsp chervil leaves
1 handful of yellow frisée lettuce
1 handful of lamb's lettuce
100g/3½oz soft goats' cheese log,
  such as Ste Maure, rind removed,
  crumbled
freshly ground black pepper
crusty bread, to serve (optional)

1 Preheat the oven to 160°C/315°F/gas 2½. Take a 50 x 30cm/20 x 12in piece of foil and sprinkle the sea salt over the centre in a thick layer. Put the beetroot on top of the salt, then fold the foil over and scrunch the edges to make a parcel. Put the parcel on a baking tray and roast for 1½ hours until the beetroot is just tender when pierced with the tip of a knife. Remove from the oven and leave the beetroot, still wrapped in its foil parcel, until cool enough to handle. Open the parcel, discard the salt, then peel the beetroot and leave to one side until ready to use.

2 While the beetroot is cooking, make the dressing. Pour the beetroot juice into a small saucepan over a medium heat and bring to a simmer, then turn the heat down to low and cook for about 10 minutes until the juice has reduced by just over half to about 2 tablespoons. Whisk in the balsamic vinegar and season with salt and pepper to taste, then leave the mixture to cool.

3 Thinly slice 3 of the cooked beetroot, put on a serving plate and brush with the oil. Season with salt and pepper and scatter the chives and chervil over the top.

4 Using a mandolin or sharp knife, cut the remaining beetroot into very fine julienne strips to make 'tagliatelle', then spoon half the beetroot dressing over the strips. Spoon neat piles of beetroot 'tagliatelle' in the centre of the beetroot carpaccio. Toss the frisée and lamb's lettuce in a bowl, spoon the remaining dressing over and toss until the leaves are coated. Scatter the leaves over the top of the beetroot, sprinkle with the goats' cheese and serve with crusty bread, if you like.

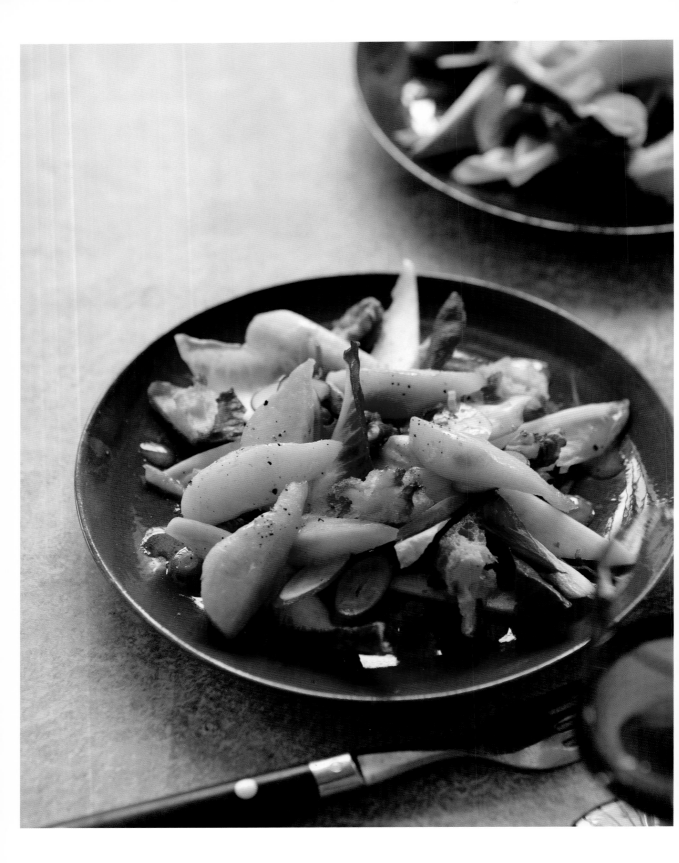

Radish, Chicory and **Marinated Pear Salad**

This is the perfect salad for autumn and the best season for buying pears. In France, there are lots of different varieties of pear, so there is a wide selection to choose from. I'm a fan of the Pascatan, but I guess it's best to choose your own favourite. Using two colours of chicory makes the salad particularly attractive, but you can just use yellow chicory if you like. You can serve the salad as a meal on its own, or it goes very well with a charcuterie board, or even a chicken liver terrine.

SERVES 4
PREPARATION TIME 15 minutes,
  plus 2 hours marinating
COOKING TIME 10 minutes

25g/1oz unsalted butter
2 large slightly under-ripe pears,
  peeled, cored and each cut into
  8 wedges
1 tbsp light soft brown sugar
4 tbsp white balsamic vinegar
1 shallot, halved lengthways and
  thinly sliced
2 tsp Dijon mustard
80ml/2½fl oz/⅓ cup light olive oil,
  plus 1 tbsp for the croûtons
50g/1¾oz stale sourdough bread,
  torn into bite-sized pieces
1 tbsp olive oil
12 small radishes, finely sliced
2 large yellow chicory, outer leaves
  discarded and leaves separated,
  cut into 3 diagonally
2 large red chicory, outer leaves
  discarded and leaves separated,
  quartered lengthways
4 spring onions, green part only,
  roughly chopped
50g/1¾oz/½ cup walnuts, toasted
  and lightly crushed

1 Melt the butter in a non-stick frying pan over a medium heat. Add the pears and cook for 3–4 minutes, turning once, until just tender and light golden. Sprinkle with the sugar, then turn the pears to coat them in the sugary butter. Transfer the pears to a dish, spoon over the balsamic vinegar and shallot and stir together. Cover and leave to marinate at room temperature for 2 hours.

2 Pour off the marinade from the pears and put 2 tablespoons in a small bowl, discarding the rest. Whisk the mustard into the marinade, then slowly add the light olive oil, whisking until it thickens and becomes glossy. Leave to one side.

3 Preheat the grill to high. Scatter the bread in the grill pan, then drizzle with the olive oil and mix until combined. Grill for 2–3 minutes, turning halfway, until golden and crisp. Tip the bread and any crumbs into a bowl, carefully wipe the pan clean and put the pears in the pan. Grill for about 1–2 minutes until just warmed through.

4 Toss the warm pears gently with the radishes, chicory and spring onions. Scatter the croûtons and walnuts over the top, drizzle with the dressing and serve while the pears are still warm.

Goats' Cheese and Dandelion Salad

This is definitely a salad to try as it's both interesting and very different. We used to eat a more traditional version at my aunt's house and she would send us into the garden to collect the dandelion leaves – called *pissenlit* in French! We would bring back loads and then prepare them with my uncle. His version of this salad included lardons but my vegetarian alternative features a crumbly goats' cheese and tangy orange to go with the bitterness of the dandelion leaves. It's a lovely summer dish to serve with a glass of Viognier.

SERVES 4
PREPARATION TIME 15 minutes, plus making the croûtons
COOKING TIME 3 minutes

1 tbsp blanched hazelnuts
4 handfuls of dandelion leaves, washed thoroughly
150g/5½oz soft goats' cheese log, such as Golden Cross or Ste Maure, rind removed, crumbled
1 small bunch of chives, cut into 5cm/2in lengths
1 tbsp chopped chervil leaves
2 small oranges
1 tbsp small Croûtons (see page 18)

FOR THE DRESSING
1 tbsp clear honey
2–3 tbsp Chardonnay vinegar or white wine vinegar
3 tbsp extra virgin olive oil
sea salt and freshly ground black pepper

1 To toast the hazelnuts, put them in a small, dry frying pan over a medium heat. Toast for 2–3 minutes, shaking the pan occasionally, until the nuts are lightly browned all over. Tip out onto a plate, leave to cool, then lightly crush.

2 Put the dandelion leaves on four large plates. Scatter the goats' cheese over the top, then the chives and chervil.

3 Peel the oranges, removing all the pith. Cut into segments, then cut each segment into 3 pieces, reserving the juice. Scatter the pieces over the salad, then finish with the toasted hazelnuts and croûtons.

4 To make the dressing, whisk together the honey, reserved orange juice, vinegar and oil in a small bowl until almost opaque, or you can blitz it with a hand-held blender. Season with salt and pepper to taste, then drizzle the dressing over the salad and serve immediately.

Jerusalem Artichoke Velouté with **Truffle Oil** and **Chive Cream**

Jerusalem artichokes are a delightful root vegetable that can be roasted, puréed or served, as here, in a velouté. When cooked this way, with a delicious chive cream, they become beautifully velvety and nutty and make a lovely creamy soup for a special occasion.

SERVES 4
PREPARATION TIME 25 minutes,
  plus making the stock
COOKING TIME 30 minutes

25g/1oz unsalted butter
1 shallot, finely diced
600g/1lb 5oz Jerusalem artichokes,
  peeled and chopped
1–1.2l/35–40fl oz/4–4¾ cups
  Chicken or Vegetable Stock (see
  pages 16–17)
400g/14oz white asparagus, peeled
  and woody ends discarded
125ml/4fl oz/½ cup whipping cream
1 tbsp finely chopped chives
6 drops of truffle oil
1 baguette, sliced, to serve
sea salt and freshly ground black
  pepper

1 Melt the butter in a large saucepan over a low heat. Add the shallot and artichokes and cook for 5 minutes, stirring occasionally. Turn the heat up to high, add 1l/35fl oz/4 cups of stock and bring to the boil. Turn the heat down to low and simmer for 10–12 minutes or until the artichokes have just softened.

2 Meanwhile, cut off the asparagus tips and leave to one side. Roughly chop the stems, add to the soup and cook for 4 minutes until just tender. Whip half the cream, using an electric whisk, until soft peaks form.

3 Transfer the soup to a blender, season with salt and pepper and blend until smooth (you may have to do this in batches depending on the size of your blender). Add the whipped cream and blend once more, then pass through a fine sieve, using a ladle to help you, into the cleaned saucepan. Leave to one side.

4 Whip the remaining cream until soft peaks form, then fold in the chives and half the truffle oil and season with salt and pepper to taste. (You could use a hand-held blender to add the chive cream to the soup at this stage, or keep it separate and serve on top of the soup as below.)

5 Bring a saucepan of salted water to the boil, add the reserved asparagus tips and cook briefly for 2–3 minutes until just tender when pierced with the tip of a knife. Drain and season with the remaining truffle oil and with salt and pepper to taste. Put into four soup bowls.

6 Gently reheat the soup, adding the remaining stock if it is too thick, until bubbles just start to form on the top. Do not allow it to boil. Ladle the soup over the asparagus and top with a spoonful of the truffle oil and chive cream. Serve with slices of baguette.

Swede and Butternut Squash Soup with Caramelized Chestnuts

SERVES 4
PREPARATION TIME 20 minutes,
 plus making the stock
COOKING TIME 55 minutes

1 swede, about 400g/14oz total
 weight, peeled and diced
2 tbsp olive oil
1 butternut squash, about 500g/
 1lb 2oz total weight, peeled,
 deseeded and diced
50g/1¾oz unsalted butter
1 small onion, chopped
1.2l/40fl oz/4¾ cups Vegetable
 Stock (see page 17), plus extra
 for thinning, if necessary
200ml/7fl oz/scant 1 cup whipping
 cream
200ml/7fl oz/scant 1 cup full-fat
 milk
75g/2½oz cooked whole chestnuts
1 tbsp caster sugar
2 tbsp extra virgin olive oil
sea salt and freshly ground black
 pepper

I think swede has been ignored for too long, but I feel it's making a bit of a comeback. It certainly makes a great warming winter soup, which goes brilliantly with the sliced caramelized chestnuts.

1 Preheat the oven to 200°C/400°F/gas 6. Put the swede in a roasting tray, drizzle over the olive oil and season with a little salt and pepper. Roast for 5 minutes, then add the squash, stir to coat in the oil, then continue to roast for a further 7–10 minutes until they are just beginning to colour around the edges but are not cooked through. Remove from the tray and drain on kitchen paper.

2 Meanwhile, heat a large saucepan over a medium heat. Add half the butter and the onion and cook for 3–4 minutes until just softened but not coloured. Add the roasted swede and squash to the pan and toss together, then pour in the stock, cream and milk and bring to a simmer. Turn the heat down to low and simmer gently for about 30 minutes, uncovered, until the vegetables are very soft. The soup must not boil or the cream will curdle.

3 While the soup is cooking, make the caramelized chestnuts. Heat a non-stick frying pan over a medium heat. Add the remaining butter and when foaming, add the chestnuts and sugar. Cook for 3–4 minutes, turning once, until the chestnuts start to caramelize but take care they don't burn. Tip the chestnuts onto baking paper and leave to cool and become crisp, then roughly slice them.

4 When the soup is ready, ladle it into a blender and blend until very smooth (you may have to do this in batches depending on the size of your blender), then pass it through a fine sieve into the cleaned saucepan; it should be very creamy and velvety. Season with salt and pepper to taste and warm the soup through. If you feel it is a little thick, add some more stock. Serve drizzled with extra virgin olive oil and topped with the caramelized chestnuts.

Goats' Cheese, Summer Vegetable and **Herb Quiche**

This quiche says summer to me – the warmth and sun of the Mediterranean – with its colourful mix of artichokes and red chard and aromatic lemon thyme. Not forgetting the crumbly goats' cheese, which, when cooked slowly, adds an almost almondy flavour to the quiche. Do try it with the Reduced Balsamic Vinegar as it gives the tart an added depth of flavour. Enjoy the quiche with a red chard salad and pickled shallots.

SERVES 4

PREPARATION TIME 20 minutes, plus making the pastry and vinegar and 30 minutes chilling

COOKING TIME 1 hour

15g/½oz unsalted butter, plus extra for greasing

250g/9oz Savoury Short Pastry (see page 22)

plain flour, for dusting

200ml/7fl oz/scant 1 cup double cream

100g/3½oz soft goats' cheese log, such as Golden Cross or Ste Maure, rind removed, crumbled

2 lemon thyme sprigs

2 tbsp olive oil

1 onion, finely chopped

75g/2½oz drained bottled artichokes, thinly sliced

75g/2½oz carrot, peeled and finely diced

50g/1¾oz red chard leaves

25g/1oz watercress leaves

2 eggs, lightly beaten

¼ tsp freshly grated nutmeg

1 tbsp Reduced Balsamic Vinegar (see page 19)

sea salt and freshly ground black pepper

1 Lightly grease a 20cm/8in loose-bottomed tart tin. Roll out the pastry on a lightly floured work surface until 25cm/10in diameter x 3mm/⅛in thick and use to line the base and the sides of the tart tin, pressing it into the edges without overstretching the dough. Trim any excess pastry, prick the base with a fork and chill for 30 minutes to prevent the pastry shrinking during baking.

2 Meanwhile, make the filling. Pour the cream into a saucepan, add two-thirds of the goats' cheese and the lemon thyme and warm over a low heat for 3–5 minutes, whisking until smooth and silky. Remove from the heat and leave to cool while you make the rest of the filling.

3 Heat a non-stick frying pan over a medium heat. Add the butter, oil and onion and fry for 5 minutes, stirring occasionally, until softened but not browned. Add the artichokes and carrot, mix well and cook for 5 minutes until softened, then add the red chard and watercress and cook for a further 2 minutes until wilted. Tip out onto kitchen paper and press dry.

4 Add the eggs and nutmeg to the cooled cream mixture, season with salt and pepper, then whisk to combine.

5 Preheat the oven to 170°C/325°F/gas 3. Line the pastry case with baking paper and cover with baking beans. Put the tart tin on a baking sheet and bake for 12 minutes, then remove the paper and baking beans and turn the oven up to 180°C/350°F/gas 4. Brush the base of the pastry case with the reduced balsamic vinegar. Spoon the vegetable mixture over the base of the pastry case and sprinkle with the remaining goats' cheese. Pour in the egg mixture and bake for 35 minutes, or until firm to the touch. Serve warm or at room temperature.

Pumpkin and Goats' Cheese Lasagne

This 'lasagne' is made with very thin layers of pumpkin, rather than pasta as you would traditionally expect. For me, goats' cheese is perfect with pumpkin, while the addition of pumpkin seeds and a drizzle of pumpkin oil make this a delicate, light and surprisingly lovely meal. I have also included a tasty little salad that you might like to serve with the pumpkin.

SERVES 4
PREPARATION TIME 40 minutes
COOKING TIME 50 minutes

2kg/4lb 8oz pumpkin, skin removed and deseeded
100ml/3½fl oz/scant ½ cup full-fat milk
500ml/17fl oz/2 cups whipping cream
1 rosemary sprig
a pinch of freshly grated nutmeg
300g/10½oz soft goats' cheese log, such as Golden Cross, rind removed, crumbled
40g/1½oz unsalted butter
2 pinches of toasted pumpkin seeds
1 tbsp toasted pumpkin seed oil
100g/3½oz firm ewes' cheese, such as Ossau Iraty, diced
sea salt and freshly ground black pepper

FOR THE GOATS' CHEESE AND PUMPKIN SALAD
75g/2½oz lamb's lettuce leaves
1 tbsp toasted pumpkin seeds
50g/1¾oz soft goats' cheese log, such as Golden Cross, rind removed, crumbled
1 tsp toasted pumpkin seed oil
2 tbsp extra virgin olive oil
1 tbsp Chardonnay vinegar or white wine vinegar

1 Cut a 13 x 7.5cm/5 x 3in rectangle 5cm/2in thick from the pumpkin, then cut it into 12 x 2mm/¹⁄₁₆in slices using a mandolin or sharp knife. Chop the remaining pumpkin (about 750g/1lb 10oz) into bite-sized cubes.

2 Put the cubed pumpkin in a saucepan with the milk, half the cream, the rosemary sprig and the nutmeg and cook over a very low heat for 10–15 minutes until the pumpkin is just tender but with a little resistance. Using a slotted spoon, lift out the pumpkin and leave to one side. Reserve the milk mixture in the pan.

3 Meanwhile, bring a saucepan of salted water to the boil over a high heat. Add the thin slices of pumpkin, a few at a time, and cook for 2–3 minutes until just tender and pliable, then use a slotted spoon to transfer them to a bowl of iced water and leave for 1 minute. Lift out and drain on kitchen paper, keeping the slices separate, then season with salt and pepper.

4 Return the saucepan containing the milk mixture to a medium heat, add the remaining cream and the goats' cheese. Turn the heat down to low and cook, whisking continuously, until the cheese has melted and the sauce thickened to a silky texture. Discard the rosemary sprig.

5 Meanwhile, preheat the oven to 180°C/350°F/gas 4 and grease a 22 x 18cm/8½ x 7in baking dish with the butter. Overlap 4 slices of the pumpkin in the base of the dish. Scatter with half the pumpkin cubes, then add half the toasted pumpkin seeds and pumpkin oil and finish with one-third of the sauce. Repeat with another 4 slices of pumpkin, then the rest of the pumpkin cubes, seeds and oil. Spread another one-third of the sauce over the top, then finish with the remaining pumpkin slices. Add the remaining sauce and sprinkle with the ewes' cheese. Bake for 20 minutes until golden and bubbling, then turn the oven up to maximum and cook for a further 5–8 minutes until golden brown. Leave to rest for 2–3 minutes.

6 Meanwhile, prepare the salad, if you like. Toss the lamb's lettuce, pumpkin seeds and crumbled cheese together in a bowl. In a separate bowl, whisk together the oils and vinegar and season with salt and pepper. Drizzle the salad with the dressing, toss and serve with the lasagne.

Glazed Chicory and Thyme Tart

Chicory is a very versatile vegetable and while it is perfect uncooked in a salad, it also tastes delicious cooked in a tart. Here, it is combined with orange juice, a drop of honey and fresh thyme, which lift the chicory to new heights. The orange zest and walnuts sprinkled over the top to finish the dish beautifully.

SERVES 4
PREPARATION TIME 25 minutes, plus 30 minutes chilling and 20 minutes cooling
COOKING TIME 1 hour

75g/2½oz unsalted butter, plus extra for greasing
250g/9oz ready-made puff pastry
plain flour, for dusting
6 heads of chicory, trimmed and halved lengthways
finely grated zest and juice of 1 orange
2 tbsp clear honey
¼ tsp thyme leaves
25g/1oz/¼ cup walnuts, chopped
2 tbsp chopped celery leaves
¼ eating apple, peeled, cored and diced
sea salt and freshly ground black pepper

1 Lightly grease a 20cm/8in loose-bottomed tart tin. Roll out the pastry on a lightly floured work surface until 25cm/10in diameter x 3mm/⅛in thick and use to line the base and the sides of the tart tin, pressing it into the edges without overstretching the dough. Trim any excess pastry, prick the base with a fork and chill for 30 minutes to prevent the pastry shrinking during baking.

2 Meanwhile, make the filling. Heat a large sauté pan over a medium heat. Add 50g/1¾oz of the butter and the chicory, cut-side down, and cook for 4–5 minutes until slightly coloured. Take care not to let the butter burn. Pour enough water into the pan to fill by 1cm/½in, then add the remaining butter. Pour in the orange juice, season with salt and pepper and stir to combine. Cover the chicory with a *cartouche* (see page 218), turn the heat down to very low and simmer for 35–40 minutes until very tender and caramelized. Check occasionally to make sure that it is not burning and add more water, if necessary.

3 While the chicory is cooking, preheat the oven to 170°C/325°F/gas 3. Line the pastry case with baking paper and cover with baking beans. Bake for 12 minutes, then remove the paper and baking beans and bake for a further 3–5 minutes until the pastry is cooked and just golden. Remove from the oven and leave to cool in the tin on a wire rack. Turn the oven up to 200°C/400°F/gas 6.

4 Lift the chicory out of the pan onto a clean tea towel to dry and leave to cool. Add the honey and thyme to the pan and warm through, gently stirring, until you have a light syrup. Remove from the heat.

5 When the chicory has cooled, lay it tightly together in the pastry case, then brush generously with the orange-honey syrup. Bake for 10–12 minutes until warmed through. Remove the tart from the oven and the tin. Scatter the walnuts, orange zest, celery leaves and apple over the top and serve warm.

Sous-Vide Little Gems with Ewes' Cheese

With this dish, I'm trying to encourage you to cook more salad vegetables as it is a much-neglected style of cooking. My home-style 'vacuum-packed' Little Gem lettuces are topped with a slightly crumbly ewes' cheese, crunchy croûtons and a drizzle of olive oil and are just delicious. Enjoy this recipe as a vegetable dish with sourdough bread or as an accompaniment to roast pork. If you have a small vacuum-pack machine, follow the instructions in the method using vacuum bags instead of cling film. Alternatively, you can use small freezer bags with a seal, making sure that the air is squeezed out before you close them. You can also cook the parcels in a microwave for just 40 seconds on full power.

SERVES 4
PREPARATION TIME 15 minutes, plus making the croûtons
COOKING TIME 20 minutes

4 baby Little Gem lettuces, outer leaves removed and quartered lengthways
125ml/4fl oz/½ cup olive oil
120g/4¼oz ewes' cheese, such as Ossau Iraty, crumbled
1 tbsp small Croûtons (see page 18)
sea salt and freshly ground black pepper

1 Put four 20cm/8in square sheets of cling film on a work surface. Top each sheet with a quartered Little Gem, putting the pieces in a pile in the centre. Drizzle 1 tablespoon of the oil over each pile, then season with a little salt and pepper. Tightly wrap the Little Gem in the cling film to make 4 small parcels, pressing out any air.

2 Put a saucepan of water on to simmer, with a steamer insert on top. Put the parcels in the steamer, cover and cook for 12–14 minutes until they are just tender.

3 Remove the parcels from the steamer and unwrap over a small saucepan to catch any juices. Pat dry with kitchen paper and put in a grill pan, putting the contents of each parcel closely together so you have four separate portions. Scatter the ewes' cheese over the lettuce, then season with more salt and pepper and leave to one side.

4 Preheat the grill to high. Put the pan of reserved cooking juices over a medium-high heat and cook until reduced by half, then whisk in the remaining oil. Drizzle the sauce over the Little Gems and put under the grill for 2–3 minutes until the cheese is golden brown and a little puffed up. Sprinkle with the croûtons and serve hot.

SOUS-VIDE COOKING

I am sure everyone is familiar with using *sous-vide* – a vacuum – as a way of storing food, as we see vacuum-packed food all over the place, from spices and coffee to cured meats and rice. It is a great way of packing food for transport. But, although it has been around for a while now and is used a lot in professional kitchens, you may not be so familiar with cooking *sous-vide*.

At The Vineyard

In The Vineyard kitchen, we sometimes use this method, and we have a professional vacuum-pack machine that seals the food ready to go in a special water bath. It's usually a great way of cooking, although I have to confess it has gone wrong once or twice and given us all a good laugh – although laughter is not quite the reaction if it happens in the middle of a busy service! If a bag is not sealed properly – or the cling film isn't tied securely if you are trying it at home – and no one notices in time, it can cause a mini disaster, and you could find yourself with an empty bag or a chicken breast swimming in water. So just watch those knots and tie them tightly!

Why would you prepare food this way?

So what are the advantages of cooking in this way? Well, to start with, you can prepare dishes one or two days ahead and keep them refrigerated, or portioned up and frozen ready to cook when you need them. Imagine how useful that would be when you have a party coming up and you can spread the preparations so you have less to do on the day.

Then there's the fact that, when prepared this way, the food develops some beautiful flavours as it cooks in its own juices, with all the flavours locked in. As nothing is lost, there's an intensity of flavour in the finished dish.

Then we come to temperature, which is critical in *sous-vide* cooking. When you cook *sous-vide*, you can cook at a low temperature, around 70°C/158°F. This is important because meat, in particular, can be adversely affected when cooked at very high temperatures as the collagen fibres within the meat can become tough. This is less important with fish but it can still happen. So to keep the meat tender, it is recommended that you cook at less than 70°C/158°F. This makes this style of cooking perfect for the cheaper cuts of meat and also for offal. Many people don't like to cook offal in case they overcook and ruin it, but with *sous-vide* cooking that's not a problem because the cooking method is so gentle. You'll be sure to get perfectly tender results every time.

Sous-vide cooking at home

So how can you try out *sous-vide* cooking at home without a professional vacuum-packing machine? I will show you how to cook a chicken breast, and you can use the same procedure for other foods. Just glance through the recipe options in the book that I've listed on page 107 and you'll see how versatile the technique is.

Firstly, make sure you use cling film and not 'food wrap'. Cling film is perfect for cooking as it can withstand the necessary temperatures, whereas food wrap will not.

• Put four layers of cling film on your work surface. Put a boneless chicken breast in the centre of the cling film, then roll it tightly in the cling film, pressing out the air to each side as you roll. Make a knot in one end, then press the air out the other side before you knot that end. This will give you a partial *sous-vide*.

• Of course, you cannot keep the product as though it had been properly vacuum-packed because you have not created a full vacuum. Therefore you need to treat the parcel as you would any non-vacuumed product and store it properly in the fridge or freezer for the recommended time only. If you follow your common sense, then you'll be fine.

- For most *sous-vide* dishes, there are two alternative cooking methods, boiling and steaming. To boil, place the parcel in a saucepan large enough to hold it comfortably, then just cover it with water. Put the pan on a medium heat and bring the water up to 70°C/158°F. Keep it at that temperature for the time indicated in the recipe, as that will depend on the size of the portion. A 180g/6¼oz chicken breast will take about 20 minutes; if it is stuffed, it will take a further 5–10 minutes.
- Alternatively, you can steam the parcel. Put a large saucepan of water on to simmer, with a steamer insert on top. Put the chicken in the steamer, cover and cook for 20–25 minutes.
- When the food is ready, just cut off one end of the cling film, push the meat through and pat it dry on kitchen paper or a clean tea towel.
- Then, to regain the crisp skin, just heat a non-stick frying pan over a medium heat and pan-fry the chicken, skin-side down, for a minute or so until crisp and browned. Then serve it with a lovely sauce, or *jus*.

Just as a reminder, if you only want to prepare the parcel in advance, make sure you do keep it refrigerated and for a maximum of 2 days. Do not cook it in advance.

Since some meats have a stronger texture, I usually wrap them in cling film in the same way but cook them as a confit, in hot fat. This method is suitable for chicken leg meat, or the dark meat from poultry or game birds.

Now you understand the technique of *sous-vide* cooking, I hope you'll try some of my recipes, such as Sous-Vide Little Gems with Ewes' Cheese (see page 105), Stuffed Chicken Breasts with Cabbage and Chestnuts (see page 111), Pork Loin with Mushrooms, Figs and Chestnuts (see page 118), Salmon in Cabbage Leaves with Lemon Butter Sauce (see page 126), Steamed Cabbage with Pork and Hazelnut Stuffing (see page 177), Pancetta-Wrapped Monkfish with Carrot and Mandarin Purée (see page 186).

Enjoy a quail salad – or perhaps a poussin

Quail is the quickest and easiest option if you want to try out cooking *sous-vide* at home, or this recipe will work equally well with poussins, which are readily available in the supermarket. This is one example of when it is best if you cook the legs as a confit as the texture of the meat is different.

Simply wrap 2 quail legs and 2 quail breasts separately in cling film, as described in the general instructions on page 106. Cook the legs very gently in goose or duck fat for 40 minutes until the meat is super-tender and falls off the bone. When the legs are almost cooked, steam the breasts very gently for about 4 minutes until tender and cooked through. You can test the meat by piercing through the cling film with a sharp knife and the juices should run clear.

Once unwrapped, heat a non-stick frying pan over a high heat, add the breasts, skin-side down, and brown for 2 minutes, then turn them over and cook for a further 2 minutes. Deglaze the pan with a splash of white wine vinegar and a little salt and pepper, stirring to remove any caramelized bits stuck to the bottom.

I make a delicious salad to serve with the quail by tossing together a handful of rocket leaves, a handful of pea shoots and a few red chicory leaves. Then I sprinkle over some shredded tarragon leaves and a quartered boiled new potato. That's just enough per person. Cut the legs and the breasts in half, then put on top of a pile of fresh salad. As an extra bonus, you could finish the dish with a quail's egg per portion, boiled for just 2½ minutes so the yolk is perfectly runny.

Stuffed Chicken Breasts with Cabbage and Chestnuts

SERVES 4
PREPARATION TIME 20 minutes, plus
  making the stock
COOKING TIME 35 minutes

120g/4¼oz unsalted butter
4 tbsp olive oil
165g/5¾oz button mushrooms,
  thinly sliced
4 chicken breasts, skin on
1 large Savoy cabbage, shredded
12 cooked whole chestnuts
4 tbsp Chicken Stock (see page 16)
4 tbsp whipping cream
1 tbsp chopped tarragon leaves
sea salt and freshly ground black
  pepper

1 Heat a large, non-stick frying pan over a high heat. Add 30g/1oz of the butter and 1 tablespoon of the oil and when the butter is foaming, add the mushrooms and sauté for 4–5 minutes until they have released all their juices and are just golden. Remove and tip onto kitchen paper to dry. Wipe the frying pan, then return it to a medium heat, add another 30g/1oz of the butter and 1 tablespoon of the oil and when the butter is foaming, add the chicken breasts, skin-side down. Cook one side only over a medium heat for 5 minutes until the skin is golden, then remove them from the pan and put, skin-side up, on a board.

2 Cut the chicken breasts horizontally through the middle and three-quarters of the way through so that you can open them out like a book. Spread half the mushrooms over the bottom half of each breast, season with salt and pepper, then fold the top half back over to make a chicken-mushroom sandwich. Tightly wrap each chicken breast in cling film to make a sausage shape. Twist and secure each end with a knot, pushing out any air.

3 Put a large saucepan of water on to simmer, with a steamer insert on top, and bring another saucepan of salted water to the boil. Put the chicken parcels in the steamer, cover and cook for 12 minutes until cooked through. Remove and leave to rest on a plate for 6 minutes.

4 While the chicken is cooking, blanch the cabbage in the boiling salted water for about 3–4 minutes until only just tender, then drain well and pat dry. While the chicken is resting, heat a further 30g/1oz of the butter and 1 tablespoon of the oil in the frying pan over a medium heat and when the butter is foaming, add the blanched cabbage. Cook for 2–3 minutes, then add the remaining cooked mushrooms and the chestnuts and toss for a further 2–3 minutes until heated through. Transfer to a warm bowl, cover and leave to one side.

5 Once the chicken has rested, remove the cling film and pour any cooking juices into a small pan over a medium-high heat. Add the stock and cook for 2–3 minutes until reduced by half. Whip the cream until soft peaks form, add it to the pan and let it melt into the sauce, without stirring. As soon as the sauce starts to simmer, remove it from the heat. Season with salt and pepper to taste, then stir in the tarragon.

6 Meanwhile, heat the frying pan over a medium-high heat. Add the remaining butter and oil and fry the chicken, skin-side down, for about 3 minutes until crisp and golden. Quarter the chicken rolls and serve on top of the braised cabbage with the sauce spooned over.

Chicken and Cucumber En Papillote with Toasted Almonds

SERVES 4
PREPARATION TIME 20 minutes
COOKING TIME 30 minutes

4 chicken breasts, about
   165g/5¾oz each, skin on
20g/¾oz unsalted butter
2 tbsp sunflower oil
1 cucumber, peeled, halved
   lengthways and deseeded
2 tbsp olive oil
1 tsp smoked sweet (mild) paprika
185ml/6fl oz/¾ cup whipping cream
1 tbsp chopped flat-leaf parsley
   leaves
2 tbsp flaked almonds, toasted
sea salt and freshly ground black
   pepper

1 Season the skin of the chicken with salt and pepper. Heat a large frying pan over a medium-high heat. Add the butter and sunflower oil and when the butter is foaming, add the chicken, skin-side down, and cook for about 5 minutes until the skin is golden and crisp. Remove from the pan and leave to one side.

2 To prepare the cucumber, cut each piece in half crossways about the same length as the chicken breasts, then slice into julienne strips, about 3mm/⅛in thick. Wipe the frying pan clean, then heat over a medium-high heat. Add the olive oil and cucumber, season with salt and pepper and sauté for 4–5 minutes, tossing continuously, until the cucumber is translucent but still retaining its crunch. Add the paprika and stir to coat the cucumber, then drain on kitchen paper.

3 Preheat the oven to 180°C/350°F/gas 4. Lay four large sheets of baking paper, about 30cm/12in square, on a work surface. Put one-quarter of the cucumber on one of the sheets, putting it lengthways in the centre. Put the chicken lengthways on top and fold in the sides and the bottom end of the paper so the top is still open. Pour 3 tablespoons of the cream into the top, then fold the paper over and tightly fold the top to seal and make a parcel. Repeat to make 4 parcels in total.

4 Put the parcels in a roasting tray and roast for 8–10 minutes. Remove from the oven and leave for 2 minutes until cool enough to handle. Turn the oven off and leave the door ajar (this will keep the chicken warm without cooking it.) Carefully open one end of each parcel and pour the juices into a small sauté pan. Close the parcels again and return the chicken to the oven. Put the sauté pan over a medium heat and bring to the boil, then turn the heat down to low and simmer, uncovered, for about 5 minutes until reduced by half.

5 Meanwhile, whip the remaining cream until soft peaks form. Remove the pan from the heat and whisk the cream into the reduced chicken juices. Return to the heat and bring to a simmer, then immediately remove from the heat. Stir in the parsley and season with salt and pepper to taste. Slide the parcels carefully onto plates and open the tops. Spoon any sauce over the chicken and sprinkle with the toasted almonds before serving.

Pan-Roasted Duck Breast with Spiced Peaches

Wild duck goes very well with lots of different fruits and spices. I like to use peaches, and you should still be able to find them in early autumn when wild duck comes into season. If you buy your duck from a butcher, ask if it is female as it is generally more tender. I also like to use whole spices rather than ground, but don't overdo the spices as they can be overpowering.

SERVES 4

PREPARATION TIME 15 minutes, plus making the stock

COOKING TIME 40 minutes

100g/3½oz/scant ½ cup caster sugar

2.5cm/1in piece of cinnamon stick, broken

4 unripe peaches

4 duck breasts, preferably wild

2 pinches of roasted, crushed Szechuan peppercorns (see page 69)

4 tbsp sunflower oil

50g/1¾oz unsalted butter

1 shallot, chopped

4 tbsp sherry vinegar

125ml/4fl oz/½ cup Chicken Stock (see page 16)

sea salt and freshly ground black pepper

1 Put the sugar in a large sauté pan and add the cinnamon stick and 750ml/26fl oz/3 cups of water over a medium heat. Cook until the sugar dissolves, stirring occasionally, and the syrup comes to a simmer. Add the peaches and poach for 10 minutes. Using a slotted spoon, lift the peaches out of the syrup, leave to cool slightly, then remove the skins. Transfer the poaching syrup and cinnamon to a bowl and leave to one side. Halve the peaches, remove the stones, then cut each half into 4 long slices.

2 Preheat the oven to 180°C/350°F/gas 4. Season both sides of the duck, then sprinkle the Szechuan pepper over the skin. Heat an ovenproof frying pan over a medium heat. Add the oil and when it starts to shimmer, add the duck, skin-side down. Cook for 4–5 minutes until golden brown, then turn the duck over and put the pan in the oven for 4–5 minutes. Remove from the oven and put the duck in a small baking tray; cover and leave to rest for 5 minutes. Reserve the fat and turn the oven up to maximum.

3 Meanwhile, put the cleaned sauté pan over a medium heat, add half the butter and the peaches and cook for 5 minutes, turning occasionally, until lightly brown. Remove and leave to one side on a plate. Add the cinnamon and 125ml/4fl oz/½ cup of the reserved poaching syrup to the pan. Cook over a medium heat for 3–4 minutes until the syrup just starts to turn a caramel colour, then return the peaches, toss to coat in syrup, then remove from the heat. Cover the pan with foil and leave to one side.

4 Discard all but 1 tablespoon of the fat in the duck pan and return it to a medium heat. Add the shallot and cook for 5 minutes until softened, then pour in the sherry vinegar and deglaze the pan by stirring to remove any caramelized bits stuck to the bottom. Add the stock, bring to the boil, then simmer, stirring, for about 5 minutes until reduced by half. Add the remaining butter and swirl the pan to combine and make a shiny sauce. Add the juices from the rested duck, cover and leave to one side.

5 Reheat the duck in the hot oven for 2 minutes. If the peaches have cooled, warm them through. Cut the duck in half lengthways, Pour the peach juices into the sauce and bring it quickly to the boil. Serve the duck surrounded by the peaches, with the sauce spooned over the top.

Guinea Fowl with **Buckwheat Spaetzle**

Spaetzle means 'little sparrow' and this type of pasta traditionally comes from Baden in Germany, but it is also very popular near my home region of Alsace in the east of France, which is where I first tried it. The dough for the *spaetzle* can be made with spinach purée or cheese and it is often served with meat, but at The Vineyard restaurant we serve it with guinea fowl.

SERVES 4
PREPARATION TIME 30 minutes
COOKING TIME 35 minutes

250g/9oz/scant 2 cups buckwheat flour
6 large eggs
¼ tsp roughly chopped tarragon leaves
½ garlic clove, finely chopped
25g/1oz Parmesan cheese, very finely grated
4 tbsp olive oil
4 guinea fowl breasts, skin on
50g/1¾oz unsalted butter
½ tsp finely chopped rosemary leaves
sea salt and freshly ground black pepper

1 To make the *spaetzle*, put the flour, eggs, tarragon, garlic and Parmesan in a large mixing bowl and whisk with a strong whisk or wooden spoon for 5 minutes, or until the mixture starts to become elastic. Finish the dough by hand, almost slapping the mixture on the side of the bowl for about 3 minutes until it becomes an elastic, sticky dough. Meanwhile, bring a large saucepan of water to the boil and stir in 3 tablespoons of the oil. Fill a large bowl with iced water. Preheat the oven to 180°C/350°F/gas 4.

2 Put one-third of the dough in a large metal colander then, holding it about 5cm/2in above the saucepan of gently boiling water, press the dough through the holes of the colander into the water using either your hand or a spatula; they look like little worms going through and will break off naturally, so you don't need to cut them. Cook the *spaetzle* for about 1–2 minutes, or until they float to the surface. Scoop them out with a slotted spoon and drop straight into the iced water. When they are cold, lift out with a slotted spoon and dry on a clean tea towel. Repeat with the remaining dough until it is all used. Leave to one side on the tea towel.

3 Heat a large, ovenproof frying pan over a medium heat. Season the skin of the guinea fowl with salt. Add the remaining oil and half the butter and when the butter is foaming, add the guinea fowl, skin-side down, and cook for 2–3 minutes until golden. Turn the breasts over, transfer the pan to the oven and cook for 8–10 minutes until cooked through. Cover with foil and leave to rest in a warm place.

4 Return the frying pan to a medium heat and heat until the cooking juices and butter start to turn a hazelnut brown colour. Add the *spaetzle* and cook for 2–3 minutes, turning once, until golden and crisp on the outside but still soft inside, then carefully lift out with a slotted spoon and drain on kitchen paper.

5 Add 100ml/3½fl oz/scant ½ cup of water to the pan and deglaze by stirring to remove any caramelized bits stuck to the bottom. Add the remaining butter and the rosemary, then simmer for 1 minute, then season with salt and pepper to taste. Thickly slice the guinea fowl, top with the *spaetzle* and spoon over the cooking juices to serve.

Pomme Farcie with **Braised Pork Shoulder**

I love all the less expensive, and often forgotten, cuts of pork, beef or lamb. Here I'm using pork shoulder, which isn't so rare these days, but it's so much better braised than roasted. Be sure to ask your butcher to cut the pork into large cubes and to keep the fat on as it will make the dish much more tasty and also keep it moist, which for me is essential. For the best texture, remember to crush the cooked meat partially using a fork – you are not making a rillette so you don't want it too smooth.

SERVES 4
PREPARATION TIME 30 minutes, plus making the stock
COOKING TIME 2 hours 25 minutes

20g/¾oz unsalted butter
2 tbsp olive oil
600g/1lb 5oz boneless fatty pork shoulder, cut into large cubes
2 small carrots, peeled and chopped
2 shallots, chopped
2 garlic cloves, unpeeled, lightly crushed
100ml/3½fl oz/scant ½ cup dry white wine
500ml/17fl oz/2 cups Chicken Stock (see page 16)
4 floury potatoes, such as King Edward or Agria, about 200g/7oz each, peeled
1 tbsp chopped sage leaves
sea salt and freshly ground black pepper
green salad, to serve

1 Preheat the oven to 140°C/275°F/gas 1. Heat the butter with 1 tablespoon of the oil in a large, flameproof casserole dish over a high heat. When the butter is foaming, add the pork, carrots, shallots and garlic and cook for 5 minutes until just beginning to brown. Add the white wine and simmer, deglazing the pan by stirring to remove any caramelized bits stuck to the bottom, until the liquid has reduced by two-thirds. Pour in the stock and bring to a simmer. Reduce the heat to low, partially cover and cook for 2 hours, stirring every 30 minutes until the meat is very tender but not quite falling apart. The sauce should be thick enough to coat the back of the spoon.

2 While the pork cooks, make a horizontal cut along the length of each potato, about one-quarter of the way down, to make a lid. Set its lid next to each potato. Using a teaspoon, scoop out the insides of the potatoes, leaving a 5mm/¼in shell. (You can use the inside flesh for another recipe.) Season the insides with salt and pepper and divide the remaining oil between them. Put the lids back on and tightly wrap in cling film. Put a large saucepan of water on to simmer, with a steamer insert on top. Put the potatoes in the steamer, cover and cook over a very low heat for 1–1¼ hours until just tender. Turn off the heat, then leave the potatoes in the steamer to cook in the residual heat for 10–15 minutes.

3 When the meat is nearly ready, remove the cling film from the potatoes, lift off the lids and turn the potatoes upside-down on a clean tea towel to absorb any condensation. Turn the potatoes over and put in a roasting tin.

4 Remove the pork from the heat, spoon out 100ml/3½fl oz/scant ½ cup of the cooking juices into a bowl and leave to one side. Lightly crush the meat with a fork, stir in the sage and season with salt and pepper. Fill each potato with the mixture, taking care not to break them, cover with the potato lid, then spoon the reserved juices over the top. Put in the oven for 15 minutes until hot and bubbling. Serve with a green salad.

Pork Loin with Mushrooms, Figs and Chestnuts

Not only is autumn the mushroom season, but it is also the best time for figs and chestnuts. They all have an 'earthy' quality but with different textures. Remember to look out for ready-cooked and peeled chestnuts, which are really good and save a lot of time, too! I have given you the option of cooking the pork in different ways and I hope you'll try both methods to appreciate the differences in flavour, colour and texture.

SERVES 4
PREPARATION TIME 20 minutes, plus making the stock
COOKING TIME 15 minutes

4 pork tenderloin fillets, about 150g/5½oz each, trimmed
80g/2¾oz unsalted butter
2 tbsp sunflower oil
200g/7oz mixed wild or cultivated mushrooms
12 cooked whole chestnuts
4 tbsp sherry vinegar
2 medium-firm figs, quartered
200ml/7fl oz/scant 1 cup Chicken Stock (see page 16)
1 tbsp chopped chives
sea salt and freshly ground black pepper
boiled rice (optional), to serve

1 Season the pork fillets with pepper, then tightly wrap each one in cling film. Twist and secure each end with a knot, pushing out any air. Put a large saucepan of water on to simmer, with a steamer insert on top. Put the pork parcels in the steamer, turn the heat down to low, cover and cook for 12 minutes, then remove and leave to rest for 1 minute until cool enough to handle. Remove the cling film and pat the pork dry with kitchen paper.

2 Heat a frying pan over a medium-high heat. Add 20g/¾oz of the butter and 1 tablespoon of the oil and when the butter is foaming, add the pork and cook for 3–4 minutes, turning occasionally, until browned all over. The pork should still be slightly pink in the centre, which is perfect. (Alternatively, brown in an ovenproof frying pan as above, instead of steaming, then transfer the pork to an oven preheated to 140°C/275°F/ gas 1 for 7–9 minutes. Remove and leave to rest for 1 minute.)

3 While the pork is cooking, heat 20g/¾oz of the butter and the remaining oil in a frying pan over a medium-high heat. When the butter is foaming, add the mushrooms and fry for 2 minutes until they have released all their juices and are golden. Add the chestnuts and cook for 2 minutes. Add the sherry vinegar and deglaze the pan by stirring to remove any caramelized bits stuck to the bottom. Add the figs, pour in the stock and cook for 3–4 minutes until reduced by one-quarter, then add the remaining butter. Cook for a further 2 minutes until the sauce has reduced and is thick enough to coat the back of a spoon. Season with salt and pepper to taste and stir in the chives.

4 Cut each pork fillet into diagonal slices and spoon the mushroom mixture over the top before serving with rice, if you like.

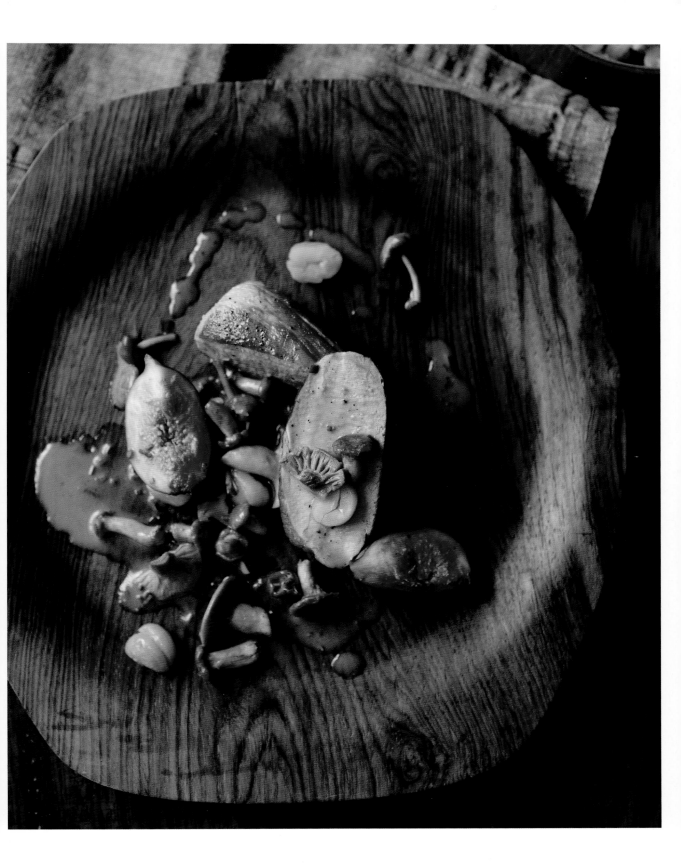

Morteau Sausage and **Warm Borlotti Bean Salad**

The town of Morteau gave its name to this famous sausage and it comes from the same part of France as I do, which is Franche-Comté to the east of the country next to the Jura mountains. Local cooks only use pork from the region because the animals are fattened traditionally. In addition, to be permitted to use the label *saucisse de morteau*, **the sausage must be smoked for at least 48 hours over sawdust from conifer and juniper trees. In this recipe, the borlotti beans bring a nuttiness, which is complemented by the sweet flavour of the oven-dried tomato. Throw in some garlic and herbs and a drizzle of French dressing and this dish is sure to impress!**

SERVES 4

PREPARATION TIME 15 minutes, plus overnight soaking and 30 minutes infusing

COOKING TIME 2½ hours

3 tbsp olive oil

6 garlic cloves, 3 unpeeled, lightly crushed, plus 1 whole and 2 chopped

250g/9oz cherry tomatoes, cut in half crossways and gently squeezed

1 tsp icing sugar

leaves from 1 thyme sprig

150g/5½oz/¾ cup dried borlotti beans, soaked overnight, drained and rinsed

1 large carrot, peeled

1 shallot

1 flat-leaf parsley sprig, plus 1 tbsp chopped leaves

2 morteau sausages or other smoked sausage, about 300g/10½oz each, pricked with a knife

3 tbsp French Dressing (see page 18)

sea salt and freshly ground black pepper

1 Preheat the oven to 110°C/225°F/gas ½. Put the oil and the whole unpeeled garlic in a small roasting tray in the oven for 30 minutes to infuse. Remove and leave the garlic to one side. Add the tomatoes to the tray, cut-side up, then sprinkle with the icing sugar and season with salt and pepper. Scatter the thyme over the top and roast for 2½ hours until the tomatoes are dried and wrinkly.

2 After the tomatoes have been cooking for 1 hour, put the soaked borlotti beans in a saucepan and cover with plenty of cold water. Bring to the boil over a high heat, then skim off any foam that rises to the surface. Add the carrot, shallot, parsley sprig and the peeled whole garlic clove. Turn the heat down to low, partially cover and simmer gently for 30 minutes. Add the sausages to the pan and simmer for a further 30 minutes until the beans are tender and the sausages cooked through.

3 Lift the sausages out of the beans into a bowl and cover with cling film. Strain the beans, reserving the cooking liquor in a separate pan. Tip the beans into a bowl. Discard the garlic clove and parsley sprig, then cut the carrot into small dice and add to the beans. Return the cooking liquor to the heat, bring to a the boil, then cook for about 5 minutes, uncovered, until reduced by half. Whisk in one-third of the French dressing.

4 Add the oven-dried tomatoes to the beans along with the remaining chopped garlic, chopped parsley and another one-third of the dressing and mix gently. Discard the skin from the sausage and cut the sausage into thick slices. Spoon the sausage on top of the beans and drizzle with the remaining dressing to serve.

Lamb Sweetbread and **Wild Mushroom Vol-au-Vents**

For a while now I've wanted to cook lamb sweetbreads in a puff pastry case and here it is. This is a very tasty dish but it's best to ask your butcher to prepare the sweetbreads for you as they can be a bit fiddly. Serve two per person for a generous portion with vegetables of your choice. Mine would be pan-fried courgettes, steamed spinach or red chard.

SERVES 4
PREPARATION TIME 15 minutes
COOKING TIME 25 minutes

500g/1lb 2oz all-butter puff pastry
2 tbsp plain flour, plus extra for
  dusting
1 egg, beaten
300g/10½oz prepared lamb
  sweetbreads
40g/1½oz unsalted butter
2 tbsp olive oil
1 tbsp very fine dry breadcrumbs
300g/10½oz mixed wild or button
  mushrooms
4½ tbsp whipping cream
1 tbsp chopped chives
sea salt and freshly ground black
  pepper
vegetables of your choice, such as
  pan-fried courgettes or steamed
  spinach or red chard, to serve

1 Preheat the oven to 190°C/375°F/gas 5 and line a baking tray with baking paper. Roll out the pastry on a lightly floured work surface and cut out 8 x 9cm/3½in diameter x 5mm/¼in thick rounds. Put 4 of the pastry rounds on the prepared baking tray. Using a 7.5cm/3in cutter, cut out a circle in the remaining rounds, leaving an outer ring. (Use the cut out circles for another recipe.) Brush the top of the rounds with beaten egg, making sure the egg does not go over the edge, then lay a pastry ring neatly on top of each one. Carefully brush with egg, then bake for 20 minutes, turning halfway, until risen and golden.

2 While the pastry cooks, bring a saucepan of salted water to the boil. Add the sweetbreads and cook for 1½ minutes, then refresh in a bowl of iced water, pat dry and remove the skin. Cut the sweetbreads into large cubes. Toss in the flour to coat and tap off any excess.

3 Heat a large frying pan over a medium heat. Add half the butter and oil and when the butter is foaming, add the sweetbreads and fry for 4–5 minutes, or until golden brown and crisp. Add the breadcrumbs, toss to combine and cook for a further 1 minute until the crumbs are crunchy, then drain on kitchen paper.

4 When the vol-au-vent cases are cooked, turn the oven down to 100°C/200°F/gas ½. Lift off the centre top layer to of each vol-au-vent to make a hollow. Keep them warm in the oven, with the door ajar, while you finish the filling.

5 Heat the remaining butter and oil in the cleaned frying pan over a medium heat. When the butter is foaming, add the mushrooms and fry for 1–2 minutes until softened. Add the cream and bring to the boil, then after 2–3 minutes when it starts to coat the mushrooms, add the cooked sweetbread mixture and the chives, toss to combine and season with salt and pepper to taste. Spoon the mixture into the cooked vol-au-vent cases and serve with your favourite vegetables.

Braised Ox Cheeks with Crushed Potatoes

Up until a few years ago, ox cheeks were a forgotten cut of meat, but they're becoming very popular again and no wonder – they are so delicious. They can be a little tricky to prepare as you need to trim them carefully, removing all the sinew before cooking, but if you have a butcher, ask him to do this for you. Crushed new potatoes are perfect with this dish and I would recommend Vitelotte, Jersey Royal or Charlotte, or even Ratte – just don't forget a good glug of olive oil and the herbs.

SERVES 4
PREPARATION TIME 25 minutes, plus making the stock
COOKING TIME 5 hours

2 cloves
4 tbsp olive oil
2 garlic cloves
2 carrots, peeled and cut into 1.5cm/⅝in chunks
2 shallots, cut into 2cm/¾in rings
1.25kg/2lb 12oz large ox cheeks, sinew and fat trimmed
6 tbsp sherry vinegar
300ml/10½fl oz/scant 1¼ cups red wine
300ml/10½fl oz/scant 1¼ cups Chicken Stock (see page 16)
200ml/7fl oz/scant 1 cup Beef Stock (see page 16)
¼ star anise
8 large new potatoes, such as Charlotte, Jersey Royals, Vitelotte or Ratte, scrubbed
1 tbsp chopped chives
sea salt and freshly ground black pepper

1 To blanch the cloves, bring a small saucepan of water to the boil, add the cloves, then return to a simmer for 1 minute. Drain, refresh in cold water and leave to one side.

2 Heat a large, flameproof casserole dish over a medium-high heat. Add 1 tablespoon of the oil and the garlic, carrots and shallots and cook for about 5 minutes until softened. Remove with a slotted spoon and leave to one side.

3 Add the beef to the casserole dish and cook for 15–20 minutes, turning the meat occasionally until browned all over. Add the sherry vinegar and deglaze the pan by stirring to remove any caramelized bits stuck to the bottom. When the vinegar has evaporated, add the red wine and cook for a further 5 minutes until reduced by half. Add the stocks, the star anise and cloves, return the cooked vegetables to the pan and bring the stock to a low simmer. Turn the heat down to low, partially cover with a lid and cook for 4½ hours, stirring every 30 minutes until the beef is very tender.

4 While the beef is cooking, prepare the potatoes. Put the potatoes in a saucepan, cover with water and bring to the boil over a medium-high heat. Turn the heat down to low and simmer for 30 minutes until very tender when pierced with the tip of a knife. Remove from the heat and leave to cool in the water.

5 Fifteen minutes before the beef has finished cooking, drain the potatoes, peel them carefully and return them to the pan. Drizzle with the remaining oil, season with salt and pepper and cover with a lid. Put the pan over a very low heat for 5–10 minutes until just heated through. Remove the lid and lightly crush the potatoes with the back of a fork until just broken up but not mashed, then add the chives and stir through. Serve the ox cheeks, carrots and sauce on top of the crushed potatoes.

Salmon in Cabbage Leaves with Lemon Butter Sauce

SERVES 4
PREPARATION TIME 25 minutes
COOKING TIME 45 minutes

4 large Savoy cabbage leaves,
  for wrapping
4 salmon fillets, about 120g/4¼oz
  each
25g/1oz unsalted butter
12 baby onions, peeled
1 tsp caster sugar
55g/2oz thick pancetta, cut into
  5mm/¼in lardons
1 tbsp olive oil
500g/1lb 2oz fresh podded peas
sea salt and freshly ground black
  pepper

FOR THE LEMON BUTTER SAUCE
4 tbsp whipping cream
100g/3½oz unsalted butter, cut into
  small pieces
finely grated zest and juice of
  1 lemon

1 Bring a large saucepan of salted water to the boil over a high heat, add the cabbage leaves, then turn the heat down to medium and cook for 5 minutes, or until tender. Using a large slotted spoon, lift out the leaves and transfer to a bowl of iced water for 1 minute. Remove and pat dry. Cut along either side of the central stem, about three-quarters of the way up the leaf from the stem end. Discard the stem, leaving the leaf still attached at the top. Repeat with the remaining leaves. Season the leaves with a little salt and pepper, then put the leaves, stem-end facing up, on a work surface. Lay a salmon fillet horizontally on the bottom half of a leaf, fold in the sides and wrap up to make a parcel. Repeat to make 4 parcels. Wrap each parcel tightly in cling film. Twist and secure each end with a knot, pushing out any air. Leave in the fridge until ready to cook.

2 Melt the butter in a pan over a medium heat. When foaming, add the baby onions and cook for 4–5 minutes, stirring occasionally, without browning. Season with salt and pepper, add enough water to cover and cook for 15 minutes until the onions have softened and the liquid has reduced by half. Add the sugar and cook, stirring, for 3–4 minutes until the onions become glazed and transparent, then leave to one side.

3 Meanwhile, bring a small pan of water to the boil. Add the pancetta and blanch for 1–2 minutes until just cooked. Drain, then refresh in cold water, tip onto kitchen paper and pat dry. Heat the oil in a frying pan over a medium heat and sauté the pancetta for 7–8 minutes until crisp and golden brown. Leave to one side.

4 Put a large saucepan of water on to simmer, with a steamer insert on top. Put the salmon in the steamer, cover and cook for 9 minutes until cooked but still slightly pink in the centre, then leave to rest in a warm place for 2 minutes.

5 Meanwhile, make the lemon butter. Pour the cream into the cleaned small pan and bring to the boil over a high heat. Remove from the heat, add 1 tablespoon of cold water, then whisk in the butter, a little at a time (if becomes too thick, add a little lemon juice to thin it), then continue until all the butter has been incorporated. Season with salt and pepper to taste, then add the lemon zest, cover with cling film and leave to one side.

6 Add the peas to the pan with the onions and simmer for 3–4 minutes, stirring occasionally, until tender. Add the pancetta and season with salt and pepper to taste. Remove and discard the cling film from the salmon and serve with the pea mixture and the lemon butter sauce spooned over the top or served separately.

Poached Pollock
with **Lemongrass**
and **Coconut Milk**

In this recipe, I have poached the pollock in coconut milk with lemongrass to add an Asian accent, but not too much as I'm still influenced mainly by the cooking of my home country, France. This is a favourite of my wife, Claire – say no more, the girl knows! You can mash any leftover sauce into your mashed potatoes to go with this dish if you like.

SERVES 4
PREPARATION TIME 10 minutes
COOKING TIME 20 minutes

600ml/21fl oz/scant 2½ cups
   whipping cream
400ml/14fl oz/scant 1⅔ cups
   coconut milk
25g/1oz unsalted butter
1 tbsp olive oil
4 pollock fillets, skin on, about
   150g/5½oz each
4 garlic cloves, unpeeled, lightly
   crushed
1 lemongrass stalk, bruised
sea salt and freshly ground black
   pepper
Creamed Mashed Potatoes (see
   page 20), to serve

1 Put the cream and coconut milk in a wide, shallow sauté pan over a medium heat and bring to a simmer.

2 Meanwhile, heat the butter and oil in a large, non-stick frying pan over a medium heat until the butter turns golden. Season the skin of the pollock with salt and pepper. Put in the frying pan, skin-side down, with the garlic and cook for 3–4 minutes until the skin is crisp and golden.

3 Turn the pollock over and put in the pan of simmering cream and coconut milk – the liquid needs to be just below the height of the fish so the skin doesn't soften. Add the garlic cloves and lemongrass to the liquid and simmer for 8 minutes, or until the fish is cooked. To check that the fish is ready, press lightly on the skin and you will see the flesh at the side of the fillet just start to flake away.

4 Lift the fish out of the pan, cover and keep it warm. Return the sauté pan to the heat and simmer for 5–8 minutes until the liquid has reduced by at least half and is thick enough to coat the back of a spoon. Add any juices from the resting fish, season with salt and pepper to taste, then pass the sauce through a fine sieve, using a ladle to help you. Spoon the sauce over the fish and serve with mashed potatoes.

Pan-Fried Cod Loin with White Bean Purée and Garlic Crisps

This dish is similar to one I make at The Vineyard restaurant and it always goes down well. Make sure the cod is super-fresh and line-caught, if possible, but you can use hake or pollock instead. The white bean purée is lovely and smooth in contrast to the crisp garlic chips and delicate, tender loins of cod.

SERVES 4
PREPARATION TIME 20 minutes, plus overnight soaking
COOKING TIME 40 minutes

8 garlic cloves, unpeeled
4 cod loins, skin on, about 150g/5½oz each, patted dry
40g/1½oz unsalted butter
2 tbsp olive oil

FOR THE WHITE BEAN PURÉE
150g/5½oz/¾ cup dried butter beans, soaked overnight, drained and rinsed
1 carrot, peeled
1 shallot
1 garlic clove
2 tbsp extra virgin olive oil
1 tbsp chopped flat-leaf parsley leaves
finely grated zest and juice of 1 lime

FOR THE GARLIC CRISPS
sunflower oil, for deep-frying
100ml/3½fl oz/scant ½ cup full-fat milk
4 large garlic cloves, thinly sliced
3 tbsp plain flour
sea salt and freshly ground black pepper

1 To make the white bean purée, put the soaked butter beans in a saucepan, cover with cold water and bring to the boil over a high heat, skimming off any foam that rises to the surface. Add the carrot, shallot and garlic, turn the heat down to a simmer, partially cover and cook for 40 minutes until tender.

2 While the beans are cooking, make the garlic crisps. Heat enough sunflower oil to deep-fry the garlic to 160°C/315°F, or until a cube of bread browns in 45 seconds. Bring the milk to a gentle boil in a small saucepan, add the sliced garlic and blanch for 2–3 minutes until softened slightly but not breaking up. Remove and pat dry with kitchen paper, discarding the milk. Lightly dust the garlic in the flour, then drop a few slices at a time into the hot oil and fry for 2–3 minutes until golden brown and crisp. Drain on kitchen paper. Season with salt and leave to one side.

3 Blanch the 8 garlic cloves in a small saucepan of boiling water for 4–8 minutes until softened, then drain, refresh in cold water and pat dry with kitchen paper.

4 Season the skin of the cod with salt and pepper. Heat a lidded, non-stick frying pan over a high heat. Add the butter and olive oil and when the butter is foaming, add the cod, skin-side down, and cook for 3–5 minutes until the skin is crisp and golden. Turn the heat down to medium-low, add the blanched garlic cloves, partially cover with a lid and cook for 3–4 minutes. Remove the lid, turn the fish over and cook for a further 2–3 minutes until just cooked through.

5 Meanwhile, strain the beans, reserving 3–4 tablespoons of the cooking liquor, then discard the carrot, shallot and garlic. Put the beans in a blender with 3 tablespoons of the reserved cooking liquor and blend to a smooth purée. Add the extra virgin olive oil and blend once more. Add the remaining cooking liquid if the purée is too thick. Season with salt and pepper to taste, then stir in the parsley, half the lime zest and all the lime juice. Serve the cod on a bed of the bean purée with the buttery garlic sauce spooned over the top. Sprinkle with the garlic chips and the remaining lime zest before serving.

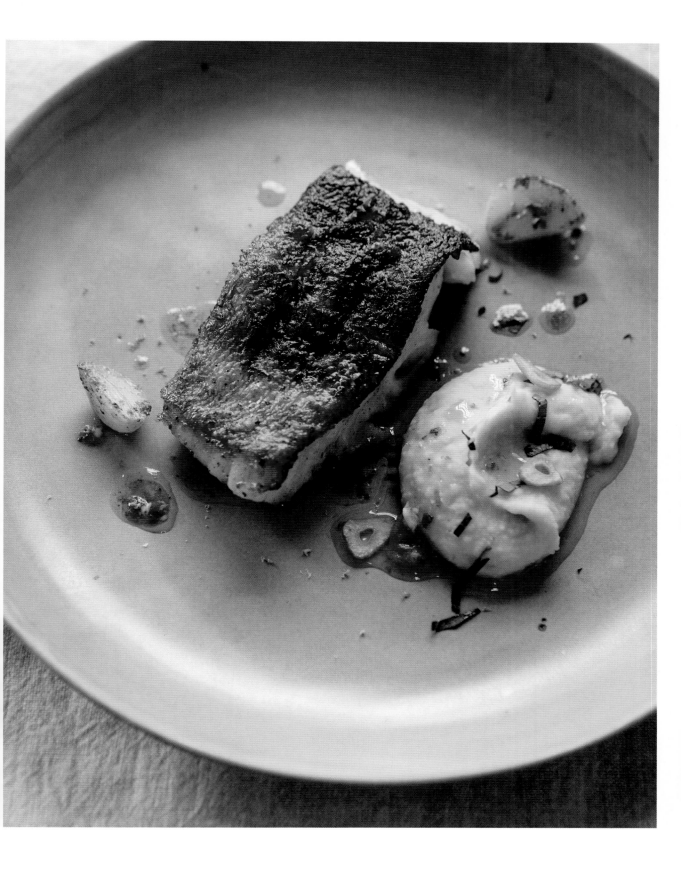

Plaice with Celeriac and Pancetta Galette

This is my alternative to the classic *sole meunière* using plaice. The plaice must be in prime condition and I would recommend your fishmonger skin it for you as it is quite fiddly. Celeriac is a beautiful root vegetable, which I personally love when it's roasted or, like here, grated with potatoes and mixed with pancetta to make a crisp and golden galette.

SERVES 4
PREPARATION TIME 15 minutes
COOKING TIME 30 minutes

50g/1¾oz pancetta lardons
200g/7oz floury potatoes, peeled and grated
200g/7oz celeriac, peeled and grated
1 tbsp chopped flat-leaf parsley leaves
120g/4¼oz unsalted butter
3 tbsp olive oil
3 tbsp plain flour
2 plaice, skinned and left on the bone
finely grated zest and juice of 1 lime
sea salt and freshly ground black pepper

1 Preheat the oven to 160°C/315°F/gas 2½. To make the galette, bring a small pan of water to the boil. Add the pancetta and blanch for 1–2 minutes until just cooked. Drain and refresh in cold water, tip onto kitchen paper and pat dry. Mix the potatoes, celeriac and pancetta in a bowl with half the parsley and season with pepper.

2 Heat a large, non-stick, ovenproof frying pan over a medium heat. Add 20g/¾oz of the butter and 1 tablespoon of the oil and when the butter is foaming, add the potato mixture and lightly press it down with a spatula into an even layer. Fry for 5 minutes until golden brown, then put the pan in the oven for 3 minutes. Remove from the oven and put a large plate on top to cover the pan, carefully turn the pan upside-down to flip the galette over onto the plate, then slide it back into the pan.

3 Return the pan to a medium heat, add another 20g/¾oz of the butter and cook the galette for 3 minutes, then return the pan to the oven for a further 3 minutes. Slide the galette onto kitchen paper to drain for a few seconds, then wrap in kitchen foil to keep warm while you cook the fish.

4 Turn the oven up to 180°C/350°F/gas 4. Put the flour on a plate, season with salt and pepper, then dust the fish in the seasoned flour, patting to remove any excess. Heat 20g/¾oz of the butter and 1 tablespoon of the oil in the cleaned frying pan over a high heat. When the butter is foaming, add the fish and cook for 6 minutes, then turn it over, add a further 20g/¾oz of the butter and, when melted, spoon it over the fish. Put the pan in the oven for 6 minutes until the fish is cooked. (Alternatively, if you have a smaller pan, cook the fish one at a time.)

5 Remove the fish from the oven, cover and leave to rest on a warm plate. Return the frying pan to the hob, add the remaining butter and oil and stir in the remaining parsley and the lime zest and juice. Heat through briefly. Spoon the sauce over the fish and serve with segments of the galette.

Casserole of **Autumn Vegetables** with **Pears** and **Ceps**

At home, I often make casseroles and it is very much the way my mother likes to cook. It is not by accident that I have chosen pears and ceps; not only do I love them but they bring so much to the casserole with their superb flavour and texture.

SERVES 4
PREPARATION TIME 30 minutes, plus making the stock
COOKING TIME 1 hour 10 minutes

80g/2¾oz unsalted butter
1 tbsp sunflower oil
200g/7oz carrots, peeled and cut into 2cm/¾in chunks
200g/7oz swede, peeled and cut into 2cm/¾in chunks
2 firm pears, peeled, cored and cut into 8 wedges
2 large shallots, cut into thick rings
40g/1½oz dried ceps or porcini, soaked in 150ml/5fl oz/scant ⅔ cup warm water
2 thyme sprigs
200g/7oz celeriac, peeled and cut into 2cm/¾in chunks
12 garlic cloves, unpeeled
200g/7oz butternut squash, cut into 2cm/¾in chunks
4 small new potatoes, such as Charlotte or Ratte, scrubbed and each cut into 3 pieces
125ml/4fl oz/½ cup Chicken or Vegetable Stock (see pages 16–17)
1 tbsp chopped flat-leaf parsley leaves
sea salt and freshly ground black pepper

1 Heat a large, flameproof casserole dish over a medium-high heat. Add 20g/¾oz of the butter and the sunflower oil and when the butter is foaming, add the carrots. Immediately turn the heat down to medium, partially cover and cook for 12–15 minutes, stirring occasionally, until the carrots just start to soften around the edges but not colour. Add the swede, cover again with the lid and cook for a further 10–12 minutes, stirring occasionally.

2 Meanwhile, heat a large, non-stick frying pan over a medium heat. Add 20g/¾oz of the butter and when foaming, add the pears and shallots and cook for 8–10 minutes until just tender and starting to caramelize.

3 Using a small slotted spoon, remove the ceps from their soaking water, taking care not to stir the bowl, then put on kitchen paper and pat dry. Strain and reserve the soaking water. Add the ceps to the pan with the pears and shallots, then stir in the thyme sprigs and sauté for a further 3–4 minutes over a medium-low heat until the ceps have softened. Season well with salt and pepper, remove from the heat and leave to one side.

4 Add another 20g/¾oz of the butter to the casserole dish with the celeriac and garlic, partially cover and cook for 8–10 minutes, stirring occasionally, until slightly softened. Add the butternut squash and potatoes and cook for a further 8–10 minutes, stirring occasionally. Turn the heat up to high, remove the lid and add the remaining butter, the stock and reserved cep water, making sure there is no sediment from the ceps in the water. Cook for 5–8 minutes until the liquid has reduced enough to just coat the vegetables; do this quickly so that the vegetables don't overcook. Remove the casserole dish from the heat, add the pear mixture and parsley, stir gently to combine and heat through, then serve hot.

Jerusalem Artichoke and Red Chard Omelette with Pickled Shallots

Red chard is a salad leaf that's not used so much in the home kitchen, but is popular with chefs. It's almost like spinach, but less buttery and cooks very quickly so you want to add the leaves at the very last minute, just before the eggs. Also, to intensify the flavour of the dish, I have added pickled shallots, which bring a touch of acidity and crunch. But the main feature is the Vacherin Mont d'Or, which is a soft, rich, creamy cow's milk cheese from the Jura region in Franche-Comté. It is made by traditional methods and is only available during the September to April season. My region, I love it, and what memories it brings...

SERVES 4
PREPARATION TIME 10 minutes,
 plus 10 minutes cooling
COOKING TIME 20 minutes

20g/¾oz unsalted butter
200g/7oz Jerusalem artichokes,
 peeled, quartered lengthways and
 thinly sliced
1 large red onion, sliced
90g/3¼oz red chard leaves
8 eggs, lightly beaten
50g/1¾oz soft, creamy cheese,
 such as Vacherin Mont d'Or
olive oil, for dressing
sea salt and freshly ground black
 pepper

FOR THE PICKLED SHALLOTS
100ml/3½fl oz/scant ½ cup
 Chardonnay vinegar or white wine
 vinegar
20g/¾oz/scant ¼ cup caster sugar
1 large banana shallot, finely sliced
 into rings

1 To make the pickled shallots, put the vinegar and sugar in a small saucepan over a medium heat, stirring to dissolve the sugar, then bring to the boil. Put the shallots in a heatproof bowl and when the liquid is boiling, pour it over the shallots. Leave to cool for about 10 minutes, which is long enough to pickle the shallots perfectly.

2 Preheat the oven to 160°C/315°F/gas 2½. While the shallots are pickling, make the omelette. Heat a large, non-stick, ovenproof frying pan over a medium heat. Add the butter and when foaming, add the Jerusalem artichokes and onion and cook for 4–5 minutes until just softened and slightly caramelized. Add 50g/1¾oz of the red chard leaves and toss twice to mix.

3 Season the eggs with salt and pepper, then pour them over the vegetables in the pan. Turn the heat up to high and spoon the cheese in small dollops all over the top. When the edges of the omelette start to bubble and thicken slightly, run the edge of a rubber spatula quickly around the pan to loosen, then put the pan in the oven for 4–5 minutes until just cooked. Check the omelette is cooked by gently pressing the top to see if it springs back lightly. If it doesn't, then return it to the oven for a further 2 minutes and check again.

4 Dress the remaining chard with a little olive oil and a touch of salt and pepper. Drain the shallots. Serve the omelette topped with the shallots and finished with the dressed chard on top.

Spiced Autumn Fruits with Pan-Fried Brioche

I've chosen my favourite fruits for this recipe – including yellow peaches, which I love – but be adventurous as it's a great way of using up any surplus stone fruits or apples or pears you may have. You can also use vanilla instead of star anise, or even black pepper to substitute for the cinnamon, but use them with care to avoid overpowering the fruit. I like to use Drambuie but you can use whisky instead, if you like.

SERVES 4
PREPARATION TIME 15 minutes
COOKING TIME 10 minutes

4 Victoria plums, halved and stones removed
4 greengages, halved and stones removed
1 yellow peach, quartered and stone removed
1 nectarine, quartered and stone removed
2 figs, quartered
75g/2½oz/heaped ⅓ cup light soft brown sugar
2 small cinnamon sticks
2 star anise
generous 4 tbsp Drambuie
juice of ½ lime
2 large eggs
4 slices of brioche loaf, about 1.5cm/⅝in thick
50g/1¾oz unsalted butter
Real Vanilla Ice Cream (see page 23), to serve

1 Heat a large, non-stick frying pan over a medium-high heat. Add the fruit in a single layer, cut-side down, and cook for 1 minute. Sprinkle one-third of the sugar over the top, add the cinnamon and star anise, then continue to cook for 3–4 minutes until the fruits start to release their juices and soften slightly; they should still keep their shape.

2 Pour the Drambuie into the pan and immediately set it alight (it should burn for a few seconds), then turn the heat down to low so some of the Drambuie remains in the pan and cook for a further 1–2 minutes, taking care not to let the fruit soften too much. Stir in the lime juice and remove from the heat. Cover the pan to keep the fruit warm while you cook the brioche.

3 Beat the eggs with the remaining sugar in a large, shallow bowl until thick and creamy. Dip each side of the brioche briefly into the egg mixture until just coated, then leave to one side.

4 Heat a second large, non-stick frying pan over a medium-high heat. Add the butter and when foaming, add the brioche and cook for a few minutes on each side until just golden brown and slightly crisp. Serve with the fruits and juice spooned over the top and with vanilla ice cream.

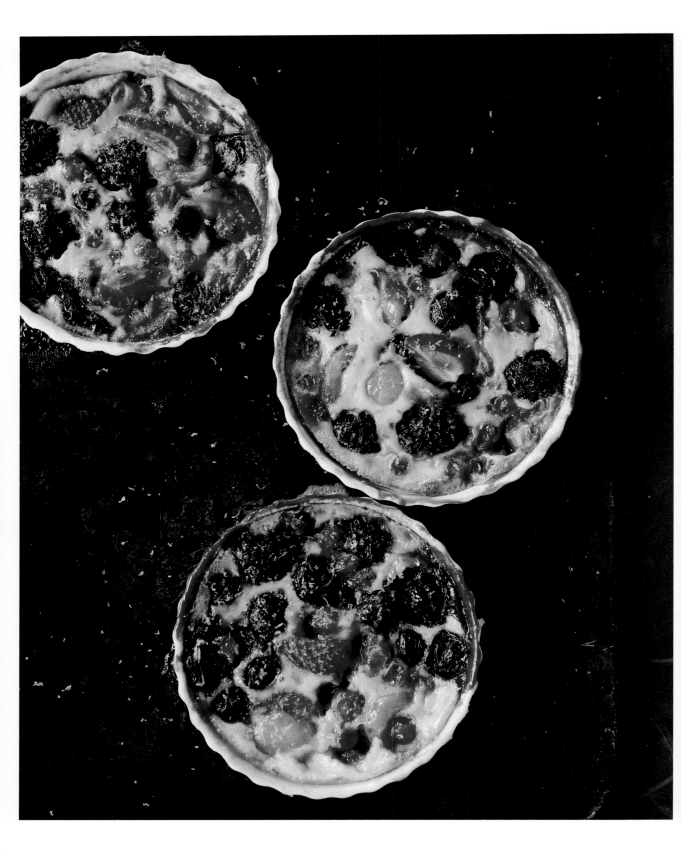

Red Fruit Clafoutis
with **Flavoured
Greek Yogurt**

Imagine all the colours and flavours of these lovely summer berries in a rosemary-infused clafoutis. And the individual clafoutis are really just as good made with thyme or lavender flowers, but make sure the flowers are edible and untreated. Another great flavour combination is crushed black pepper and grated lime zest — enjoy experimenting!

SERVES 4
PREPARATION TIME 15 minutes, plus
  1 hour macerating
COOKING TIME 12 minutes

60g/2¼oz/heaped ⅓ cup
  blueberries
60g/2¼oz/heaped ⅓ cup
  blackberries
60g/2¼oz/½ cup redcurrants
60g/2¼oz/scant ⅓ cup cherries,
  pitted
60g/2¼oz/heaped ⅓ cup
  strawberries, hulled and quartered
80g/2¾oz/⅓ cup caster sugar
½ tsp very finely chopped young
  rosemary leaves (from the tips)
4 tbsp Greek yogurt
50g/1¾oz unsalted butter, half
  softened and half melted
60g/2¼oz/½ cup plain flour, sifted
a pinch of salt
1 egg
2 egg yolks
200ml/7fl oz/scant 1 cup full-fat
  milk

1 Wash the fruit, drain and put into a bowl. Add 2 tablespoons of the caster sugar and the rosemary and turn to coat. Cover and leave to macerate at room temperature for 1 hour to release some of the juices from the fruit.

2 Preheat the oven to 180°C/350°F/gas 4. Strain the fruit and add half of the juices to the yogurt, reserving the other half. Mix well, then cover and chill until ready to serve.

3 Grease four large ramekins with the softened butter and sprinkle with 2 tablespoons of the caster sugar, carefully turning the ramekins to make sure the sugar coats the insides, then tipping out any excess.

4 Sift the flour and salt into a mixing bowl. In a separate bowl, whisk together the egg, egg yolks and remaining sugar, then slowly add to the flour, mixing until incorporated and smooth. Gradually add the milk and the reserved fruit juices, stirring until the mixture has the consistency of a pancake batter, then add the melted butter and mix well until combined.

5 Divide the berries into the prepared ramekins and pour the batter over to just below the top. Bake for 10–12 minutes until set and golden brown. Serve with a dollop of the flavoured Greek yogurt, if you like, or you can serve it separately.

Honey Parfait with Poached Rhubarb

There are so many types of honey to choose from, so do experiment to find the ones you like the best. The subtle flavours of flower honeys I find delicious, and they perfectly complement the flavour of delicate pink rhubarb.

SERVES 4
PREPARATION TIME 20 minutes, plus at least 8 hours freezing
COOKING TIME 10 minutes

5 egg yolks
1 vanilla pod, split in half lengthways and seeds scraped out
300g/10½oz clear honey, such as lavender, thyme, chestnut or acacia
160ml/5¼fl oz/⅔ cup whipping cream
4 rhubarb sticks, chopped into large pieces
a few edible lavender flowers, to serve

1 Line a 500g/1lb 2oz loaf tin or terrine with cling film, leaving a generous overhang. Put the egg yolks in a mixing bowl and add the vanilla seeds, reserving the pod for another recipe. Put 50g/1¾oz of the honey in a saucepan over a low heat and heat gently until melted, then scrape into the egg yolks and whisk for about 10 minutes, using an electric whisk, until the mixture has cooled and forms a light ribbon when the beaters are lifted out of the bowl.

2 Whip the cream, then fold it into the cold egg and honey mixture. Pour into the prepared loaf tin, cover with the overhanging cling film and put in the freezer for at least 8 hours until firm.

3 To poach the rhubarb, pour 500ml/17fl oz/2 cups of water and the remaining honey into a saucepan and bring to the boil over a high heat. Turn the heat down to low and simmer for 3–4 minutes until it forms a very light syrup. Add the rhubarb and poach gently for about 5 minutes until just soft. Using a slotted spoon, scoop out the rhubarb and put on a plate to cool. At the same time, leave the syrup to cool. When both have cooled, return the rhubarb to the syrup, then sprinkle with the lavender flowers and serve with a slice of the honey parfait.

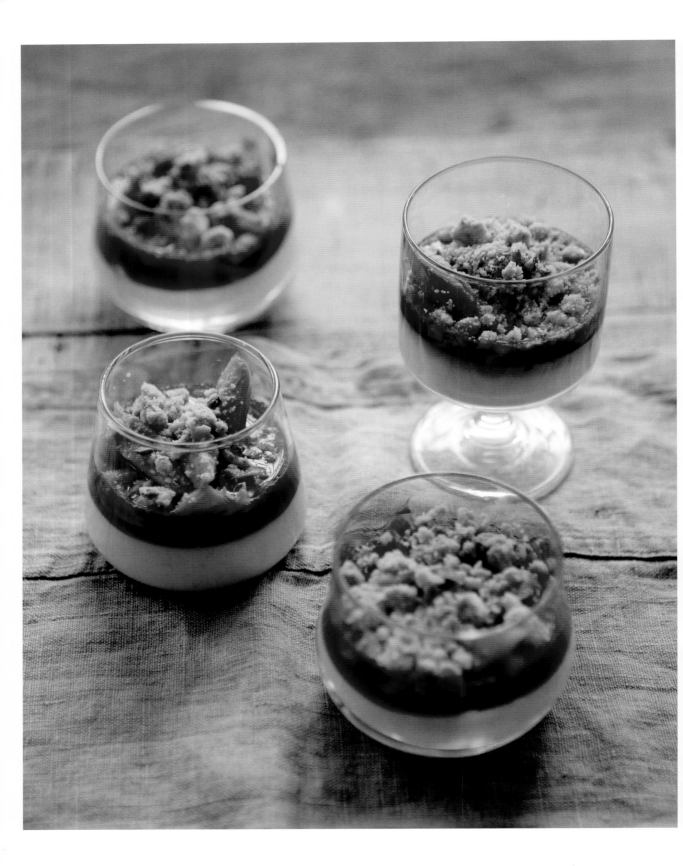

Deconstructed Poached Rhubarb and **Pistachio Crumble**

This is a very different type of crumble from the one your grandmother used to make, as the rhubarb is gently poached in a lemongrass-infused syrup and then elegantly layered in a glass with a lemon and lime cream and topped with a crispy pistachio crumble. It makes a deliciously elegant and modern twist on an old favourite.

SERVES 4

PREPARATION TIME 20 minutes, plus at least 3 hours chilling

COOKING TIME 50 minutes

400g/14oz rhubarb, peeled, peelings reserved, cut into 2.5cm/1in long pieces
100g/3½oz/scant ½ cup caster sugar
1 lemongrass stalk, split and bruised

FOR THE LEMON AND LIME CREAM
185ml/6fl oz/¾ cup double cream
2 tbsp caster sugar
2 tbsp lemon juice
finely grated zest of ½ lemon
finely grated zest of ½ lime

FOR THE PISTACHIO CRUMBLE
100g/3½oz/heaped ¾ cup icing sugar
100g/3oz/heaped ¾ cup plain flour
a pinch of salt
75g/2½oz/¾ cup ground almonds
40g/1½oz/scant ⅓ cup shelled pistachios, roughly chopped
100g/3½oz unsalted butter, softened

1 To make the lemon and lime cream, put the cream and sugar in a small saucepan over a high heat and bring to the boil. Put the lemon juice and both zests in a small jug and as soon as the cream comes to the boil, pour it into the jug and mix quickly to combine. Pour the hot cream mixture into four small sundae glasses, leave to cool, then chill in the fridge for at least 3 hours.

2 Put the rhubarb, rhubarb peelings, sugar and lemongrass in a sauté pan and just cover with water. Heat over a low heat until simmering, then cook for 15–20 minutes until the rhubarb is just tender but keeps its shape. Strain through a fine sieve into the cleaned pan, then return the syrup to the heat and cook until it has reduced by half and is thick and syrupy. Meanwhile, discard the rhubarb peelings and the lemongrass and put the rhubarb in a shallow non-metallic dish. Pour the reduced syrup over the top of the rhubarb and leave to cool while you make the crumble.

3 Preheat the oven to 160°C/315°F/gas 2½. Put all the crumble ingredients in a large mixing bowl and rub gently with your fingertips to make a coarse crumb mixture. Tip onto a baking tray in an even layer and bake for 20–25 minutes until golden brown. Turn the crumble mixture, bringing the edges into the centre and spreading it out into an even layer again every 6–8 minutes to make sure it cooks evenly. Remove from the oven and leave to cool completely until crunchy.

4 Take the cream-filled glasses out of the fridge and top with the rhubarb. Drizzle with the syrup and finish with the crumble, gently sprinkling it over the top. Serve immediately while the crumble is still crunchy.

Confit Tomato Marmalade with Goats' Milk Yogurt and Langues de Chat

Langues de chat are thin, crisp biscuits that we normally serve at The Vineyard restaurant with afternoon tea or coffee. As I'm a lover of goats' milk I wanted to see if I could make a version of the biscuit with goats' butter and goats' crème fraîche, and here it is. They are delicious dipped into the sweet and slightly acidic confit tomato marmalade and goats' milk yogurt dessert.

SERVES 4
PREPARATION TIME 30 minutes, plus cooling
COOKING TIME 40 minutes

125g/4½oz vine cherry tomatoes, halved
50g/1¾oz/scant ¼ cup caster sugar
2 basil leaves
1 tsp balsamic vinegar
450g/1lb/heaped ¾ cup natural goats' milk yogurt
finely grated zest of 1 lime

FOR THE LANGUES DE CHAT
100g/3½oz goats' butter, softened, plus extra for greasing
100g/3½oz/scant ½ cup caster sugar
3 egg whites
125g/4½oz/1 cup strong white flour, sifted, plus extra for dusting
½ vanilla pod, split in half lengthways and seeds scraped out
90g/3¼oz/generous ⅓ cup goats' milk crème fraîche

1 To make the confit tomato marmalade, put the tomatoes, sugar, 1 basil leaf and the vinegar in a sauté pan with 100ml/3½fl oz/scant ½ cup of water over a medium heat. Bring to the boil, then turn the heat down to low and simmer for 20–30 minutes until thickened to the consistency of marmalade. Remove from the heat and spoon into a bowl, cover and leave to cool. When fully cold, strain through a fine sieve into a bowl to collect the juices (leave the marmalade to one side).

2 Roughly chop the remaining basil leaf and add to the goats' milk yogurt with the strained juices, then mix until just combined. Cover and leave in the fridge until ready to serve.

3 Preheat the oven to 200°C/400°F/gas 6. To make the *langues de chat*, beat together the butter and sugar, using an electric whisk, for 5 minutes until light and well blended. Whisk in the egg whites, one at a time as the mixture will split if you add them all at once, until incorporated. Gradually fold in the flour, then beat in the vanilla seeds and crème fraîche until the mixture is soft, pale and creamy. Spoon into a piping bag.

4 Grease and flour a large baking tray. Trim the end off the piping bag to a 1cm/½in diameter, then carefully pipe biscuits 7.5cm/3in in length onto the tray, leaving a 10cm/4in gap between each one as they spread during cooking. Bake for 5–6 minutes, turning the tray halfway, until dark golden around the edges and pale in the centre. Remove from the oven, transfer to a wire rack and leave to cool and become crisp.

5 To serve, spoon the confit tomatoes into the bottom of small sundae glasses, top with the yogurt and a sprinkling of lime zest and serve with the biscuits.

Strawberry Jelly Purée with Elderflower Yogurt and Sesame Nougatine

I recommend that you wait for the strawberry season before making this dish – the quality of the fruit will make a massive difference to the taste of the jelly. I also use a lovely elderflower cordial, which is not as sweet as some cordials. To finish the dessert, I use black and white sesame seeds made into a lovely transparent, glass-like type of nougatine, which is very crunchy, but absolutely delicious! If you have not come across liquid glucose before, you'll find it in your supermarket in the baking aisle.

SERVES 4

PREPARATION TIME 35 minutes, plus at least 30 minutes chilling and cooling

COOKING TIME 25 minutes

FOR THE STRAWBERRY JELLY PURÉE
2 leaves of gelatine, about 3g/¹⁄₁₆oz total weight
500g /1lb 2oz/3⅓ cups strawberries, hulled
1 tbsp caster sugar
2 tbsp white balsamic vinegar

FOR THE ELDERFLOWER YOGURT
300g/10½oz/scant 1¼ cups Greek yogurt
150g/5½oz cream cheese
3 tbsp elderflower cordial
1 tbsp icing sugar, sifted

FOR THE SESAME NOUGATINE
50g/1¾oz/⅓ cup black sesame seeds
50g/1¾oz/⅓ cup white sesame seeds
2 tbsp liquid glucose
90g/3¼oz/heaped ⅓ cup caster sugar
70g/2½oz unsalted butter

1 To make the jelly, put the gelatine in a medium-sized bowl with enough cold water to cover, then leave to soften for 5 minutes. Drain and return the gelatine to the bowl. Heat a large, non-stick frying pan over a high heat, add 280g/10oz/scant 2 cups of the strawberries and the sugar and cook for 2 minutes, tossing to coat the strawberries in the sugar. Remove from the heat, cover and leave for 3 minutes.

2 Transfer the strawberries and any juices in the pan to a blender and blend to a purée, then pass through a fine sieve, using a ladle to help you, directly onto the soaked gelatine and whisk briskly until it dissolves. Put the bowl directly in a larger bowl of iced water to cool rapidly. When the jelly starts to set, divide it equally into four whisky tumblers. Put them in the fridge to set for at least another 30 minutes. Meanwhile, cut 120g/4¼oz of the remaining strawberries into a fine dice, put in a bowl with the vinegar and leave to macerate for 20 minutes.

3 Put all the elderflower yogurt ingredients in a separate bowl and mix well to combine, then leave in the fridge until needed.

4 When the jelly has set, spoon the yogurt into the four glasses. Using a slotted spoon, add the macerated strawberries on top, then leave in the fridge to set while you make the nougatine.

5 Preheat the oven to 180°C/350°F/gas 4 and line a baking tray with baking paper. Put all the nougatine ingredients in a non-stick frying pan. Add 1 tablespoon of water and stir to combine, then heat over a medium heat for 3 minutes, or until the butter melts and the sugar dissolves. Turn the heat up and cook for 4–5 minutes until it just starts to turn golden. Pour onto the prepared tray and spread out with a wet spatula. Bake for 12 minutes until golden brown – it shouldn't be as dark as caramel. Remove from the oven and leave to cool on the tray until crisp. Break the nougatine into large pieces. Remove the glasses from the fridge and balance a piece of nougatine in the top of each dessert, then put the rest in a bowl to share.

Balsamic and Lime Raspberries with Goats' Milk Ice Cream

This was a bit of a discovery for me. I've been thinking about making a goats' milk ice cream for a while and I was really pleased with the results as it is easy to make and the lift from the lime zest is perfect. Buy raspberries in season for the best flavour and you need a very good, aged balsamic vinegar for the marinade – one that is slightly syrupy but not too acidic. It will specify the age on the label. The Langues de Chat (see page 139) go really well with this too. The finished dessert is summer itself!

SERVES 4

PREPARATION TIME 20 minutes, plus at least 3½ hours freezing

COOKING TIME 5 minutes

Langues de Chat (see page 139), to serve
1 tbsp fennel seeds
1 tbsp icing sugar

FOR THE GOATS' MILK ICE CREAM
300ml/10½fl oz/scant 1¼ cups goats' milk
100ml/3½fl oz/ scant ½ cup goats' cream
200g/7oz/heaped ¾ cup natural goats' milk yogurt
120g/4¼oz/scant 1 cup icing sugar
finely grated zest of ½ lime

FOR THE BALSAMIC AND LIME RASPBERRIES
200g/7oz/scant 1⅔ cups raspberries
3 tbsp good-quality balsamic vinegar
finely grated zest of ½ lime, plus extra for sprinkling
2 drops of lime juice

1 Line a medium-deep freezerproof tray with baking paper. Put all the ice cream ingredients in a bowl and whisk together until smooth. Pour into the prepared tray and freeze for at least 3 hours, or until hard. Remove and break into small chunks, put into a food processor and blend briefly to a smooth, firm purée – you don't want the mixture to defrost too much. Spoon into a small freezerproof container, smooth the top, cover and return to the freezer for 25–30 minutes until hard again.

2 Meanwhile, put the raspberries in a large bowl with 2 tablespoons of the balsamic vinegar, the lime zest and juice. Gently stir until combined, cover with cling film and put in the fridge.

3 Preheat the oven to 200°C/400°F/gas 6 and line a baking sheet with baking paper. Put the fennel seeds on the prepared baking sheet and dust with the icing sugar until lightly coated. Put in the oven for 4–5 minutes until light golden and caramelized. Return to the oven for a couple of minutes at a time if they are not ready. Remove and leave to cool, breaking up any seeds that may have stuck together.

4 Remove the raspberries from the fridge and, using a slotted spoon, spoon into serving bowls and put a small scoop of ice cream one on top of each bowl of raspberries. Drizzle any of the liquid from the raspberries and the remaining balsamic over the top and finish with a scattering of caramelized fennel seeds and a little extra lime zest. Serve with *langues de chat*.

Pain de Gênes with **Rosemary** and **Tonka Bean Crème Anglaise**

I have loved *pain de gênes* since I was a boy. It was an afternoon cake at home and often served when we had visitors and is similar to a genoise sponge but with toasted flaked almonds on top. For an exotic twist, I'm serving it with a chilli, rosemary and tonka bean crème anglaise and sprinkling it with hazelnuts. Tonka beans, by the way, are wrinkled black seeds with an aroma reminiscent of vanilla and almond – you can buy them online if they are not available in your supermarket.

SERVES 4–6
PREPARATION TIME 40 minutes, plus 30 minutes infusing and cooling
COOKING TIME 50 minutes

FOR THE PAIN DE GÊNES
60g/2¼oz unsalted butter, softened, plus extra for greasing
50g/1¾oz/scant ½ cup strong white flour, sifted, plus extra for dusting
200g/7oz good-quality soft marzipan, ideally 50:50
3 eggs
1 tbsp baking powder, sifted
2 tbsp blanched hazelnuts, toasted and chopped

FOR THE ROSEMARY AND TONKA BEAN CRÈME ANGLAISE
125ml/4fl oz/½ cup full-fat milk
125ml/4fl oz/½ cup whipping cream
leaves from 1 small rosemary sprig
1 small red chilli, deseeded and finely chopped
1 tonka bean or 1 vanilla pod, split in half lengthways and seeds scraped out
3 large egg yolks
50g/1¾oz/scant ¼ cup caster sugar

1 Preheat the oven to 150°C/300°F/gas 2. Grease and flour a deep 20cm/8in loose-bottomed cake tin.

2 To make the *pain de gênes*, put the marzipan and butter in a food mixer fitted with a paddle, or use a bowl with an electric hand whisk, and beat for 5 minutes until soft and light. Add the eggs, one at a time, making sure that they are properly incorporated before adding the next one. When all the eggs have been added, continue to beat for at least 20 minutes until white and fluffy. Add the flour and baking powder and fold in very gently with a large metal spoon. Pour the mixture into the prepared cake tin and sprinkle the hazelnuts over the top. Bake for 35–40 minutes until risen and golden. To check the cake is ready, insert a skewer through the deepest part and if it comes out clean then it is cooked. If not, bake for a further 5 minutes and check again. Remove from the oven, put on a wire rack to cool slightly, then turn out of the tin and leave to cool completely.

3 While the cake is baking, make the rosemary and tonka bean crème anglaise. Put the milk and cream in a saucepan over a medium heat, bring to a simmer, then remove from the heat. Add the rosemary leaves, half the chilli and the tonka bean, stir to combine, then cover and leave to infuse for 30 minutes.

4 Put the egg yolks and sugar in a bowl and whisk until the sugar dissolves. Return the pan of infused cream and milk to a medium-high heat and bring to a simmer, then pass through a sieve onto the egg mixture, whisking continuously. Discard the solids in the sieve. Return the mixture to the pan and cook over a medium heat for 5–8 minutes, stirring continuously with a wooden spoon (otherwise you'll get scrambled eggs!) until it starts to thicken. You will be able to tell when the crème anglaise is ready if, when you run two fingers down the back of the spoon, the two lines don't immediately join. Stir in the remaining chilli. Serve the *pain de gênes* cut into wedges with a generous spoonful of the crème anglaise.

Paris-Brest with Chicory and Coffee Cream

This is a twist on the beautiful, classic Paris-Brest choux pastry dessert, which I've given a whole new dimension by filling it with a delicious mixture of chicory and coffee cream. You will find chicory and coffee online or in specialist coffee shops.

SERVES 4
PREPARATION TIME 45 minutes, plus cooling and 35 minutes resting
COOKING TIME 40 minutes

FOR THE CHOUX PASTRY
180g/6¼oz unsalted butter
¾ tsp salt
¾ tbsp caster sugar
250g/9oz/2 cups plain flour
8 small eggs
a few drops of vanilla extract
1 tsp granulated chicory and coffee

FOR THE CHICORY AND COFFEE CREAM
270ml/9½fl oz/generous 1 cup full-fat milk
2 tsp granulated chicory and coffee
3 eggs
100g/3½oz/scant ½ cup caster sugar
25g/1oz/scant ¼ cup cornflour
150g/5½oz unsalted butter, softened

1 To start the chicory and coffee cream, put the milk in a small saucepan over a medium heat and bring almost to the boil. Stir in the chicory and coffee until dissolved. Remove from the heat, cover and leave to cool.

2 To make the choux pastry, put the butter, salt, sugar and 500ml/ 17fl oz/2 cups of water in a large saucepan and bring to the boil over a medium heat. Remove from the heat and whisk in the flour. Return to the heat and stir gently with a wooden spoon until the mixture starts to come away from the sides of the pan and falls off the spoon easily. Remove from the heat and gently whisk in the eggs, one at a time, until incorporated. Stir in the vanilla, cover with cling film and leave to rest for 35 minutes.

3 Meanwhile, using an 8cm/3¼in biscuit cutter or cup as a template, draw eight circles on a large sheet of baking paper. Turn the paper over and put on a large baking sheet. Preheat the oven to 180°C/350°F/gas 4.

4 Spoon the choux pastry dough into a piping bag, snip off the end to a 2cm/¾in diameter, then carefully pipe eight circles using the rounds drawn on the baking paper as templates. Sprinkle the granulated chicory and coffee on top and bake, with the door ajar by 5cm/2in, for 30 minutes, or until a medium golden brown. (Leaving the door open allows the pastry to dry as it cooks and makes it very light.)

5 While it is cooking, complete the chicory and coffee cream. Whisk together the eggs, sugar and cornflour, using an electric whisk, for about 5 minutes until light and fluffy. Strain the chicory-coffee milk onto the egg mixture and whisk to combine, then return to the pan. Put over a medium-low heat and stir continuously for 10 minutes, or until the mixture starts to thicken. Remove from the heat and continue to stir until the mixture has cooled down and is smooth, thick and slightly trembling. Whisk the softened butter in a separate mixing bowl until very soft, then add the chicory-coffee cream, a little at a time, until incorporated. Continue to whisk for 10 minutes or until you have a very light butter cream.

6 To assemble, halve the choux rings horizontally and spoon the chicory-coffee cream into a piping bag the same size you used for the choux pastry. Pipe the cream over the bases, then gently put on the pastry tops.

Cider-Soaked Babas with Cinnamon Chantilly Cream

In my version of the classic rum baba I'm using an infusion of cider and cinnamon to give a welcome, refreshing, tangy flavour. They are served with a cinnamon Chantilly cream, or you could try ice cream – I know which one I would go for, though!

SERVES 4
PREPARATION TIME 25 minutes,
  plus 50 minutes proving and
  10 minutes cooling
COOKING TIME 12 minutes

FOR THE BABAS
200g/7oz/heaped 1⅔ cups strong
  white flour
a pinch of salt
1 tbsp caster sugar
2 eggs
60g/2¼oz unsalted butter, very soft,
  plus extra for greasing
7g/¼oz fresh yeast or 5g/⅛oz dried
  yeast mixed with 1 tbsp warm
  water

FOR THE CIDER AND CINNAMON INFUSION
1.5l/52fl oz/6 cups good-quality dry
  cider
110g/3¾oz/scant ½ cup caster
  sugar
1 cinnamon stick

FOR THE CINNAMON CHANTILLY CREAM
200ml/7fl oz/scant 1 cup double
  cream
1 heaped tbsp caster sugar
a pinch of ground cinnamon or
  ½ tsp vanilla extract

1 To make the babas, put all the ingredients in a food mixer bowl and, using the dough hook, mix slowly until it forms a soft dough, then remove the bowl from the machine. (Alternatively, put all the ingredients in a mixing bowl and mix using a wooden spoon for 2 minutes until it forms a soft dough. Tip out onto a lightly floured work surface and knead for about 6 minutes until smooth.) Cover the bowl with a clean tea towel and leave at room temperature for 30 minutes until risen by half. When risen, press it down with one hand to knock back.

2 Lightly grease a 12-hole deep muffin tin and put on a baking sheet. Divide the dough into 12 pieces, each about the size of a golf ball. Take a ball of dough in your hand, form a fist and squeeze the dough out through the bottom of your fist into a muffin hole. Repeat with all the dough. (It is important that the muffin holes are only half filled to allow the dough to rise.) Cover with a clean tea towel and leave to rise in a warm place for 20 minutes or until doubled in size.

3 Meanwhile, make the cider and cinnamon infusion. Put the cider and sugar in a large saucepan and bring to the boil over a medium heat. Stir to dissolve the sugar, then remove from the heat. Add the cinnamon stick, cover and leave to infuse for 30 minutes.

4 To make the cinnamon Chantilly cream, whip the cream with the sugar and ground cinnamon, using an electric whisk, until soft peaks form. Cover and put in the fridge until ready to serve.

5 Preheat the oven to 190°C/375°F/gas 5. Bake the babas for about 12 minutes, turning the tin once, until golden and cooked through. Remove from the oven and leave to cool in the tin for 5 minutes, then turn out onto a wire rack to cool completely.

6 Remove the cinnamon stick and check that the cider and cinnamon infusion is still warm. If not, reheat it briefly. Carefully dip the babas, two at a time, into the cider infusion, pushing them under until wet and heavy. Serve the babas with the cinnamon Chantilly cream.

FRATERNITÉ

Dishes that bring innovation and style to classic combinations of ingredients

In these recipes, you'll find a sense of originality, as I have taken ingredients that are classically put together, but combined them in innovative ways – in a kind of union, a friendship that can be achieved by modern association. There is more imagination in the construction of these dishes, so some may be more challenging to cook, but also more fun. I am sure your guests and family will enjoy these creative recipes.

There are some lovely ideas to discover in this chapter, from Smoked Duck and Lentils with Lavender (see page 154) to Chocolate, Chilli and Lemongrass Tart (see page 208). You'll find ingredients that you may not have thought of putting together, but which will lift the dish and delight you when you taste them, so I am very much hoping that you will try the recipes and give me some lovely feedback.

Chicken, Leek and Wild Mushroom Parcels

I wanted to try a twist on a *pithivier*, a puff pastry torte, and I decided filo pastry would make it both unusual and lighter. I am sure you will find this fun – especially when you get to eat the delicious results.

SERVES 4
PREPARATION TIME 20 minutes, plus making the stock and 30 minutes marinating
COOKING TIME 1 hour

270g/9½oz unsalted butter
2 boneless skinless corn-fed chicken breasts, about 180g/6¼oz each, cut into 2cm/¾in cubes
grated zest and juice of 1 lemon, plus 1 whole lemon
2 tbsp Greek yogurt
2 tsp finely chopped tarragon leaves
1 small young leek, green part cut in half lengthways and then into slices, white part reserved for something else
200g/7oz mixed wild or shiitake mushrooms
1 tbsp sunflower oil
2 x 270g/9½oz packs fresh filo pastry, cut into 16 x 22cm/ 6¼ x 8½in rectangles
1 egg, beaten
2 tbsp sherry vinegar
200ml/7fl oz/scant 1 cup Chicken Stock (see page 16)
200ml/7fl oz/scant 1 cup whipping cream
sea salt and freshly ground black pepper

1 To make the clarified butter, put 250g/9oz of the butter in a saucepan over a very low heat. Leave it for 30 minutes until the butter has melted and the solids have fallen to the bottom. Remove from the heat.

2 Mix the chicken, lemon zest and juice, yogurt and half the tarragon in a non-metallic bowl. Cover and marinate in the fridge for 30 minutes.

3 Bring a saucepan of water to the boil, add the leek, return to the boil and blanch for 1 minute. Lift out using a slotted spoon and refresh in iced water, then lift out and pat dry with kitchen paper. Add the mushrooms to the boiling water, blanch for 1 minute, then lift out, refresh and pat dry.

4 Heat a large, non-stick frying pan over a high heat. Add the remaining butter and the oil and when foaming, add the mushrooms and sauté for 2 minutes. Add the leek and chicken and sauté for 2 minutes until starting to colour. Remove from the pan and leave to cool at room temperature.

5 Preheat the oven to 180°C/350°F/gas 4. Cover the pile of filo with a clean damp tea towel and work quickly with one piece at a time. Lay a sheet of filo onto the work surface, brush lightly with clarified butter, then grate a little lemon zest from the whole lemon over the top. Lay a second sheet over the top and brush with butter as before, then season with a little salt. Put another sheet on top, brush with butter again and grate over a little lemon zest. Finish with a fourth sheet, then a little pepper. Beat together the egg and 1 tablespoon of water to make an egg wash. Brush the edges of the pastry with the egg wash, then spoon a quarter of the chicken onto the bottom half of the pastry. Gently fold the pastry over the filling, press the edges together and tuck them under to seal and form a little parcel. Put on a baking tray and put in the fridge while you repeat to make 3 more parcels, then brush the outsides with the clarified butter. Bake for 20–25 minutes until golden and crisp.

6 Meanwhile, return the frying pan to a medium heat, add the sherry vinegar and deglaze by stirring to remove any caramelized bits stuck to the bottom. Add the stock and cream, turn the heat down to low and simmer for 10–12 minutes until there is 200ml/7fl oz/scant 1 cup of sauce thick enough to coat the back of a spoon. Add the remaining tarragon and season to taste. Spoon the sauce over the parcels to serve.

Smoked Duck and **Lentils** with **Lavender**

You can hot-smoke your duck at home or use a cold-smoked, air-dried duck, sliced and served as a salad with the hot lentils. Either way, corn-fed, free-range birds will give the best results. I enjoy both and usually decide depending on the weather, but these flavour combinations always works well.

SERVES 4
PREPARATION TIME 20 minutes
COOKING TIME 35 minutes

FOR THE CRYSTALLIZED ORANGE
1 large orange, washed and
   scrubbed
2 tbsp caster sugar

FOR THE SMOKED DUCK
100g/3½oz/½ cup basmati rice
3 tbsp green tea
1 tsp caster sugar
2 small lavender sprigs
1 tbsp rapeseed oil
2 duck breasts, about 200g/7oz
   each
1 tbsp clear honey
a few chervil leaves

FOR THE LENTILS
200g/7oz/1 cup Puy lentils, picked
   over and rinsed
1 onion, finely chopped
2 cloves
1 bouquet garni, made with 1 thyme
   sprig and 1 parsley sprig, tied
   together with kitchen string
50g/1¾oz unsalted butter
sea salt and freshly ground black
   pepper

1 To crystallize the orange zest, pare the zest from the orange into fine strips using a vegetable peeler or small, sharp knife, cutting away the pith. Put the zest in a small saucepan, cover with cold water and bring to the boil over a medium heat. Remove from the heat, drain, refresh under cold water, then drain again. Repeat this blanching process.

2 Return the zest to the pan over a low heat and add the sugar and 3 tablespoons of water, stirring until dissolved. Raise the heat to medium and bring to the boil, then turn the heat down to low and simmer for 4–5 minutes, or until the zest becomes transparent. Remove from the heat and leave the strips to cool in the syrup.

3 Put a large piece of kitchen foil, shiny-side down, in the bottom of a wok or steamer. Add the rice, tea, sugar and 1 lavender sprig, and drizzle with the rapeseed oil. Cover with a wire rack or steamer insert and lid, and put over a medium heat for 5 minutes, or until the mixture starts to smoke. Quickly put the duck breasts inside, cover with kitchen foil to help seal the duck, then put the lid on, turn the heat to low and smoke for 5 minutes.

4 Meanwhile, put the lentils in a small saucepan and cover with cold water. Bring to the boil, then skim off any foam that rises to the surface. Add the onion, cloves and bouquet garni, turn the heat down to low and simmer for 5–7 minutes until only just tender. Season with salt and pepper to taste, then strain, discarding the flavourings.

5 When the duck is almost ready, heat a non-stick frying pan over a medium heat. Turn off the heat under the smoker, lift out the duck and put the lid back on the smoker. Put the duck, skin-side down, in the hot frying pan and cook for 4–5 minutes. Flip the duck over, brush the skin with the honey and sprinkle over a little of the remaining lavender, then cook for a further 5 minutes. Lift out, cover with kitchen foil and leave to rest, quickly discarding the foil with the smoking ingredients.

6 Heat a non-stick frying pan until hot, add the butter and lentils and stir-fry for a few minutes until hot. Cut the duck into chunks and serve on top of the lentils, sprinkled with the orange zest strips with a little of the syrup, the chervil leaves and a pinch more lavender.

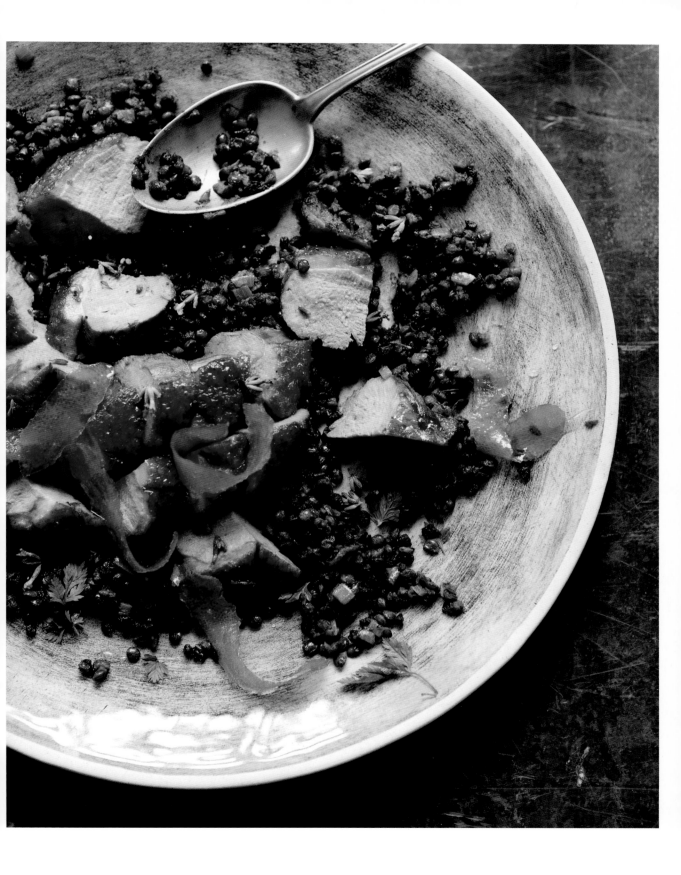

Salmon Marinated in **Fennel** and **Coriander**

I have always loved marinated salmon and sea trout. It makes for a refreshing and delicate dish, which is unusual for your guests as very few people make this at home. It is very much up to you which herbs and fruit you use, as there are many ways to make this recipe, but coriander works well, chives and chervil too. Chervil is fairly difficult to find but as it is one of the tastiest herbs around, you might like to grow your own. You can also use other citrus fruits instead of the grapefruit. Orange, lemon, blood orange or kumquat all work well, but lime is my favourite. But as long as you get the essential sugar-salt combination, you will have a great spring or summer starter.

SERVES 4

PREPARATION TIME 20 minutes, plus 24 hours curing

600g/1lb 5oz salmon fillet, skin on
2 tbsp sea salt, plus extra for seasoning
2 tbsp caster sugar
1 tsp ground cumin
1 tsp ground coriander
2 small fennel bulbs, outer sections removed
finely grated zest of 1 and juice of ½ grapefruit
2 tbsp roughly chopped coriander leaves
1 tbsp olive oil
freshly ground black pepper

1 Put the salmon, skin-side down, on a large piece of cling film. Mix together the salt, sugar, cumin and ground coriander, sprinkle the mixture over the flesh side of the salmon, then finish with a little pepper. Using a mandolin, grate one of the fennel bulbs over the top of the mixture and press it down so it totally covers the fish. Wrap the whole lot in the cling film and put, flesh-side down, in a small baking tray. Cover with another small tray and put a tin or similar weight on top, then put it into the fridge and leave to cure for 24 hours in total, following the instructions in step 2 during that time.

2 After the first 8–10 hours, remove the weight and turn the fish over, flesh-side up. Then turn it flesh-side down, then up, every following 4–5 hours. You can go to bed, just turn it before you go to bed, then again when you get up!

3 The following day, remove the salmon from the fridge and carefully rinse it under cold running water to remove the excess cure, then pat dry on a clean tea towel. Slice as thinly as you can and put on a plate, spreading the slices attractively. Season with a little pepper, a tiny touch of sea salt, some of the grapefruit zest and juice and half the coriander leaves.

4 Finely slice the second fennel bulb on a mandolin or by hand, then toss it in a small bowl with the oil, grapefruit zest and the remaining grapefruit juice and coriander leaves. Season with a little pepper to taste, then serve with the salmon.

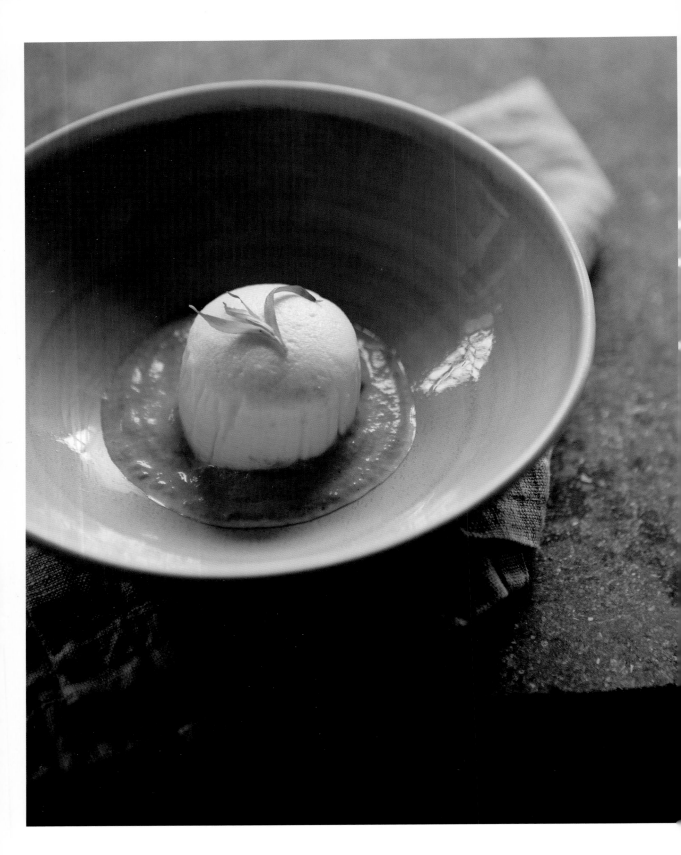

Scallop Soufflé with **Mushroom** and **Tarragon Cream**

This is one of my favourite recipes to serve to friends. Although there's egg and cream, don't think for a minute that the soufflés will be heavy – on the contrary, they are fantastically light. Add the freshness of the tarragon and the earthy mushroom cream and you'll want to make it more than once.

SERVES 4
PREPARATION TIME 30 minutes, plus
  making the stock
COOKING TIME 12 minutes

100g/3½oz scallops, rinsed
1 large egg
185ml/6fl oz/¾ cup whipping cream
20g/¾oz unsalted butter
125g/4½oz button mushrooms,
  roughly chopped
1 tbsp roughly chopped tarragon
  leaves, plus 4 tiny tarragon sprigs
4 tbsp Vegetable Stock (see
  page 17)
sea salt and freshly ground white
  pepper

1 Remove the roes from the scallops, trim off any tough flesh and remove any veins. Put the scallop, egg and 4 tablespoons of the cream into a blender. Season with salt and white pepper and blend to a very fine, smooth, shiny purée. Pass the scallop mixture through a fine sieve into a bowl. Whip 4 tablespoons of the remaining cream until soft peaks form, then whisk it into the purée. Spoon into a piping bag and put in the fridge.

2 Line a plate that will fit inside a large steamer basket with baking paper, then put four 5cm/2in diameter x 5cm/2in deep chef's rings on top, making sure that they do not touch each other. Cut four bands of baking paper 7.5cm/3in long x 5cm/2in deep and use to line the chef's rings. The paper needs to sit snugly inside the rings with the ends overlapping.

3 Remove the scallop mix from the fridge and snip the end to give a 1cm/½in opening. Pipe the filling into each ring until two-thirds full and about 1cm/½in below the rim, making sure that you hold onto the ring to stop it slipping. Cover the plate loosely with cling film so that no condensation can get in, yet the soufflés have space to rise. Put a large saucepan of water on to simmer, with a steamer insert on top. Put the plate of soufflés in the steamer, cover, then turn the heat down as low as possible and steam for 12 minutes until risen. Turn the heat off, remove the lid and leave the soufflés to rest for 2 minutes.

4 While the soufflés are cooking, make the mushroom cream. Heat a large frying pan over a high heat. Add the butter and mushrooms and sauté for 3–4 minutes until they just turn golden brown. Add the chopped tarragon and toss to combine. Add the stock and the remaining cream and bring to a simmer, then season with salt and pepper to taste. Pour into a blender and blend to a fine, light, foamy purée.

5 Divide the mushroom cream into four warm soup plates. Remove the plate from the steamer and carefully take off the cling film then, using a small palette knife, transfer a soufflé to the centre of a plate of mushroom cream. Slide out the palette knife, holding the edge of the ring so that it doesn't move around. Lift the ring off and gently peel away the paper lining. Repeat with the remaining soufflés, then top each one with a tiny tarragon sprig to serve.

Langoustine or Prawn Ceviche

So what is ceviche? It is originally a Spanish word, and is a great speciality of Peru, as well as Ecuador and Chile. It is basically raw fish or shellfish marinated in plenty of citrus juice, fresh herbs, onions, shallot and other flavourings. If you use shellfish, make sure they are fresh or freshly frozen – trust your fishmonger as he will have the expertise you need. You'll see that I use garlic here, just enough to bring a little accent to the dish. Enjoy your ceviche served with mango, perhaps, or an avocado, sweet potato and red onion salad with flat-leaf parsley. I use Chardonnay vinegar in many recipes in preference to ordinary white wine vinegar as it imparts a better flavour, so it may be worth buying a bottle.

SERVES 4
PREPARATION TIME 20 minutes,
    plus 3 hours marinating

20 medium to large raw, peeled
    langoustines or tiger prawns,
    cleaned and intestinal thread
    removed
grated zest and juice of 1 lime
1 red chilli, deseeded and finely
    chopped
2 garlic cloves, crushed
2 tbsp Chardonnay vinegar
a pinch of sea salt
1 tsp chopped tarragon leaves
1 hard, green eating apple, such as
    Granny Smith
Mayonnaise (see page 18), flavoured
    with chilli, tarragon or garlic, to
    serve

1 Reserve 4 whole langoustines, then cut the rest into 1cm/½in chunks and put in a non-metallic bowl. Add the whole langoustines, then add the lime zest and juice, chilli, garlic, vinegar and a pinch of salt and gently fold everything together. Cover and leave to marinate in the fridge for 2–3 hours.

2 Just before you are ready to serve, core the apple, then cut it into thin slices from top to bottom, discarding the ends that are all skin. Stack the slices and cut through them to form thin matchsticks.

3 When ready to serve, remove the langoustines from the fridge, take out the whole langoustines, then add the tarragon and all but 1 tablespoon of the apple and fold together. Spoon the mixture into four glasses, then hang the whole langoustines on the edge of the glasses. Scatter the remaining apple over the tops and serve immediately with mayonnaise flavoured with your chosen spice or herb.

Crab Tian with Artichoke and Pepper Confit

Spring is the time for this recipe, when you can get some lovely crab, freshly cooked for you, or why not try cooking the crab yourself? If you like, you can also use a little of the brown meat and mix it with the white, which will give the dish more strength and flavour. The red peppers need to be roasted, but that's very easy or, if you're short of time, just use a 290g/10¼oz jar of roasted Spanish piquillo peppers. The ingredients make for a brilliant combination with a light mayonnaise with a touch of tarragon for freshness.

SERVES 4
PREPARATION TIME 15 minutes, plus making the mayonnaise and dressing
COOKING TIME 12 minutes, plus 8 minutes cooling

2 small to medium red peppers
400g/14oz fresh white crab meat
60ml/2fl oz/¼ cup whipping cream, lightly whipped
4 tbsp Mayonnaise (see page 18)
2 tsp chopped tarragon leaves
1 tsp grainy mustard
grated zest and juice of 1 small lime
300g/10½oz jar whole chargrilled artichokes, drained
50g/1¾oz baby rocket leaves
a few drops of Tabasco sauce
a few drops of Worcestershire sauce
2 tbsp French Dressing (see page 18)
sea salt and freshly ground black pepper

1 Preheat the grill to high. Put the peppers on a tray under the grill and cook for about 8 minutes until charred on all sides, turning regularly. Transfer to a bowl, cover with cling film and leave to cool. When nearly cold, remove and discard the skin and seeds, then cut the cooked peppers into quarters.

2 Put the white crab meat in a bowl with the cream, mayonnaise, tarragon, mustard, lime zest and juice and mix to combine, then season with salt and pepper to taste.

3 Put a piece of the red pepper into the base of individual soup plates. Take a spoonful of the crab mixture and put on top of each piece of red pepper, then top that with a piece of artichoke, then another piece of red pepper, another quenelle of crab, and finally another artichoke. Divide the rocket leaves among the plates. Whisk the Tabasco and Worcestershire sauces into the French dressing, then drizzle over the top to serve.

Pan-Fried Chilli Squid with Garlic Mayonnaise

Squid is another of my favourite foods. In Spain it is everywhere, mainly served as tapas but cooked and flavoured in many different ways. At The Vineyard we sometimes prepare squid *sous-vide* – sealed in a bag and slowly cooked in a water bath – but I like it fried this way, too, with the squid coated in spiced breadcrumbs and fried until golden, then served with the perfect garlic mayonnaise. You can buy panko breadcrumbs in your supermarket. In fact, the name just means 'breadcrumbs' but they are processed to form flakes rather than fine crumbs so tend to give a crispier coating.

SERVES 4
PREPARATION TIME 25 minutes
COOKING TIME 6 minutes

4 squid, about 175g/6oz each
200g/7oz/2 cups panko
  breadcrumbs
1 tsp dried chilli flakes
3 eggs, beaten
2 red chillies, deseeded and finely
  chopped
100g/3½oz/heaped ¾ cup plain
  flour
2 tbsp sunflower oil
80g/2¾oz unsalted butter
4 tbsp very finely chopped flat-leaf
  parsley leaves

FOR THE GARLIC MAYONNAISE

2 egg yolks
1 tbsp white wine vinegar
1 tbsp Dijon mustard
150ml/5fl oz/scant ⅔ cup sunflower
  oil
2 garlic cloves, crushed to a paste
grated zest of 1 lime
sea salt and freshly ground black
  pepper

1 Start by preparing the squid. Wash them thoroughly, then pat dry, remove the tentacles and leave to one side, then remove and discard the beak. Cut the body in half lengthways, then rinse and pat dry again. Cut the body in half lengthways once more so you have 4 pieces for each squid, plus the tentacles. Pat dry with kitchen paper.

2 To make the garlic mayonnaise, put the egg yolks, vinegar and mustard in a medium bowl and whisk together. Whisking continuously, drizzle in the oil a little at a time until the mayonnaise is thick and creamy. Add the crushed garlic and lime zest and season with salt and pepper to taste. Cover and put in the fridge until ready to serve.

3 Put the breadcrumbs into a food processor with the dried chilli and blitz to a fine powder. Pour onto a plate. Break the eggs into a bowl and whisk with the chopped fresh chilli. Put the flour on a plate. Pass the squid through the flour, then drop into the chilli egg and finally into the chilli breadcrumbs, tossing to coat on all sides.

4 Heat a frying pan over a medium-high heat. Add the oil and half the butter and when the butter is foaming, add half the squid and pan-fry for 2–3 minutes, turning once, until golden brown and crunchy. Drain on kitchen paper, then repeat with the remaining butter and squid.

5 Pile the squid on a large plate, scatter the parsley over the top and put it in the centre of the table with the garlic mayonnaise and let everyone help themselves.

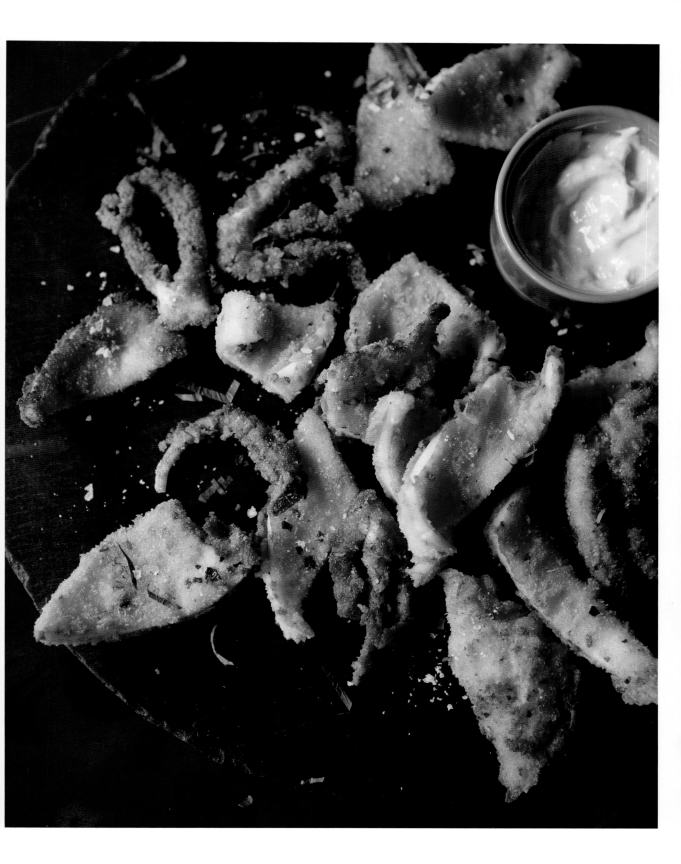

Red Onion Tarte Tatin with Goats' Cheese

This is a twist on the classic tarte tatin as it is made not with fruit, but with onions – deliciously sweet red onions, to be precise – using more or less the same principle and technique. To go with my onion tart, I have chosen goats' cheese, which for me is the perfect partner, and I have also created these as individual tarts, which means they are ideal for serving as a meal for a starter or lunch, and make a lovely dish to serve outdoors, sitting on the terrace or in your garden. My choice of accompaniment would be some fresh salad leaves, or a pea shoot or herb salad, either of which would go well.

SERVES 4
PREPARATION TIME 25 minutes, plus 30 minutes chilling
COOKING TIME 1 hour

375g/13oz ready-made puff pastry
plain flour, for dusting
200g/7oz/heaped ¾ cup caster sugar
½ tsp lemon juice
4 thyme sprigs
6 red onions, peeled, root trimmed to the level of the base and cut into quarters
1 egg, lightly beaten
100g/3½oz soft goats' cheese log, such at Ste Maure, rind removed
1 tsp black onion seeds
4 handfuls of pea shoots
1 tbsp extra virgin olive oil
sea salt and freshly ground black pepper

1 Roll out the pastry on a lightly floured work surface and cut into 4 discs, each about 20cm/8in in diameter. Put the pastry on a baking sheet, cover with cling film and chill in the fridge for 25–30 minutes to prevent the pastry shrinking during baking.

2 Meanwhile, preheat the oven to 160°C/315°F/gas 2½. Melt the sugar, lemon juice and 80ml/2½fl oz/⅓ cup of water in a non-stick frying pan over a low heat. Increase the heat to medium and cook for 10–12 minutes until it turns a rich golden brown. Divide into four 15cm/6in non-stick cake tins or ovenproof dishes. Put a thyme sprig in the centre of each tin, then put the red onion quarters, rounded-side down, into the caramel; there should be 6 quarters in each pan. Bake for 20 minutes, then remove from the oven and turn the oven up to 190°C/375°F/gas 5.

3 Take the pastry out of the fridge and quickly and carefully put the pastry over the top of the onions, pushing the edges down into the sides of the dishes. Brush the tops with the egg wash. This needs to be done really quickly as the pastry will start to melt if you take too long. Sprinkle a little sea salt over the top, then return it to the oven and bake for a further 20–25 minutes until the pastry is golden brown and crisp.

4 Remove the tarts from the oven and leave to cool for a few minutes. Put an upside-down plate the size of the dish on top of the first tart and, holding both the plate and dish, flip it over to unmould the tart onto the plate. Crumble the goats' cheese over the top of the tart and sprinkle with the black onion seeds. Repeat with the remaining tarts.

5 Toss the pea shoots with the extra virgin olive oil in a small bowl, then season with salt and pepper. Serve the tarts as the cheese just starts to melt, with the pea shoot salad served separately.

Celeriac and Apple Rémoulade with Crystallized Celeriac Leaves

What better to have as part of a fresh tray of crudités than a celeriac *rémoulade* – well, perhaps, a *rémoulade* with a little freshly cut, crunchy green apple to bring some essential acidity to cut through the richness of the mayonnaise. You'll see what I mean when you try it, as the apples really raise the dish to another level. I have also used the leaves of the celeriac, which you may be able to get if you buy your celeriac from a market, but not from a supermarket. If you can't get them, just use celery leaves. They are more tender and a touch less bitter but will work fine as they will be sprinkled with caster sugar before being dried in an oven and becoming crystallized. It is a fun idea that's worth doing if you have some time to hand, and it really finishes the dish beautifully.

SERVES 4
PREPARATION TIME 25 minutes, plus making the mayonnaise and 20 minutes marinating
COOKING TIME 6–8 hours

leaves from 1 head of celeriac or celery
1 egg white, lightly whisked
4 tbsp caster sugar
1 small celeriac, about 500g/ 1lb 2oz total weight, peeled
1 lemon, halved
grated zest of 1 lime
5 tbsp Mayonnaise (see page 18)
2 tbsp Dijon mustard
1 tbsp whipping cream, lightly whipped
1 crisp green eating apple, such as Granny Smith, cored
sea salt and freshly ground black pepper

1 Preheat the oven to 70°C/150°F/gas ¼ with the fan switched off. Line a baking sheet with baking paper.

2 Pick all the leaves from the celeriac, and leave to one side about 24–28 very fine, pale, flat leaves from the centre, then roughly chop the remaining green, slightly firmer leaves. Put the fine leaves in a single layer on the prepared baking sheet, then brush with a little egg white on one side. Sprinkle the sugar lightly over the top of the egg white and put in the oven for 6–8 hours until fully crystallized and dry. Remove from the oven and leave to one side.

3 Quarter the celeriac lengthways, then rub all over with a cut lemon to stop it from turning brown. Grate into long strips (you can use a mandolin if you have one, just take care) and put in a bowl with another squeeze of lemon juice. Add the chopped celeriac leaves and lime zest, then add the mayonnaise, mustard and cream and fold together. Cover and leave to marinate in the fridge for 20 minutes.

4 Just before the *rémoulade* finishes marinating, cut the apple into fine slices from top to bottom, discarding the end slices that are all skin, then stack the slices back up and cut through into small matchsticks.

5 When ready to serve, fold the apple through the celeriac mixture. Pile the *rémoulade* on a plate and carefully put 4–5 crystallized leaves on top. Serve immediately while the leaves are crisp.

Leek and Potato Terrine

This recipe needs a bit of care but I think you will love the result. Just follow the instructions and you'll soon get the technique right. The recipe contains wild mushrooms and I normally use a summer truffle, but they may be hard to find and quite expensive, so look out for the *trompette*, or horn of plenty mushroom as it's called in Britain, which you can buy dehydrated. If you forage in the autumn and dry your own mushrooms, you could use them.

SERVES 6–8
PREPARATION TIME 30 minutes, plus making the stock and dressing and 24 hours chilling
COOKING TIME 30 minutes

a little oil, for greasing
1l/35fl oz/4 cups Vegetable Stock (see page 17)
8 baby leeks
1.5kg/3lb 5oz floury potatoes, peeled and cut into 12 pieces
15g/½oz dried horn of plenty mushrooms
2 leaves of gelatine, about 4g/⅛oz total weight, soaked in cold water
2–5 drops of truffle oil
125–185ml/4–6fl oz/½–¾ cup French Dressing (see page 18)
2 tbsp chopped flat-leaf parsley leaves
sea salt and freshly ground black pepper

1 Lightly oil a terrine mould or 1kg/2lb 4oz loaf tin, then line with three large sheets of cling film, allowing a long overhang on all sides. Wrap two 500g/1lb 2oz/2¼ cup bags of sugar in two layers of cling film.

2 Bring the stock to the boil in a wide frying pan over a high heat, add the leeks, then turn the heat down to low and simmer for 4–5 minutes until just tender. Lift the leeks out of the stock using a slotted spoon and drain on kitchen paper. Cut in half lengthways and leave to dry.

3 Add the potatoes to the stock a few at a time, return to the boil, then simmer for 10–12 minutes until almost tender; the tip of a knife should just go through with the barest resistance. Lift the potatoes out onto kitchen paper to dry. Simmer the stock until reduced by half.

4 Put 3–4 pieces of potato directly into the bottom of the terrine, making sure that all the base is covered. Cover the potatoes with half of the prepared leeks, cut-side down, then crumble over half of the dried mushrooms. Repeat with a layer of potatoes, the rest of the leeks, the mushrooms, then a final layer of potatoes.

5 By now the stock should have reduced to about 500ml/17fl oz/2 cups. Squeeze out the soaked gelatine and add to the hot stock, whisking until melted. Season with salt and pepper, then strain through a fine sieve over the terrine so that the liquid only just covers the potatoes; you don't want it to come too high up. As you pour, press down lightly on the potatoes so there are no air pockets. Fold the cling film over the top to cover it completely, then put the prepared bags of sugar down the length of the terrine. Cool, then chill in the fridge for 24 hours until totally set.

6 Remove the terrine from the fridge and turn it out in its cling film wrapping onto a small tray. Carefully cut into thick slices with a very sharp, non-serrated knife, and only then remove and discard the cling film.

7 Add the truffle oil to the French dressing (remember, you only want a few drops of truffle oil as it is very strong), then stir in the parsley and drizzle over the terrine to serve.

Warm White Asparagus Salad with Grapefruit Zest Vinaigrette

In France we could almost change our national day to White Asparagus Day. Well, almost, but not quite! But when it comes into season, you will find asparagus on all the tables at home, in restaurants, bistros, brasseries and *auberges* – you name it, it will be on every menu for that short season. I love it, it's just superb. Here, I am serving it with some lovely white grapefruit and a boiled egg and grapefruit dressing that complements the white asparagus perfectly. If you like, you could serve it with some crusty bread and my Chicory and Radish Salad (see page 19).

SERVES 4
PREPARATION TIME 25 minutes, plus making the mayonnaise
COOKING TIME 20 minutes

1 egg
1kg/2lb 4oz white asparagus, peeled and woody ends discarded
1 white grapefruit
1 tbsp Dijon mustard
1 heaped tbsp Mayonnaise (see page 18)
6 tbsp sunflower oil
1 tsp chopped chervil leaves
sea salt and freshly ground black pepper

1 Bring a pan of water to the boil over a medium heat, add the egg, return to the boil, then turn the heat down to low and simmer for 10 minutes. Drain and refresh under cold water, then crack and peel the egg. Finely chop the cooked egg and leave to one side.

2 Divide the asparagus into 4 equal-sized bunches and tie each bunch with kitchen string to secure. Bring a large pan of salted water to the boil over a medium heat, add the bunched asparagus and simmer for 5–8 minutes, depending on the size of your asparagus, until tender but with just a little resistance when pierced with the tip of a knife.

3 Grate the zest from the grapefruit, reserve a pinch and put the rest in a small bowl. Peel the grapefruit, then take out 4 segments, cut each one in half and leave to one side. Juice the rest of the grapefruit, pressing it through a fine sieve into the bowl with the zest. Add the mustard and mayonnaise and whisk together until well blended, then whisk in the sunflower oil in a steady stream. Stir in the chopped egg and chervil and season with salt and pepper to taste.

4 Remove the asparagus from the pan and drain briefly on kitchen paper or a clean tea towel. Remove the string and put the asparagus onto serving plates. Spoon the dressing over the top and finish with the reserved grapefruit segments and a sprinkling of the reserved zest.

SMOKING FOOD

I am a big fan of smoked foods, particularly meat, as I just love those smoky flavours, and although smoking was developed as a way of preserving food, I think it is more about the wonderful flavours it creates. Originally – going back to ancient times – people used to hang their kill to dry in their caves. Since there was no way out for the smoke from the fire, they noticed that both the flavour and the preserving qualities were improved by the smoke … and so it began!

Since then, smoking foods, usually over wood smoke, has become popular in many regions of the world and has developed commercially. In particular, smokehouses were built on farms to preserve meat – well away from the farm buildings to avoid fire spreading if an accident happened – and on the coast, to be handy for the fishermen landing their catch.

The first commercial smoker in the UK was set up in Scotland in 1939. Much later, when I worked in Scotland, there was a small smokehouse just down the road from us, which I used to drive past every day. Those memories will stay with me for ever as I can still vividly recall the delightful smell of the burning wood.

Where I come from in Franche-Comté, smoking foods has always been a speciality and the technique is still very much alive today. On market day, I often used to go shopping with my mum or my sister, Dolores. They were both really good cooks – although that goes without saying in my family as we are all enthusiastic gourmands. Anyway, you will see that in this book, I like to use products from my home area and one of those is Morteau, a rather delicious smoked sausage. We often bought this from the market, along with smoked pork shoulder, bacon or neck. To serve with it, Mum used to make a lovely sauerkraut with turnip instead of cabbage – that day was one we looked forward to.

At The Vineyard

We serve some smoked dishes in my restaurant. My friend, John, has supplied our smoked salmon, haddock and mackerel for the last 20 years and, trust me, he is very good at it! I also love to use some smoked ingredients, like smoked paprika and, of course, Morteau sausage. But we also do some smoking ourselves; my particular favourites are smoked beetroot, which has a wonderful earthy flavour, to serve as a side dish or as part of a salad, and smoked duck, a meat that seems perfect to prepare in this way.

Foods for smoking

All kinds of poultry and meat can be smoked, creating a range of products from spiced pastrami to smoked bacon. Smoked fish ranges from cod or haddock to salmon, herring or mackerel. Tofu and cheeses absorb fabulous flavours in the smoker, as do nuts, vegetables like peppers and beetroot, and fruit such as prunes, which are often smoked while drying. Then there are smoked teas, like lapsang souchong, and even whisky. It is important to remember, though, that there are various methods of smoking and not all act as a preservative.

Hot and cold smoking

Whatever their size, smokers create heat and smoke by burning wood chips or sawdust, or they may have gas burners. In the UK, oak or alder are the woods of choice in most smokehouses, as well as beech and fruit-tree woods, such as apple. In the US, corncobs are popular, while in New Zealand, they like to burn the wood from the manuka tree. Some smokers also have steam coils to create humidity and maintain the correct temperature, which is obviously crucial or the results will be dry and flavourless.

Hot smoking uses both smoke and heat in a wood-fired oven, a smoke-roaster or even a barbecue. The temperature reaches 52–80°C/125–176°F so, at the higher temperatures, the food is cooked as well as absorbing the smoky flavours.

Cold smoking does not cook the food as the temperature of 20–30°C/62–68°F only imparts the wood-smoke flavour, so many cold-smoked foods are cured in brine first. For our smoked recipes, I'm using a method based on a Chinese technique known as tea smoking, as a combination of rice, tea and sugar is used to create the smoke. We'll then cook our smoke-flavoured foods afterwards. (I decided that the Icelandic tradition of smoking fish over dried sheep's dung was perhaps not one to try at home!)

How it's done

I hope you will try this method. You can buy smokers in pre-packed sets and there is a vast range of different wood chips available online for you to try. However, I would recommend you use my tea-smoking option first as you can simply adapt your steamer or wok.

Just one reminder. Do be careful of the heat and smoke, especially when disposing of the smoking ingredients as they'll stay hot for a while even after you take them off the heat.

- You need a steamer with a lid, or a wok with a lid and a metal rack, and some kitchen foil.
- Your smoking mixture is 100g/3½oz/½ cup basmati rice, 2 tablespoons of green tea and 2 teaspoons of caster sugar.
- Prepare the food as if you were going to cook it, so trimmed, stoned, left whole or sliced.
- Put a large piece of kitchen foil, shiny-side down, in the bottom of a steamer or wok. Put the rice, tea and sugar on the foil, cover with a steamer insert or wire rack, then put on the lid. Put over a medium heat for about 5 minutes until the mixture starts smoking.

- Quickly lift the lid and put the food onto the rack. Put the lid back on, turn the heat down to low and smoke for the time recommended in the recipe; that's about 5 minutes for chicken or duck pieces.
- Lift out the food and put on a plate to rest.
- Wrap the smoking ingredients in the foil and discard them carefully.

Leave the food to cool, or continue to cook, following the recipe instructions, then savour those stunning flavours. Try smoking a cod fillet following the method below, or try Smoked Duck and Lentils with Lavender (see page 154) or Smoked Chicken, Courgette, Garlic and Rosemary Casserole (see page 174).

Fennel-Smoked Cod with Warm Bean Salad

When you smoke fish with herbs such as fennel, the subtle scent permeates the fish to complement the lovely smoky flavour. Try this simple cod recipe.

Add a pinch of dried fennel to the smoking mixture (left) in the foil-lined wok, then put in the smoker 2 very fresh pieces of cod, skin-side down, season with salt and pepper, cover and smoke for 5 minutes. Remove them from the smoker and brush the skin with a little olive oil. Heat a frying pan over a medium heat and pan-fry the cod, skin-side down, for about 5 minutes until the skin is wonderfully crisp and golden. Flip it on the other side and cook for 2 minutes to finish it off. Cool and discard the smoking ingredients.

The perfect partner would be a warm white bean salad. Gently warm 300g/10½oz cooked white beans in a pan with 1 or 2 diced oven-dried tomatoes and a chopped garlic clove. Take off the heat and stir in 2 teaspoons of chopped parsley leaves, drizzle with a little extra virgin olive oil and top with your smoked cod fillet to serve. You are in paradise! Can I join you for dinner?

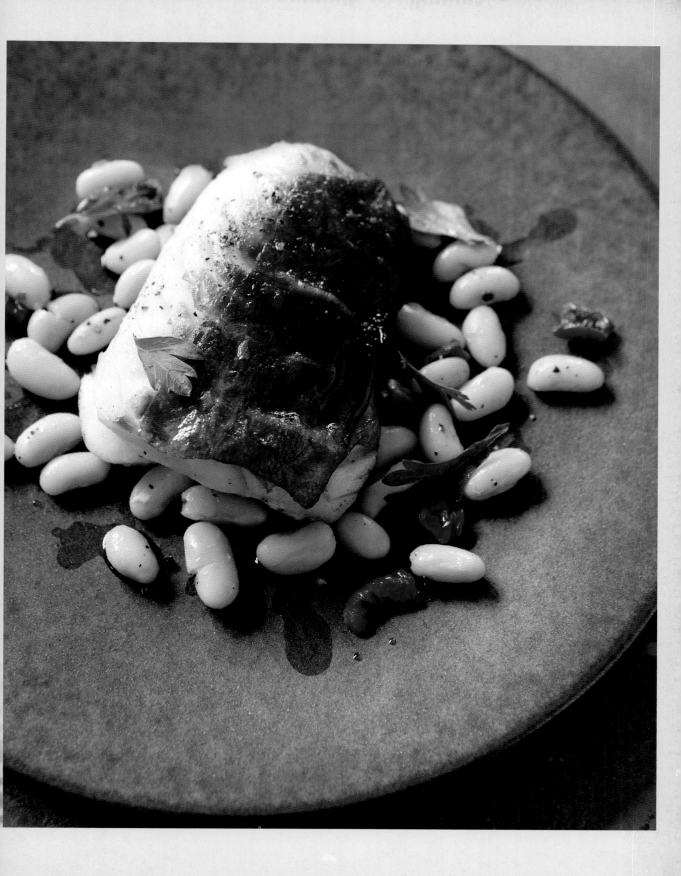

Smoked Chicken, Courgette, Garlic and **Rosemary** Casserole

A steamer works perfectly as a smoker so, if you have one, do give this recipe a try. You put the smoking mix in the bottom and the chicken in the top, but do keep it on a low heat – you don't want your smoke alarm to go off, so take it easy and don't get too excited! The green tea will bring a lovely flavour to the chicken, which will infuse into the courgettes. It's almost as if you'd grilled the courgettes as it recalls that wonderful, smoky scent.

SERVES 4
PREPARATION TIME 10 minutes, plus making the stock
COOKING TIME 50 minutes

100g/3½oz/½ cup basmati rice
2 tbsp green tea
2 tsp caster sugar
4 chicken legs, with thighs and drumsticks separated
20g/¾oz unsalted butter
2 tbsp sunflower oil
2 tbsp olive oil
400g/14oz courgettes, cut in half lengthways, then cut into 2.5cm/1in pieces
12 garlic cloves, unpeeled
4 tbsp sherry vinegar
500ml/17fl oz/2 cups Chicken Stock (see page 16)
1 rosemary sprig
1 tsp chopped rosemary leaves
sea salt and freshly ground black pepper

1 Put a large piece of kitchen foil, shiny-side down, in the bottom of a steamer, then put the rice, tea and sugar on the foil, cover with a steamer insert and lid and put over a medium heat for about 5 minutes until the mixture starts smoking. Quickly lift the lid and put all the chicken inside. Put the lid back on, turn the heat down to low and smoke for 5 minutes. Lift out the chicken and put on a plate to rest, wrapping the smoking ingredients in the foil and discarding them as quickly as you can.

2 Season the chicken with salt and pepper. Put a flameproof casserole dish over a medium-high heat. Add the butter and sunflower oil and when the butter is foaming, add the chicken, skin-side down, and cook for 6–8 minutes until golden brown all over, turning occasionally. Remove from the pan and put in a bowl, cover with cling film and leave to rest.

3 Discard the oil from the casserole dish and lightly wipe the excess away with kitchen paper, taking care not to disturb the sediment. Return the dish to a medium-low heat, add the olive oil, courgettes and garlic and cook gently for 4–5 minutes until coloured but only just tender.

4 Move the courgettes to the sides of the pan and put the chicken pieces in the centre to reheat. Turn the heat up to medium and when you can actually hear the food starting to cook, add the sherry vinegar straight away; it should evaporate immediately. Quickly pour the stock over the top and throw in the rosemary sprig. When the stock comes to a simmer, gently wriggle the pan around a little so that nothing is stuck to the bottom, then put the lid on top without closing it completely – you just want a little gap so that condensation doesn't create too much liquid, but not too large so that the liquid evaporates. Cook for 15 minutes.

5 Remove the lid and discard the rosemary. Turn the heat to high and cook for a further 5 minutes, stirring to remove any caramelized bits stuck to the bottom, until the sauce is shiny and just thick enough to coat the back of the spoon. Add the chopped rosemary and season with salt and pepper to taste, then serve hot. Guests can squeeze the garlic out of the skins into the dish.

Poached Chicken with **Lemon Zest** and **Black Olives**

Here I have modernized a classic *poulet au pot*, bringing in some Mediterranean flavours with olives and lemon. You would normally serve the bouillon first as a soup, then the garnish – the vegetables – with the chicken as a main course. But I have taken some of the liquid and reduced it to a sauce, then added olives, thyme and lemon zest – it makes it very refreshing. Try both and see which one you prefer; that would make a really interesting comparison.

SERVES 4
PREPARATION TIME 30 minutes
COOKING TIME 1½ hours

1.5kg/3lb 5oz chicken
4 carrots, peeled
4 small turnips
4 small new potatoes, such as
    Charlotte, scrubbed
4 baby leeks
1 thyme sprig
150ml/5fl oz/scant ⅔ cup whipping
    cream
1 large handful of pitted black olives
grated zest and juice of 1 lemon
1 tbsp thyme leaves
1 tbsp extra virgin olive oil

1 Tie the legs of the chicken together by the top of the cavity with a piece of kitchen string. Put the chicken in a large, flameproof casserole dish, cover with cold water and bring to the boil over a high heat. When it starts to simmer, skim off any foam that rises to the surface; this helps to keep the soup nice and clear.

2 Add the carrots and cook over a very low heat for 15 minutes, just keeping the water simmering. Add the turnips and cook for 15 minutes, then the potatoes and cook for 15 minutes, and finally the leeks and thyme sprig and cook for a further 15 minutes. It will have simmered for 1 hour in total and the chicken should be cooked through, so the juices run clear when the thickest part is pierced with the tip of a sharp knife, and the vegetables all perfectly tender.

3 Remove from the heat and ladle out 300ml/10½fl oz/scant 1¼ cups of the cooking liquor straight into a sauté pan. Put over a low heat, add 100ml/3½fl oz/scant ½ cup of the cream, bring to a simmer and simmer for 10–12 minutes until reduced by half.

4 Whip the remaining cream in a small bowl, then add it to the sauce, return to a simmer, then remove from the heat. The sauce should just be thick enough to coat the back of a spoon. Add the olives, lemon zest and a squeeze of lemon juice, then taste before adding any more lemon juice; it should just be slightly lemony, but not acidic. Add the thyme leaves and stir through.

5 Lift the chicken and potatoes out of the bouillon – you can use the bouillon and remaining vegetables for a soup. Discard the string, cut the chicken into 4 pieces and put straight onto a serving plate. Crush the potatoes with a little extra virgin olive oil and serve alongside, then spoon the sauce over the top.

Steamed Cabbage with **Pork** and **Hazelnut Stuffing** and **Creamy Mustard Sauce**

SERVES 4

PREPARATION TIME 25 minutes, plus making the stock

COOKING TIME 1 hour 20 minutes

1 large Savoy cabbage, 3 outer leaves discarded and root trimmed so it sits flat
1 tbsp sunflower oil
500g/1lb 2oz shoulder of pork, cut into small dice
1 small onion, chopped
2 small carrots, peeled and diced
6 garlic cloves, finely chopped
60g/2¼oz finely sliced pancetta, cut into julienne strips
150ml/5fl oz/scant ⅔ cup Chicken Stock (see page 16)
100g/3½oz minced pork
50g/1¾oz pig's liver, finely chopped
1 egg
2 tbsp fresh breadcrumbs
2 tbsp blanched hazelnuts, toasted and chopped
2 tbsp chopped flat-leaf parsley
sea salt and freshly ground black pepper

FOR THE CREAMY MUSTARD SAUCE

30g/1oz unsalted butter
2 tbsp sunflower oil
1 shallot, finely chopped
80ml/2½fl oz/⅓ cup dry white wine
100ml/3½fl oz/scant ½ cup Chicken Stock (see page 16)
80ml/2½fl oz/⅓ cup single cream
1 tsp wholegrain mustard
1 tarragon sprig

Sadly, cabbage is often overcooked, resulting in a brown and virtually flavourless vegetable. I aim to rectify that with this modern steamed cabbage recipe. I have used pork shoulder, but collar is good too, and both will be moister and tastier than dry pieces like loin or fillet.

1 Cut off the top one-third of the cabbage, like a lid, and leave to one side. Gently pull out the leaves so you can get to the centre, without breaking them off. Use an ice cream scoop to scoop out most of the inner leaves, giving an outer casing about 2cm/¾in thick. Use the inner leaves for another dish or serve them sautéed with a little butter.

2 Heat a large frying pan over a high heat, add the oil and diced pork and sauté for 4–5 minutes until golden. Transfer to a large bowl. Add the onion, carrots, garlic and pancetta to the pan and sauté for 4–5 minutes until the onion is just soft. Add the stock and deglaze the pan by stirring to remove any caramelized bits stuck to the bottom. Cook for 5–8 minutes until reduced by two-thirds and syrupy. Mix with the pork.

3 In a separate bowl, put the minced pork, liver, egg, breadcrumbs, hazelnuts and parsley, season with salt and pepper and mix well. Mix this into the now slightly cooled pork and vegetable mixture.

4 Put two sheets of cling film, about 50cm/20in long, on top of each other, then put another two sheets across the middle, giving you a cross-shape. Put the hollowed-out cabbage in the centre, then gently open it out and fill it with the pork mixture. Set the lid back on top and then tightly wrap in the cling film. Twist and secure each end with a knot, pushing out any air.

5 Put a large saucepan of water on to simmer, with a steamer insert on top. Put the cabbage in the steamer, cover and cook for 50 minutes until the liquid runs clear when you pierce the pork through the clingfilm with a knife, then turn off the heat and leave to rest in the pan for 10 minutes.

6 Meanwhile, to make the sauce, heat the butter and oil a non-stick frying pan over a medium heat until foaming, add the shallot and cook for 3–4 minutes, stirring occasionally, until golden brown. Add the wine, turn the heat up to high and cook until reduced by half. Add the stock and cook until reduced by half again, then turn the heat down to low, bring to a gentle simmer and slowly stir in the cream and mustard. Add the tarragon and season with salt and pepper to taste.

7 Lift out the cabbage, discard the cling film and cut the cabbage into quarters. Serve with the creamy mustard sauce.

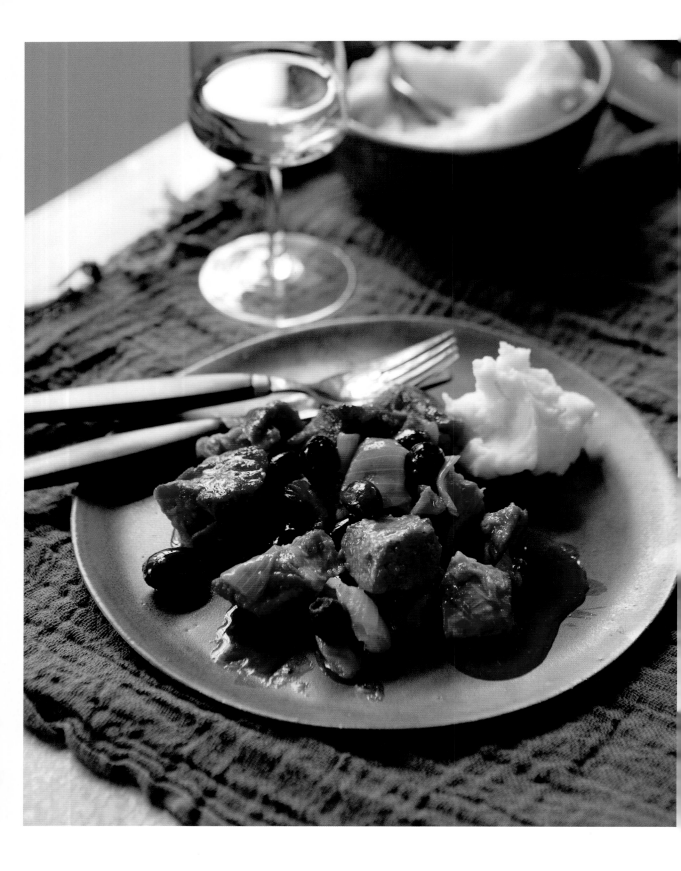

Casserole of Lamb and Pomegranate Molasses

I think this is my favourite casserole in this book. I like to use lamb shoulder as it has excellent flavour, it's moist and there is just the perfect amount of fat needed for it to be tasty – ask the butcher to trim down the fat if there is too much. I'm pairing it with pomegranate molasses, which is a reduction of pomegranate juice that's taken right down to a thick, syrupy liquid. It's slightly tangy with a delicate sweet and sour accent. Just imagine the aromas in your kitchen when this casserole has been cooking for a couple of hours. Your guests will be wondering and asking questions. But make them wait a little longer until they taste it and all will be revealed. Then you can tell them that the secret ingredient fraternizing with the lamb is pomegranate molasses, which lifts a humble lamb shoulder to new heights.

SERVES 4
PREPARATION TIME 10 minutes
COOKING TIME 2½ hours

20g/¾oz unsalted butter
2 tbsp sunflower oil
1 onion, roughly chopped
2 garlic cloves, roughly chopped
1kg/2lb 4oz boneless shoulder or
  neck of lamb, cut into large cubes
500ml/17fl oz/2 cups Lamb Stock
  or Chicken Stock (see page 16)
1 rosemary sprig
1 handful of good-quality stoned
  black olives
2 tbsp pomegranate molasses
grated zest of 1 lemon
sea salt and freshly ground black
  pepper
Creamed Mashed Potatoes (see
  page 20), to serve

1 Heat a flameproof casserole dish over a medium heat. Add the butter and oil and when the butter is foaming, add the onion and garlic, reduce the heat to low and cook for 5–8 minutes until slightly soft and translucent but not coloured.

2 Turn the heat up to high, add the lamb and sauté for 12–15 minutes until golden brown on all sides. Add the stock and rosemary and bring to a simmer, then cover with the lid without closing it completely – you just want a little gap so that the condensation does not produce too much liquid – and simmer over a very gentle heat for 1¾ hours, making sure the liquid is just shimmering but not bubbling.

3 Check that the lamb is very tender and the liquid reduced by about half, but no more. If not, then continue cooking for a further 15 minutes and check again. Add the olives and pomegranate molasses and cook for a further 10 minutes until the sauce is lovely and shiny. Add the lemon zest and season with salt and pepper to taste. Serve with deliciously creamy mashed potato.

Slow-Roasted Shoulder of Lamb with **Garlic, Basil** and **Ginger**

You might ask why I have included another recipe for lamb shoulder in this book. Firstly, because it's delicious – that goes without saying. And because, with the neck and the belly, it is the tastiest cut – flavoursome, moist and succulent. These are the cuts we use in the restaurant. You can keep the shoulder on the bone if you want, as it is slowly cooked, and the bone will come out very easily at the end. Here I have used basil, garlic and also ginger, the latter being slightly more unusual with lamb but bringing an exotic touch that goes really well. Then the Chardonnay vinegar brings a welcome sweet acidity. Make sure you brown the lamb well first, then reduce the heat and slow-cook the lamb to perfection.

SERVES 4–6
PREPARATION TIME 10 minutes
COOKING TIME 3 hours 40 minutes

1.25kg/2lb 12oz shoulder of lamb, either on or off the bone, and tied, if boned, at room temperature
1 tbsp sea salt
3 tbsp olive oil
4 large basil leaves
8 garlic cloves
5cm/2in piece of root ginger, peeled and diced
2 banana shallots
100ml/3½fl oz/scant ½ cup Chardonnay vinegar
750ml/26fl oz/3 cups Lamb Stock (see page 16)
2 tomatoes, quartered
a few small rosemary sprigs
freshly ground black pepper
fried aubergine and courgette slices, to serve

1 Preheat the oven to 220°C/425°F/gas 7. Season the lamb with the salt and plenty of black pepper, massaging the seasoning into the lamb really well. Put it in a deep-sided flameproof roasting tray, drizzle with the oil and roast for 25–30 minutes until browned all the over.

2 Add 2 of the basil leaves, the garlic, ginger and shallots to the tray and return to the oven for 5 minutes. Remove the tray from the oven again and put over a low heat. Add the vinegar, which should evaporate more or less immediately, and deglaze the pan by stirring to remove any caramelized bits stuck to the bottom. Add the stock and tomatoes and stir to combine everything, then cover with kitchen foil, leaving one edge open to allow the steam to escape.

3 Turn the oven down to 140°C/275°F/gas 1, return the lamb to the oven and roast for 30 minutes. Remove the foil, baste the lamb and cover again. Repeat after 30 minutes, then remove the foil and cook for a further 2 hours, basting every 30 minutes. The lamb should be lovely and tender, almost falling apart.

4 Remove the tray from the oven, then pour the juices through a sieve into a sauté pan. Put over a medium-high heat and cook for 5–8 minutes until thick enough to coat the back of a spoon, stirring continuously. Chop the remaining basil leaves and add to the sauce, then season with salt and pepper to taste.

5 Carve the lamb, spoon over the sauce and top with the rosemary sprigs. Serve with some fried aubegine and courgette slices.

Slow-Roast Beef Rib Eye with Carrot and Horseradish Purée

This is a lovely way of eating beef, and cooking it in a really low oven is an excellent way to get that melting texture. I like to serve this with a carrot purée but with a really gorgeous twist – a little freshly grated horseradish. Make sure that you have a good blender to hand so the purée is very smooth. Just drizzle a lovely beef or red wine sauce on it and it's perfection.

SERVES 4

PREPARATION TIME 20 minutes, plus making the stock

COOKING TIME 2½ hours

800g/1lb 12oz rib eye loin of beef, trimmed and tied into a joint, bone reserved
1 tbsp sunflower oil
1 carrot, peeled and chopped
1 onion, chopped
2 garlic cloves, chopped
2 thyme sprigs
200ml/7fl oz/scant 1 cup dry red wine
400ml/14fl oz/scant 1⅔ cups Beef Stock (see page 16)
sea salt and freshly ground black pepper

FOR THE CARROT PURÉE
80g/2¾oz unsalted butter
1 shallot, chopped
1kg/2lb 4oz carrots, peeled and roughly chopped
100ml/3½fl oz/scant ½ cup full-fat milk
200ml/7fl oz/scant 1 cup double cream
2 tbsp finely grated horseradish

1 Preheat the oven to 100°C/200°F/gas ½. Season the beef with salt and pepper. Heat a large frying pan over a medium-high heat. Add the oil and beef and cook for 10–12 minutes, turning until it is a lovely golden brown on all sides and taking care not to burn it on any side. Put the carrot, onion, garlic, thyme and reserved beef bones in a flameproof roasting tray and put the sealed beef on top. Cover loosely with kitchen foil, then roast for 1½–2 hours. Check with a meat thermometer that the temperature in the centre of the beef is 55–60°C/131–140°F, which will give you medium-rare to medium. If you don't have a thermometer, insert the tip of a sharp knife into the meat, then carefully touch it on the inside of your wrist – it should be medium hot.

2 To prepare the carrot purée, heat a saucepan over a medium-low heat. Add half the butter, the shallot and carrots and cook for 10–12 minutes until just tender and the edges are softening but not colouring. Add the milk, cream and horseradish, bring to a low simmer, then cover with cling film tightly so that no air escapes, turn the heat down as low as it will go, and cook for 1½ hours – they will be overcooked and create a delicious confit. Check occasionally and add 2 tablespoons of water if necessary.

3 Use a slotted spoon to put the carrots into a blender, then blitz to a fine purée, adding half the cooking liquor as you go to give you a light, shiny purée. Add the remaining butter and blitz once more to incorporate, then season with salt and pepper to taste.

4 Transfer the beef to a large plate, cover with kitchen foil and leave to rest in a warm place. Put the roasting tray over a medium heat and stir until the juices start to bubble. Add the red wine and deglaze the pan by stirring to remove any caramelized bits stuck to the bottom. Simmer until there is barely any liquid left. Add the stock, bring to the boil, stirring up any sediment, then turn the heat down to low and simmer for 8–10 minutes until reduced by half, shiny and thickened.

5 Remove the string from the beef, then cut it into slices. Spoon the sauce over the beef and serve with the carrot purée, putting any spare sauce into a bowl to serve at the table.

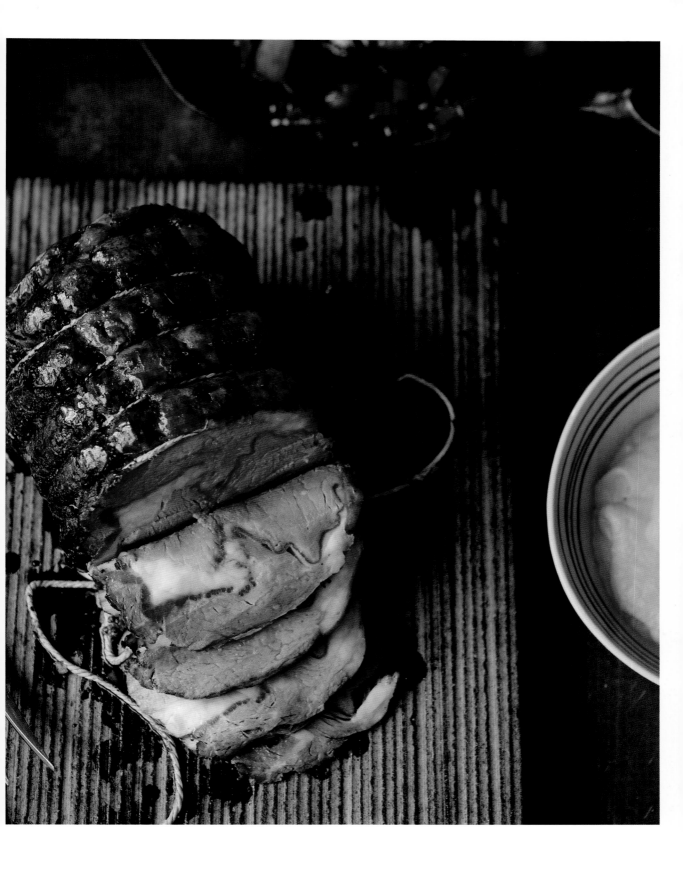

Fennel-Roasted Sea Bream with Fennel Salsa

I have used sea bream and fennel more than once in my demonstrations, although in very different ways, because these two ingredients work so well together. It surprises me that so few people cook with them. People tell me they find the aniseed flavour too strong, or they don't know how to prepare fennel or don't normally use this particular fish. That's a shame because sea bream is very much under-rated, as it is tasty, sustainable and very affordable as one is often enough for two people. So do try this lovely, refreshing recipe as it will show you just how light and pleasant this combination can be.

SERVES 4
PREPARATION TIME 20 minutes
COOKING TIME 20 minutes

4 fennel bulbs, as long as possible
25g/1oz unsalted butter
1 tbsp olive oil
2 sea bream, about 800g/
   1lb 12oz each, gills removed,
   scaled and gutted
1 small red onion, finely chopped
1 tbsp chopped coriander leaves
½ tbsp chopped dill leaves
grated zest and juice of 1 lemon
1 tbsp clear honey
3 tbsp extra virgin olive oil
1 tbsp white balsamic vinegar
sea salt and freshly ground black
   pepper

1 Preheat the oven to 200°C/400°F/gas 6 and line a baking dish with kitchen foil. Cut the top one-third off the fennel bulbs and put them in the prepared dish. Peel off the first 2 layers of the remaining fennel bulbs, chop the layers roughly, then add them to the dish.

2 Heat a large, non-stick frying pan over a medium-high heat. Add the butter and olive oil and when the butter is foaming, add the fish and fry for 3–4 minutes on each side until the skin is light golden brown and slightly crisp. (A little tip, if you're not too sure how non-stick your pan is, cut a sheet of baking paper to fit the bottom of the pan and put it into the hot pan before you add the butter and oil, then cook in the same way – this will prevent it sticking but will not make it hot enough to catch fire.) Season with salt and pepper, then put on top of the fennel in the baking dish. Spoon the cooking juices from the frying pan over the top of the fish, then roast for 12 minutes.

3 To make the fennel salsa, thinly slice the remaining fennel hearts, using a mandolin if you have one. Put them in a large bowl, add the remaining salsa ingredients, season with salt and pepper to taste, then toss together to combine.

4 By now, the fish should be ready – insert a knife into the flesh and it should slice through without any resistance. Remove from the oven and leave to rest in a warm place for 2 minutes. Serve the fish from the baking dish, with the salsa, allowing people to help themselves. The top fillet will lift off the bone very easily. Then lift off and discard the whole bone from the tail end upwards, revealing the succulent fillet on the other side.

Curry-Spiced Cod and **Mango Parcels** with **Coconut and Chervil Sauce**

I love cod, and I am always improvising new ways to cook it. My wife, Claire, always sneaks into the kitchen when I cook cod at home – it's the lovely smells wafting through the house that attracts her. Cooking it *en papillote* is one of my favourite methods – it's fun, fresh, fast and delicious. Here I am giving it a modern twist with Asian ingredients. Even if you like strong spices, stick to a mild curry powder or the cod will be overpowered and the balance of the dish will be lost. Ginger, red onion and Chardonnay vinegar set the right tone for the mango – flavoursome but not too sweet. Then all that's left is to make a light, creamy sauce with coconut milk and herbs.

SERVES 4
PREPARATION TIME 15 minutes
COOKING TIME 30 minutes

4 cod loins, about 150g/5½oz each, skin on
1 tsp light soft brown sugar
2 tbsp Chardonnay vinegar
1 small red onion, thinly sliced
1 firm mango, peeled, pitted and roughly chopped
2.5cm/1in piece of root ginger, peeled and grated
1 small red chilli, halved, deseeded and cut into julienne strips
1 tsp mild curry powder
20g/¾oz unsalted butter
1 tbsp olive oil
60ml/2fl oz/¼ cup Fish Stock (see page 17)
60ml/2fl oz/¼ cup coconut milk
100ml/3½fl oz/scant ½ cup whipping cream, lightly whipped
1 tbsp chopped chervil leaves
1 tsp lemon juice
sea salt and freshly ground black pepper

1 Preheat the oven to 200°C/400°F/gas 6 and cut four 46 x 25cm/18 x 10in rectangles of baking paper. The fish should have been pin boned but, if not, remove all small bones with a pair of fish tweezers.

2 Heat a small frying pan until medium-hot, add the sugar and Chardonnay vinegar and cook for 1–2 minutes until the sugar has dissolved. Add the onion and sauté for 3–4 minutes, then reduce the heat to low, add the mango and ginger and cook for about 8 minutes until the mango has softened but is still holding its shape. Add the chilli, stir gently to combine, then remove from the heat and leave to cool.

3 Season the cod on both sides with curry powder, salt and pepper. Heat a non-stick frying pan over a medium-high heat. Add the butter and oil and when the butter is foaming, add the cod, skin-side down, and sauté for 3–4 minutes until the skin is golden and crisp.

4 Put the baking paper rectangles on the work surface, then spoon the mango equally onto half of each sheet. Put the cod on top, skin-side up. Fold the paper over the filling and then fold along the edges to seal the liquid in securely. Put the parcels on a baking tray and bake for 12 minutes. Remove from the oven and leave to rest for 2 minutes.

5 While the fish cooks, make the sauce. Heat a sauté pan over a medium heat. Add the stock and coconut milk and bring to the boil, then turn the heat down to low and simmer for 4–5 minutes until reduced by half.

6 Carefully open one side of each parcel and pour the juices into the sauce, then put the parcels on serving plates. Whisk the cream into the sauce, return it to the boil, then remove from the heat and season with salt and pepper to taste. Add the chervil and finish with the lemon juice. Serve the parcels *en papillote* at the table with the sauce served separately, or open the parcels, slide out the filling and spoon the sauce on top.

Pancetta-Wrapped Monkfish with Carrot and Mandarin Purée

I can't stress often enough that you will really taste the difference if you buy your fish fresh from your fishmonger. It is that simple with fish. Remember, too, how delicate the flesh is so don't overcook fish; monkfish is a meaty fish and therefore dries out quickly. The pancetta needs to be very thinly sliced and, if possible, a touch longer than normal so you can overlap the slices when wrapping the fish.

SERVES 4
PREPARATION TIME 20 minutes
COOKING TIME 1 hour 20 minutes

4 monkfish fillets, about 140g/5oz
  each, trimmed
20 thin slices of pancetta
200g/7oz carrots, peeled and thickly
  sliced
250ml/9fl oz/1 cup freshly squeezed
  mandarin juice
1 lemongrass stalk, bruised
grated zest of 1 lime
2 tbsp olive oil
25g/1oz unsalted butter
a few coriander leaves
sea salt and freshly ground black
  pepper

1 Season the monkfish with pepper, then wrap each fillet in the sliced pancetta until totally covered. Lay two sheets of cling film on top of each other, then put a monkfish fillet at one edge. Tightly wrap in the cling film to make a sausage shape. Twist and secure each end with a knot, pushing out any air. Repeat with each piece of monkfish. Put in the fridge while you prepare the carrots.

2 Put a large saucepan of water on to simmer, with a steamer insert on top. Put the carrots in the steamer, cover and cook for at least 1 hour until super soft.

3 While the carrots are steaming, put the mandarin juice in a small saucepan over a medium heat, add the lemongrass and half the lime zest and bring to a gentle boil. Turn the heat down to low and simmer for about 15 minutes until the liquid has reduced by two-thirds and is syrupy. Remove from the heat and keep warm.

4 Remove the carrots from the steamer and pat dry with a clean tea towel. Put them in a blender, then strain in the reduced mandarin juice, discarding the lemongrass, and blend to a smooth, soft purée. Season with salt and pepper to taste, then leave to one side to keep warm.

5 Now put the monkfish in the steamer, cover and cook over a very low heat for 8–10 minutes. Remove from the steamer, then cut away and discard the cling film. Put the monkfish onto a clean tea towel to absorb any of the liquid released while cooking.

6 Put half the oil in a sauté pan over a medium heat. Add the monkfish and cook for 3–4 minutes until crisp and golden brown on all sides. Remove from the pan and leave to rest on kitchen paper.

7 Gently reheat the purée until hot, then whisk in the butter and season with salt and pepper to taste. Cut each piece of monkfish in half on the diagonal – if it's cooked properly then you will see a tiny rainbow on the flesh of the fish. Sprinkle the monkfish with the coriander, the remaining lime zest and oil, then serve warm with the purée.

Lemongrass-Skewered Prawns with **Sauce Vièrge**

I guess by now you have noticed that I really like Asian ingredients, perhaps because of my time in Singapore and travelling in Malaysia and the Far East. Using lemongrass as the skewer means it imparts its superb fragrance to the prawns, so do choose fresh green stalks. The *sauce vièrge* finishes the dish beautifully, so make sure you cook plenty as everyone will be asking for more!

SERVES 4
PREPARATION TIME 15 minutes
COOKING TIME 25 minutes

48 large raw peeled tiger prawns
12 lemongrass stalks
2.5cm/1in piece of root ginger,
   peeled and grated
80g/2¾oz unsalted butter
125ml/4fl oz/½ cup olive oil
sea salt and freshly ground black
   pepper
Thai-Style Pilau Rice (see page 21),
   to serve

FOR THE SAUCE VIÈRGE
125ml/4fl oz/½ cup extra virgin
   olive oil
1 tomato, peeled, deseeded and
   diced
1 tsp lightly crushed coriander
   seeds
grated zest and juice of 1 lemon
2 tbsp chopped coriander leaves

1 Preheat the oven to 140°C/275°F/gas 1 and line a baking tray with kitchen foil. Make a small hole through the centre of each prawn with a sharp knife, then thread 4 prawns onto each lemongrass stalk as a skewer. Sprinkle with the ginger, then season with salt and pepper.

2 Heat a large, non-stick frying pan over a medium-high heat. Add 20g/¾oz of the butter and 2 tablespoons of the olive oil and when the butter is foaming, add 3 skewers and fry for 2–3 minutes on each side until just cooked through and golden. You will be able to see the prawns change colour to pink as they cook. Transfer to the prepared tray and put it in the oven, but leave the oven door open – you just want to keep them warm, not for them to cook any more. Repeat with the remaining skewers, butter and olive oil.

3 While the last batch is cooking, make the *sauce vièrge*. Put the extra virgin olive oil, the tomato, coriander seeds, lemon zest and juice in a small saucepan over a low heat and season with salt and pepper. Warm through very gently for 2 minutes, stirring occasionally – you don't want the oil to actually get hot. Remove from the heat, add the coriander leaves, then stir to combine.

4 Simply serve the skewers with the sauce drizzled over the top, with an Asian-style steamed rice of your choice.

Crushed Pea and Mint Tortellini with Pea Shoots

Not only is the pea one of Britain and France's favourite vegetables, but it's also my wife and my son's too – although, botanically speaking, a pea is actually a fruit! The salad is optional but I like it with this dish.

SERVES 4
PREPARATION TIME 40 minutes,
  plus 60 minutes resting
COOKING TIME 15 minutes

FOR THE PASTA
300g/10½oz/2¾ cups pasta flour
1 egg
1 egg yolk
1 tbsp olive oil

FOR THE TORTELLINI
50g/1¾oz unsalted butter
300g/10½oz/scant 2 cups fresh
  podded peas or frozen, defrosted
  (if there are no really fresh ones
  around)
1 tbsp chopped mint leaves
semolina flour, for dusting
100g/3½oz soft goats' cheese log,
  such as Ste Maure, rind removed
sea salt and freshly ground black
  pepper

FOR THE PEA SHOOT SALAD
75g/2½oz pea shoots
1 tbsp olive oil
1 tbsp pumpkin seeds

1 Blitz the pasta ingredients in a food processor until small granules form, then tip out onto a work surface and gather together quickly to form a firm dough. Wrap in cling film and put in the fridge for 30–60 minutes.

2 To make the filling, pour 3½ tablespoons of water into a saucepan over a medium heat, add the butter, season with salt and pepper and bring to the boil. Add the peas and cook for 4–8 minutes for fresh or 2–3 minutes for frozen, or until just tender. Taste one and it should be sweet but with the merest hint of a crunch. Using a slotted spoon, lift the peas out of the water and put 200g/7oz/1⅓ cups in a bowl. Crush them lightly with a fork, season with salt and pepper to taste, then fold in the mint. The mixture should be really moist. Cover with cling film and leave to one side.

3 To make a pea coulis, put the remaining peas in a food processor and blitz until very smooth, then add a little of the cooking liquor and blitz until thick enough to coat the back of a spoon. Pass through a fine sieve into flameproof pasta bowls, cover and leave to one side.

4 Lightly dust a work surface and a baking tray with semolina flour. Roll out the pasta to 1cm/½in thick, then cut into 2 rectangles big enough to fit through your pasta machine. Roll through the machine, decreasing the thickness gauge each time until it reaches the thinnest setting possible, dusting with semolina flour to prevent it sticking. Cut out 20 x 7.5cm/3in discs of pasta. Put a teaspoon of crushed peas onto each disc, just below the centre. Brush the edges of the pasta lightly with water, then fold the top half over the filling and press the edges lightly to seal. Pick up the pasta crescent and twist the edges together, forming a lip on the outside edge, and put the tortellini on the prepared baking tray.

5 To make the salad, toss the pea shoots, oil and pumpkin seeds in a small bowl, then season with salt and pepper to taste.

6 Bring a large pan of salted water to the boil over a high heat, add the tortellini and cook for 4–5 minutes until the pasta floats to the top of the pan. Drain the tortellini, then spoon on top of the coulis on serving plates. Crumble the cheese over the top and top with a little of the salad and a twist of black pepper to serve. Alternatively, you can grill it for a few moments until light gold.

Spring Vegetables with **Watercress** Dressing

I am not a vegetarian, but I do eat a lot of vegetarian dishes, especially in the spring and summer when I really like the colours, taste and freshness of them. The only downside is I am often left wanting more, so I like to make generous portions. That's what you'll find with these spring vegetables complemented with a modern watercress dressing and some perfectly poached quail's eggs.

SERVES 4
PREPARATION TIME 20 minutes,
  plus making the dressing
COOKING TIME 50 minutes

2 bunches of watercress, main
  stems discarded
250ml/9fl oz/1 cup French Dressing
  (see page 18)
120g/4¼oz Chantenay carrots,
  scrubbed
100g/3½oz baby leeks, trimmed
100g/3½oz baby turnips, trimmed
100g/3½oz baby courgettes
100g/3½oz baby corn
2 small bunches of fine asparagus,
  trimmed and cut in half
200g/7oz fine green beans, cut in
  half
100g/3½oz baby new potatoes,
  scrubbed
1 bunch of spring onions, white part
  only, green part kept for another
  dish
175g/6oz baby chargrilled
  artichokes, drained
16 quail's eggs
2 tsp white wine vinegar
sea salt and freshly ground black
  pepper

1 Put 2 small handfuls of watercress leaves to one side. Bring a small saucepan of salted water to the boil, add the remaining watercress and blanch for 30 seconds. Drain and refresh in iced water, then drain briefly so that there's still water on the leaves. Put into a spice grinder or small blender and blitz to a fine purée. Pass through a fine sieve, pressing down into the sieve to release as much juice as possible; there should be about 6 tablespoons of juice. Whisk the juice into the French dressing, season with salt and pepper and leave to one side.

2 Bring a large saucepan of salted water to the boil, add the carrots and blanch for 2–5 minutes until just tender. Use a slotted spoon to lift them out of the pan, then drain and refresh in iced water, drain once more and tip carefully into a bowl. One at a time, blanch all the other vegetables except the artichokes in the same way and put them in the bowl. Keep the saucepan of water for reheating when you are ready to serve.

3 Bring another small saucepan of salted water to the boil, add the vinegar and then crack the eggs into the water and return it to just above a simmer – you want the water to be bubbling so that the eggs don't stick to the bottom of the pan. Simmer for 2 minutes, then lift out the eggs and refresh in a bowl of iced water. Drain on kitchen paper, then season with salt and pepper.

4 Return the saucepan of vegetable water to the boil, add all the vegetables, including the artichokes, and cook for 2 minutes until hot. Lift out of the pan using a slotted spoon and put onto kitchen paper to drain. Add the quail's eggs to the pan of water and heat through for 15–20 seconds until hot, then drain and pat dry.

5 Drizzle the vegetables with the watercress dressing, and top with the quail's eggs, then serve with a scattering of watercress leaves.

Stuffed Courgettes with Camargue Rice and Melted Cheese

My mum often used to make stuffed vegetables to use up leftover food, as when I was growing up, life was hard and food could not be wasted. But actually, we really liked it and sometimes the mix was fantastic – potatoes, tomatoes, aubergines, all with different fillings, lined up on the tray. Served with a freshly made tomato coulis tossed through with fresh herbs, I remember how delicious it was as though it were yesterday. You can try different cheeses, such as a mature farmhouse Comté or Gruyère, which are readily available, or a Tomme de Savoie, which you should find at the deli.

SERVES 4
PREPARATION TIME 20 minutes, plus making the stock and coulis
COOKING TIME 50 minutes

4 large courgettes, trimmed
4 tbsp olive oil
1 large onion, diced
1 small bouquet garni, made with 1 thyme sprig and 1 parsley sprig, tied together with kitchen string
150g/5½oz/heaped ¾ cup Camargue rice or mixed white and wild rice
300ml/10½fl oz/scant 1¼ cups Vegetable Stock (see page 17)
100g/3½oz unsalted butter, chopped
1 recipe quantity Tomato Coulis (see page 21)
60g/2¼oz semi-soft ewes' milk cheese, such as Ossau Iraty, rind removed, grated
sea salt and freshly ground black pepper

1 Preheat the oven to 150°C/300°F/gas 2. Put a saucepan of water on to simmer, with a steamer insert on top large enough to hold all the courgettes. Carefully cut a strip of the smallest amount lengthways down each one, so that they will sit flat on the work surface, then cut lengthways again, taking off the top one-third as a lid. Use a teaspoon to scoop out the inside of the courgettes, taking care not to make a hole in the bottoms or break the sides, and leave the courgettes to one side. If they don't have too many seeds, chop the flesh to use in the pilau.

2 Put the lids back on the courgettes and tightly wrap each one in cling film. Twist and secure each end with a knot, pushing out any air, to keep the lid on top of the courgette. Steam for 12–15 minutes. Turn off the heat, remove the steamer lid and leave to rest while you make the rice.

3 Heat an ovenproof frying pan over a medium heat. Add the oil, onion, chopped courgette, if using, and the bouquet garni and fry for 5 minutes until just softened. Turn the heat down to low, add the rice and fold in gently, then fry for 3–4 minutes. Add the stock, bring to a simmer and season with salt and pepper. Dot the butter over the top of the rice, then cover with a lid or a *cartouche* (see page 218) and put in the oven for 25 minutes. Check to see if the rice is tender and the liquid has all been absorbed. If the rice is not quite tender, then return it to the oven for a further 5 minutes and check once more.

4 Preheat the grill. Run a fork through the rice, discard the bouquet garni and season with salt and pepper to taste. Remove the courgettes from the cling film and turn hollow-side down on a clean tea towel to drain. Turn the bases the right way up in a baking dish and season with salt and pepper. Fill with the rice, pressing down lightly, then put a large spoonful of tomato coulis on top of the rice, sprinkle with the cheese, then put the whole dish under the grill for 2–3 minutes until the cheese has melted and started to colour. Top with the lids and serve with extra tomato coulis.

Caramelized Pineapple and Rum with Vanilla and Szechuan Peppercorns

This is such a lovely dessert, full of an exotic mix of flavours. The pineapple is caramelized with rum – just imagine the aromas rising from the pan. There's also the delicate vanilla flavour and, to finish, the dry-roasted Szechuan pepper, my favourite of all the spices, with its slightly lemony overtones. Only the husks are used, as the seed is discarded. You will find it used a lot in traditional Chinese cuisine, and here I use it to enhance the dish and raise the pineapple to new heights.

SERVES 4
PREPARATION TIME 15 minutes
COOKING TIME 25 minutes

1 large pineapple, peeled, cored, quartered lengthways and halved widthways
200g/7oz/heaped 1 cup light soft brown sugar
2 small vanilla pods, cut in half widthways, then lengthways and seeds scraped out
300ml/10½fl oz/scant 1¼ cups dark rum
50g/1¾oz unsalted butter
20g/¾oz/scant ¼ cup sultanas
½ tsp Szechuan peppercorns, lightly toasted and gently crushed (see page 69)
1 red chilli, deseeded and finely chopped
coconut ice cream, coconut cake or Pistachio Madeleines (see page 75), to serve

1 Roll the pineapple pieces in the brown sugar to coat all sides. Add the vanilla seeds to the rum and mix well.

2 Heat the butter in a large, non-stick frying pan over a medium heat. Add the pineapple and cook for a few minutes on each side. Add the vanilla pods and cook for a further 8–10 minutes until the pineapple is golden brown. Add 100ml/3½fl oz/scant ½ cup of the rum and the sultanas, turn the heat down to low and leave to simmer for a few minutes to reduce, basting the pineapple continuously, until it just forms a light syrup and starts to caramelize.

3 Repeat this three more times, adding one-quarter of the remaining rum each time, then add the remaining rum and the Szechuan peppercorns and repeat once more until you have a lovely thick, light caramel-brown syrup that coats the pineapple. Finally, add the chilli and baste a few more times to fully coat the pineapple. Serve with coconut ice cream, coconut cake or madeleines.

Caramelized Apricots with Pistachio Nuts and Peach Sauce

If there is a season I wait for with impatience, it is spring. Why? One of the reasons is the start of the apricot season; I love this fruit so much. When they are very fresh and ripe, they smell like fresh girolles – sweet, with a hint of dry leaf scent and a touch of flower blossom – gorgeous! So imagine what they are like when pan-fried and then served with crushed pistachio nuts and a lemony peach syrup. You know what, I think I should stop talking about them now – let's just make and enjoy them! By the way, fruit will always cook better when it has either been brought back to room temperature before cooking or has been stored at room temperature. Never cook fruit straight from the fridge as the shock of the heat will quite often make the fruit split or stick to the pan.

SERVES 4
PREPARATION TIME 10 minutes
COOKING TIME 25 minutes

100g/3½oz/scant ½ cup caster sugar
2 large ripe peaches, stone removed and roughly chopped
juice of 1 lemon
1 tbsp chopped pistachio nuts
2 tbsp clear honey
8 large, firm apricots, halved and stone removed
20g/¾oz unsalted butter
Pain de Gênes (see page 146), to serve

1 Heat a non-stick frying pan over a medium heat, add the sugar and 300ml/10½fl oz/scant 1¼ cups of water and heat until the sugar has dissolved and the liquid has just started to simmer. Add the peaches and lemon juice, return to a simmer and poach for 8–10 minutes until very soft and almost puréed, but still holding a little shape. Strain through a sieve, catching the syrup in a clean bowl, and leave to one side so that the juices can drip into the syrup.

2 Put the pan that you've just used for the peaches back over a medium heat, add the pistachios and cook gently for a few minutes until golden and slightly sticky. Drain on a clean tea towel, fold the tea towel over and gently crush the nuts using a rolling pin so they are just partially crushed.

3 Put the same frying pan back onto the heat again. Add the honey and when it is just foaming, add the apricots, cut-side down, and instantly start gently swirling the pan around so that the apricots don't stick or burn. Add the butter and when foaming, turn the apricots over and cook for a few minutes until they are nicely caramelized. Add about 100ml/3½fl oz/scant ½ cup of the syrupy peach juices and cook for a further 3–4 minutes until the apricots are lovely and tender but are still holding their shape.

4 Spoon the apricots over the peaches and drizzle with the last of the peach syrup. Sprinkle with the crushed pistachio pieces and serve with *pain de gênes*.

Cinnamon and Honey-Baked Figs with Sweet Ginger Slices

When I lived in the Algarve in Portugal, I used to eat figs all the time because it is such a favourable climate, the *figier* grew everywhere. As a result of a particularly bad drive on the golf course one day, I found myself off the fairway surrounded by fig trees loaded with fruit ... so ripe, so good, that I ate one fig, then another and another until I completely forgot the game! Meanwhile, my friend – totally intent on the game – marched ahead. That shows you how much I like figs. The best ones for me are the purple-black ones, with their succulent flavour that is perfect in this gratin. The spiced crisp cake is just what you need to complement the dish, while the smooth yogurt with honey – well, imagine how good that is.

SERVES 4
PREPARATION TIME 10 minutes, plus freezing
COOKING TIME 40 minutes

about 9cm/3½in piece of ginger cake, frozen until almost hard
12 firm purple-black figs, cut into quarters from top to bottom but not all the way through, so the figs are held together
2 tbsp clear honey
½ tsp ground cinnamon
75g/2½oz/scant ⅓ cup Greek yogurt
2 egg yolks

1 Cut the cake into 8 thin slices. Freezing the cake until it is nearly hard makes it easier to slice thinly and also gives a much better crisp. Preheat the oven 140°C/275°F/gas 1, line a baking sheet with baking paper and have another sheet of baking paper and a second baking sheet ready.

2 Put the cake slices on the prepared baking sheet, cover with the second sheet of paper, then the second baking sheet so that the cake is held flat, and bake for 6–8 minutes. Carefully lift off the top sheet and paper, checking that the cake is not too coloured, then put back in the oven for 3–4 minutes to dry out. Remove from the oven and leave to cool. Turn the oven up to 180°C/350°F/gas 4.

3 Put the figs in a baking tray, cut-side up, drizzle over the honey and 4 tablespoons of water and sprinkle with 2 pinches of the cinnamon. Roast for 12–15 minutes until they are soft. There will be a lovely liquid left in the baking tray. Pour half into a large, heatproof bowl and leave to one side, and the other half into a serving bowl with the yogurt and mix well. Preheat the grill to medium.

4 Add the egg yolks to the juices in the heatproof bowl and mix together. Rest the bowl over a saucepan of gently simmering water, making sure the bottom of the bottom of the bowl does not touch the water. Beat the mixture for 8–10 minutes, using an electric whisk, until it turns pale, thickens and forms ribbon-like shapes when you lift the whisk out of the mixture. Spoon straight over the figs, then put under the grill for a few minutes until just browned. You don't want it too close to the top of the grill, or for too long, just until it is light golden brown.

5 Sprinkle the yogurt with the remaining cinnamon. Serve the figs hot with the spiced crisp slices to dip into the yogurt.

Pan-Fried Plums and **Almond Biscotti** with **Amaretto Cream**

Pan-fried plums are always tasty, with its touch of acidity and lovely, delicate texture, so I thought a biscuit would be good with it – and a biscotti seemed just the right choice. It's unusual, perhaps not often baked at home, and the almonds give it a good nutty crunch. For a change, try serving the dish with some silky Greek-style yogurt with a sprinkling of cinnamon.

SERVES 4
PREPARATION TIME 30 minutes
COOKING TIME 40 minutes

FOR THE ALMOND BISCOTTI
100g/3½oz unsalted butter, softened
75g/2½oz/scant ⅓ cup caster sugar
3 eggs
½ vanilla pod, halved lengthways and seeds scraped out
250g/9oz/2 cups plain flour, plus extra for dusting
grated zest of ½ lemon
a pinch of ground star anise
20g/¾oz/scant ¼ cup ground almonds
½ tsp baking powder
4 tbsp whole blanched almonds, toasted
a pinch of salt

FOR THE PLUMS
100g/3½oz/scant ½ cup caster sugar
10 plums at room temperature, halved, stoned, then each cut into 8 segments
1 tbsp amaretto

FOR THE AMARETTO CREAM
30g/1oz/¼ cup icing sugar
1 egg
125g/4½oz mascarpone, brought to room temperature
125ml/4fl oz/½ cup double cream
2 tbsp amaretto

1 Preheat the oven to 180°C/350°F/gas 4 and line a baking sheet with baking paper. To make the biscotti, whisk together the butter and sugar, using an electric whisk, until very pale and fluffy. Add 2 of the eggs, one at a time, beating in between each addition, then add all the vanilla seeds and all the remaining biscotti ingredients except the remaining egg and the salt. Continue to mix on a slow speed until the mixture just comes together to form a dough. Scoop the dough out onto a lightly floured work surface and form into a log about 20 x 7.5cm/8 x 3in. Using the palms of your hands, roll the log until it is 2.5cm/1in thick, then put on the prepared baking sheet – it should just fit.

2 Whisk the remaining egg with the salt and 1 tablespoon of water. Brush over the top of the loaf, then bake for 8 minutes. Turn the tray around front to back, turn the oven down to 150°C/300°F/gas 2 and cook for a further 20–25 minutes until pale golden.

3 To cook the plums, put a frying pan over a low heat, add the sugar and cook gently for a few minutes until it turns to a light golden caramel. Add the plums a few pieces at a time, mix them into the caramel and cook for 5 minutes until they are soft, then drizzle over the amaretto and stir gently. Leave to cool to room temperature.

4 To make the amaretto cream, whisk the icing sugar and egg in a large bowl until very light and pale. Mix the mascarpone and cream in a separate bowl, then whisk in the amaretto. Fold the mixtures together, then whisk until smooth, silky and very soft but just holding soft peaks.

5 Remove the biscotti from the oven, transfer to a chopping board and cut off both ends of the loaf, then cut the rest into 1cm/½in slices and put them flat on the baking tray. Return them to the oven and bake for a further 5–8 minutes until they are just dry and a light golden colour. Crumble the ends of the biscotti into 5mm/¼in pieces in a small bowl.

6 Sprinkle half the plums with the crumble and half the amaretto cream, then spoon some more plums on top and finish with the rest of the amaretto cream. Balance a biscotti on top and serve the rest separately.

Apple, Raspberry and **Thyme Puffs**

Depending on whether I had time to pop into the baker, I used to eat these *chaussons* **– literally 'slippers' – on the way to or from school, but we used to make them at home too. They are like apple turnovers – the same idea, but made in a slightly different way. The puff pastry gives them a beautifully warm, buttery crunch just before you reach the fruit, full of sweet acidity. There should be more fruit than pastry, so make sure the mix is not too runny or they may be tricky to close. And I can assure you that apple, raspberry and freshly picked thyme leaves are fabulous together!**

SERVES 6
PREPARATION TIME 30 minutes, plus cooling
COOKING TIME 15 minutes

80g/2¾oz/⅓ cup caster sugar
4 large Bramley apples or similar cooking apples, peeled, halved, cored and roughly chopped
a little flour, for dusting
750g/1lb 10oz ready rolled all-butter puff pastry, cut into 12 x fluted 7.5cm/3in discs
1 egg
a pinch of salt
125g/4½oz/1 cup fresh raspberries
leaves from 1 thyme sprig

1 Heat a large, non-stick frying pan over a medium heat, add the sugar, 2 tablespoons of water and all the apples, cover and cook gently for 8–10 minutes until the apples are cooked but not completely puréed. Remove the lid, then turn the heat up slightly so the liquid just starts to evaporate. Keep moving the apple around the pan with a spatula to help drive off the moisture and dry out the apple until you have a dry purée. Transfer to a bowl and leave to cool completely. (The purée must be dry and cold before you start to make your *chaussons*, otherwise the pastry will just melt and collapse.)

2 Preheat the oven to 180°C/350°F/gas 4 and line a baking sheet with baking paper. Dust a work surface with a very little flour, then lay a pastry disc on the dusted surface and roll with a rolling pin just once to the top and the bottom. You want the disc to be slightly oval. Repeat with the other discs. Lay all the discs out in front of you on the work surface with the oval shape top to bottom. Mix the egg and salt with 1 tablespoon of water in a small bowl to make an egg wash.

3 Put a spoonful of apple purée on the bottom one-third of the oval, 1.5cm/¾in from the sides. Put 4 raspberries on top of the purée and a little sprinkle of the thyme, then brush the egg wash around the bottom edge of the oval – nothing so far has come above the halfway mark. Fold the top half of the pastry over to cover the filling, then gently press the edges together to seal. Brush the top of the pastry with the egg wash, taking care not to get any on the back of the folded pastry – this will run down and make the pastry stick to the tray. Using a spatula, carefully lift each one onto the prepared baking sheet. Use the back of a fork to make a criss-cross pattern on top.

4 Bake for 12 minutes until the pastry is golden brown. If not, return them to the oven for a further 2–3 minutes. Remove from the oven and serve warm with a cup of coffee or Earl Grey tea, ideally in front of the fire!

Cherry and Almond Cream Tarts

Kirsch was originally made from Morello cherries, grown in the Black Forest in Germany, although it is now made from many types of cherry. Where I come from in eastern France, kirsch is a speciality of a town called Fougerolles. It is a clear fruit brandy made with a double-distillation of whole cherries – hence the slight taste of bitter almond. That hint of bitterness is just what we are looking for in this tart, for which we are using almonds, cherries, of course, and a lovely sabayon made with this beautiful *eaux de vie*. On top of the nutty crunchiness of the pastry, all these elements are from the same note – the almond! This dessert is best enjoyed warm as it releases all those wonderful flavours. But when I finished I thought something was missing – and it was a spoonful of creamy vanilla or almond ice cream!

SERVES 8
PREPARATION TIME 40 minutes, plus 50 minutes chilling
COOKING TIME 20 minutes

FOR THE SWEET PASTRY
grated zest of ½ blood orange
90g/3¼oz unsalted butter, softened, plus extra for greasing
a pinch of salt
70g/2½oz/heaped ½ cup icing sugar
25g/1oz/¼ cup ground almonds
1 egg
175g/6oz/heaped 1⅓ cups plain flour

FOR THE ALMOND CREAM
100g/3½oz unsalted butter, softened
75g/2½oz/heaped ½ cup icing sugar
75g/2½oz/¾ cup ground almonds
3 eggs
1 tbsp kirsch

FOR THE TOPPING
225g/8oz cherries, pitted and halved or quartered, depending on the size
50g/1¾oz/⅓ cup flaked almonds

Real Vanilla Ice Cream (see page 23), to serve

1 To make the pastry, beat the orange zest, butter, salt, sugar, ground almonds and egg in a bowl until light and fluffy. Sift in the flour and fold through and as soon as the dough is formed, stop! You don't want to work this pastry at all. Wrap in cling film and put in the fridge for 20 minutes.

2 Grease eight 9 x 4cm/3½ x 1½in loose-bottomed individual tart tins with a little butter if they are not non-stick. Roll the pastry between two sheets of baking paper until 3mm/⅛in thick, then cut out 8 discs, each about 18cm/7in in diameter. One at a time, roll each pastry disc over the rolling pin and lift over a tart tin. With one hand, lift the pastry edge and with the other, gently tuck the pastry into the bottom and sides of the tin so that it fits tightly. Don't overstretch it or it'll break, just press gently to push out any bubbles. Trim off any excess pastry by rolling the pin over the top edge of the tin. Prick the bases with a fork and chill for 30 minutes to prevent the pastry shrinking during baking.

3 Preheat the oven to 160°C/315°F/gas 2½. To make the almond cream, whisk together the butter, sugar and ground almonds in a large bowl, using an electric whisk, or in a food mixer, until light and fluffy. Add the eggs one at a time so that the mixture doesn't split. Add the kirsch, then mix for about 8–10 minutes until very light and smooth. Spoon the mixture into the pastry cases, taking care to leave a good 1cm/½in clear from the top of the pastry. Cover the mixture with the cherry pieces (if you feel like it, you can arrange them perfectly, but random is fine!) and sprinkle some flaked almonds on top. Sit the tins on a baking sheet.

4 Bake for 20 minutes until a skewer inserted through the deepest part comes out clean. If not, return it to the oven for a further 3–5 minutes and check again. Serve warm with a lovely vanilla ice cream.

Earl Grey Rice Pudding with Blackberry Marmalade

Most of my childhood memories are great – except for rice pudding. My mum used to make it so often that I did not want to eat it any more for a long time. But this recipe somehow brings it to life. In the restaurant, we use Carnaroli rice – I think it is the perfect grain for it – strong enough, nutty enough, too. So cook it very gently with all the other ingredients and it will taste delicious, but take note that I said gently. It must be cooked that way otherwise the grain will explode and the mixture burn if you have the heat too high. Then, of course, the lovely blackberry marmalade is perfect drizzled over the top to finish the dish.

SERVES 4
PREPARATION TIME 5 minutes
COOKING TIME 40 minutes

FOR THE BLACKBERRY MARMALADE
250g/9oz/1⅔ cups blackberries
60g/2½oz/heaped ¼ cup caster
    sugar

FOR THE RICE PUDDING
110g/3¾oz/½ cup Carnaroli risotto
    rice
500ml/17fl oz/2 cups full-fat milk
200ml/7fl oz/scant 1 cup whipping
    cream
4 Earl Grey teabags
2 tbsp caster sugar

1 Start by making the blackberry marmalade. Put the blackberries and sugar in a non-stick frying or sauté pan over a low heat and cook for 30–40 minutes, depending on how soft the berries are, stirring occasionally, until there is no juice left and the blackberries are fully cooked. You want the blackberries to release their juices as they cook so don't be tempted to increase the heat. Eventually, they will dehydrate and turn into a marmalade.

2 Meanwhile make the rice pudding. Put the rice, milk, cream and teabags in a saucepan, stir once to make sure that all the rice is dispersed through the liquid, then bring to the boil over a medium heat. Turn the heat down to low and simmer for 18 minutes – you shouldn't need to stir, but just check a couple of times.

3 Remove the rice from the heat. There should be a little liquid left in the saucepan. Remove the teabags and squeeze them dry over the saucepan so the liquid goes into the rice, but be careful not to pierce the teabags. Only then do you add the sugar and fold it delicately into the cooked rice, adding a little more to taste. Keep turning the rice very gently for about 5 minutes to cool it down.

4 Serve the rice topped with a spoonful of the fresh blackberry marmalade.

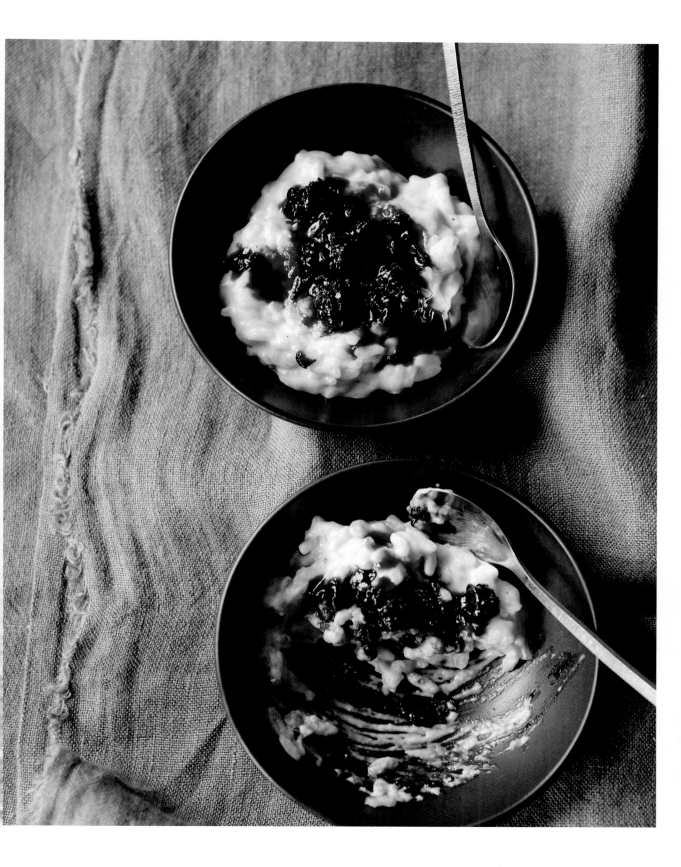

Rosemary-Infused Crêpes Suzette with Pink Grapefruit and Rosemary Syrup

Created in the late nineteenth century, both the name and origin of this dish are disputed, although everyone does agree that a girl called Suzette was involved! In my new twist on this classic, we will make a syrup with grapefruit juice infused with rosemary, and you will see how different and delicious it is.

SERVES 4
PREPARATION TIME 20 minutes,
  plus 45 minutes infusing
COOKING TIME 25 minutes

FOR THE ROSEMARY-INFUSED CRÊPES
300ml/10½fl oz/scant 1¼ cups milk
2 rosemary sprigs
125g/4½oz/1 cup plain flour
2 tbsp caster sugar
a pinch of salt
2 eggs
25g/1oz unsalted butter, melted,
  plus extra for frying (optional)

**FOR THE GRAPEFRUIT AND ROSEMARY
  SYRUP**
100g/3½oz/scant ½ cup caster
  sugar
100g/3½oz unsalted butter
grated zest of 1 and juice of 2 pink
  grapefruits (150ml/5fl oz/
  scant ⅔ cup juice)
leaves from 1 small rosemary sprig,
  finely chopped

1 Bring the milk to the boil in a saucepan over a medium heat. Add the rosemary sprigs, then remove the pan from the heat, cover with cling film and leave to infuse for 45 minutes until just cool. Discard the rosemary.

2 While the milk infuses, make the syrup. Put a frying pan over a low heat, add the sugar and cook gently for a few minutes until it turns to a light golden caramel. Add the butter and when it is foaming, add the grapefruit zest and juice, mix well and bring to a simmer. Cook for about 3 minutes until it forms a syrup, then remove from the heat, toss in the chopped rosemary and leave to infuse in a warm place.

3 Put the flour, sugar, salt, eggs and 125ml/4fl oz/½ cup of the rosemary-infused milk in a bowl. Add the melted butter and whisk, using an electric whisk, until smooth, then whisk in the remaining milk until smooth, quite runny and lump free. Adding the milk gradually means there is no need to rest the batter.

4 Heat a 15–18cm/6–7in non-stick pancake or frying pan over a medium heat. If you use a non-stick pan, you won't have to add butter, though it can make flipping easier if you do. If you are not using a non-stick pan, add a little butter first to keep the pancake from sticking.

5 Using a ladle, pour enough batter into the pan to cover the base thinly, swirling the pan around to spread the batter, then cook for 1–1½ minutes until the underside is golden. Now comes the fun part: try to flip it over, or turn it with a spatula. Cook for a further 1–2 minutes until the other side is golden. Remove the pancake from the pan and keep it warm, then repeat with the remaining batter, adding more butter if necessary.

6 Fold the warm pancakes in half one at a time, pick them up with tongs and dip them into the syrup, swirling them around to make sure the pancake is coated, then fold over into quarters and serve immediately. Repeat with the remaining pancakes and syrup. If you're really lucky the last one will be for you.

Gluten-free Chocolate and Ginger Fondant

Chocolate fondant is often served in restaurants in many different ways with many different flavours or spices added to it or infused into it. The main idea is always the same – when cooked and turned out, the warm chocolate must find its way out, running slowly like lava coming down the slopes of a volcano. That is a must, but there is also no compromising when it comes to the chocolate you are using – it must be good quality, not too sweet, not too bitter, and it must be dark. And in this recipe it is scented with ginger confit, which I love. If that is not to your taste, try it with star anise, cinnamon, cardamom or Szechuan pepper, but whatever the spice, you just want a hint of it, so do use it carefully.

SERVES 4
PREPARATION TIME 25 minutes,
 plus 30 minutes resting
COOKING TIME 8 minutes

100g/3½oz unsalted butter, plus
 extra for greasing
a little good-quality dark cocoa
 powder, for dusting
100g/3½oz dark chocolate,
 70% cocoa solids, broken into
 pieces
3 eggs
4 tbsp caster sugar
4 tbsp cornflour
1 ball of stem ginger, finely chopped
Chilli Crème Anglaise (see page 23),
 to serve

1 Butter four small ramekins or pudding moulds and dust with cocoa powder. Put the chocolate and butter in a heatproof bowl and rest it over a pan of gently simmering water, making sure that the bottom of the bowl does not touch the water. Heat, stirring occasionally, until the chocolate has melted. Alternatively, melt very gently in short bursts in the microwave, stirring regularly. Remove from the heat.

2 Whisk together the eggs and sugar, using an electric whisk, for at least 15 minutes until they are almost white in colour, very shiny and almost forming soft peaks. This will give a really light, crusty outside to the fondant, but the inside will be meltingly soft. Pour the melted chocolate and butter into the mix and whisk to combine. Sift the cornflour over the top and fold in, then finally fold in the stem ginger, taking care not to overmix at this point. Divide the mixture into the prepared ramekins, filling them only three-quarters full. Put on a baking tray in a cool place to rest for 30 minutes.

3 Preheat the oven to 220°C/425°F/gas 7. Bake the chocolate fondants for 5–6 minutes until the fondant has risen above the moulds and has formed a light crust on top and around the edges. Remove from the oven and turn out straight onto a serving plate, then serve immediately with chilli crème anglaise.

Chocolate, Chilli and **Lemongrass Tart**

Infused with lemongrass and chilli and made with the finest cocoa, this superb chocolate tart has a rich texture, a silky silhouette and lovely crisp pastry, which is a combination bound to make you happy. I almost decided not to give any of the details away, but it was just too good to keep to myself!

SERVES 4–6
PREPARATION TIME 15 minutes, plus 50 minutes chilling and 1½ hours setting
COOKING TIME 15 minutes

FOR THE CHOCOLATE PASTRY
90g/3¼oz/¾ cup plain flour
1 tbsp good-quality dark cocoa powder
60g/2¼oz unsalted butter, softened, plus extra for greasing (optional)
30g/1oz/¼ cup icing sugar
a pinch of salt
1 large egg yolk

FOR THE CHOCOLATE FILLING
250ml/9fl oz/1 cup whipping cream
1 large really fresh lemongrass stalk, cut in half lengthways and bruised
2 small red chillies, deseeded and roughly chopped
200g/7oz dark chocolate, 70% cocoa solids, roughly chopped
20g/¾oz unsalted butter, softened

Orange, Cardamom and Thyme Salad (see page 214) made with ordinary oranges, to serve

1 To make the sweet pastry, sift the flour and cocoa powder into a bowl. In a separate bowl, beat together the butter, sugar, salt and egg yolk until light and fluffy. Sift in the flour mixture, then fold it through gently until it just begins to form a dough, then stop! You don't want to work this pastry at all. Wrap in cling film and put in the fridge for 20 minutes.

2 Grease an 18cm/7in non-stick, loose-bottomed flan tin with a little butter, if necessary. Roll out the pastry between two sheets of baking paper until 3mm/⅛in thick, then roll the pastry over the rolling pin and lift it over the flan tin. With one hand, lift the pastry edge and with the other, gently tuck the pastry into the bottom and sides of the tin so that it fits tightly. Don't overstretch it or it will break, and press down gently to push out any bubbles. Trim off any excess pastry by rolling the pin over the top edge of the tin. Prick the base with a fork and chill for 25–30 minutes to prevent the pastry shrinking during baking.

3 Meanwhile to make the filling, put the cream in a saucepan over a medium heat and bring just to a simmer. Remove from the heat, add the lemongrass and chilli, cover with cling film and leave in a warm place to infuse for 30 minutes.

4 Towards the end of the chilling/infusing time, preheat the oven to 180°C/350°F/gas 4. Line the pastry case with baking paper and cover with baking beans. Bake for 6 minutes, then remove the paper and baking beans, turn the oven down to 160°C/315°F/gas 2½ and bake for a further 3–4 minutes until the pastry is cooked through and light brown.

5 Put the chocolate and butter in a heatproof bowl and rest it over a saucepan of gently simmering water, making sure the bottom of the bowl does not touch the water. Heat, stirring, until the chocolate has melted. Remove the cling film from the cream and strain to discard the lemongrass and chillies. Pour the cream slowly into the chocolate mix, whisking all the time until you have a soft, shiny, chocolate ribbon. Pour it into the pastry case and leave to one side in a cool place for 1½ hours until just set. Do not put it in the fridge as this will take the shine off the chocolate. Serve sliced with the orange salad.

Raspberry Tart with **Crème Pâtissière** and **Rosemary**

SERVES 4
PREPARATION TIME 25 minutes,
  plus 20 minutes infusing
COOKING TIME 30 minutes

300g/10½oz/heaped 2⅓ cups
  raspberries (36 raspberries)
icing sugar, to decorate
grated zest of ½ lime
1 tsp chopped rosemary leaves
2 tbsp crème fraîche

FOR THE SABLÉ PASTRY
90g/3¼ oz/¾ cup plain flour
1 tsp baking powder
70g/2½oz/heaped ½ cup icing sugar
60g/2¼oz unsalted butter, softened
a pinch of salt
2 egg yolks
grated zest of ½ lime

FOR THE CRÈME PÂTISSIÈRE
250ml/9fl oz/1 cup full-fat milk
½ vanilla pod, split lengthways
3 egg yolks
50g/1¾oz/scant ¼ cup caster
  sugar
25g/1oz/scant ¼ cup cornflour
1 tbsp unsalted butter
juice of ½ lime

I have included a few recipes with raspberries in this chapter, and with herbs too, but I can assure you they are totally different. Here, for example, the touch of grated lime, the crème fraîche and rosemary bring a unique balance to the dessert with its crunchy Breton *sablé* pastry.

1 Preheat the oven to 170°C/325°C/gas 3. To make the *sablé* pastry, sift together the flour and baking powder in a bowl. Whisk together the sugar, butter, salt and egg yolks, using an electric whisk, until light and fluffy. Fold in the flour mixture and lime zest to make a soft dough. Flatten between two sheets of baking paper to about 1cm/½in thick, then transfer to a baking sheet, lifting off the top sheet of baking paper. Bake for 12–18 minutes until light golden brown. Remove from the oven and cut immediately into an 18cm/7in square while it is still soft and pliable, but then leave it to cool before lifting off the tray.

2 To make the crème pâtissière, put the milk in a saucepan over a low heat. Use a sharp knife to scrape the vanilla seeds into the milk, whisk the milk, then add the vanilla pod as well. Heat the milk until it is almost simmering, then remove from the heat, cover with cling film and leave to infuse for about 20 minutes. Remove the vanilla pod from the milk, rinse and dry on kitchen paper as you can use it again.

3 Meanwhile, whisk the egg yolks and sugar until light, thick and creamy. Gradually add the cornflour, a spoonful at a time, whisking well after each addition to avoid any lumps forming. Slowly pour half the infused milk into the egg mixture, beating as you pour, then transfer the mixture back into the saucepan with the remaining milk. Put over a medium-low heat and stir continuously and quickly for about 10 minutes, or until the mixture begins to thicken. Remove from the heat, whisk in the butter and lime juice and continue to stir until the mixture has cooled down and is lovely and smooth, thick and slightly trembling.

4 Spread the crème pâtissière about 5mm/¼in thick over the pastry, leaving a small margin clear around the edge. Put the raspberries in lines over the top of the crème pâtissière to cover it completely. Dust with a shake of sifted icing sugar, and sprinkle with the lime zest and a little of the chopped rosemary. Mix the remaining rosemary with the crème fraîche and spoon into a piping bag, then pipe a small dot of crème fraîche on the top of every other raspberry all over the tart. Add a tiny piece of rosemary to each crème fraîche dot.

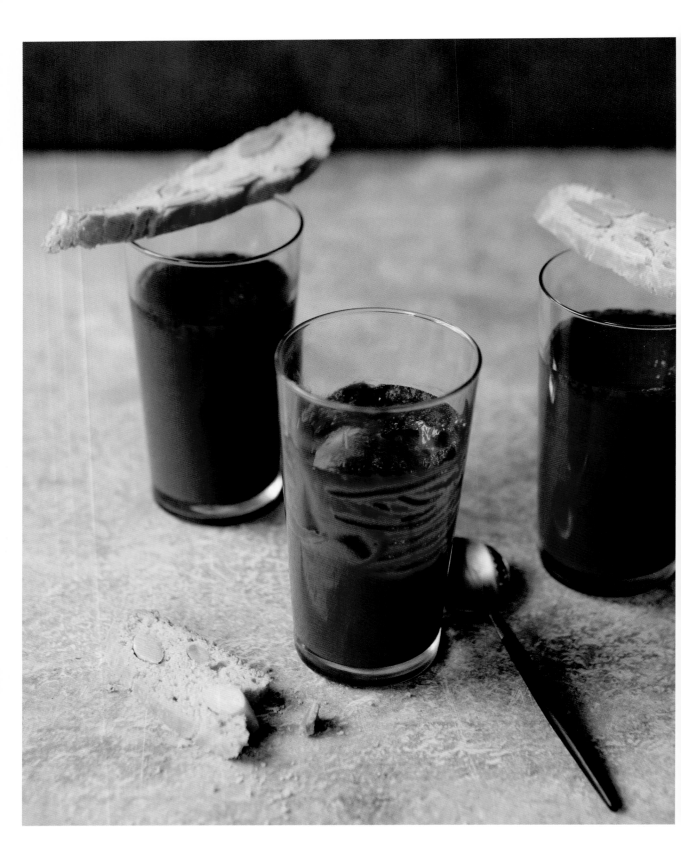

Thyme-Infused Chocolate Pots with **Biscotti**

I love the subtle hint of thyme in this rich chocolate dessert – it adds an elegant and unexpected touch that will surprise your guests. Serving the chocolate with your favourite biscuit provides a welcome contrast.

SERVES 8
PREPARATION TIME 15 minutes, plus 10 minutes infusing and 3 hours chilling
COOKING TIME 1 hour

250ml/9fl oz/1 cup full-fat milk
250ml/9fl oz/1 cup whipping cream
1 thyme sprig
70g/2½oz clear honey
4 egg yolks
250g/9oz dark chocolate, 70% cocoa solids, roughly chopped
Almond Biscotti (see page 200), Pain de Gênes (see page 146) or Pistachio Madeleines (see page 75), to serve

1 Preheat the oven to 150°C/300°F/gas 2 and line a deep baking dish with baking paper to direct the bubbles away from the pots, making the cooking process more gentle so the custard won't curdle. Have ready eight 150ml/5fl oz/scant ⅔ cup ovenproof glasses or pots. Bring the milk and cream to a simmer in a small saucepan over a medium heat. Remove from the heat, add the thyme, cover with cling film and leave to infuse for 10 minutes.

2 Whisk together the honey and eggs in a bowl for 1–2 minutes until the sugar has dissolved. Put the chopped chocolate in a separate heatproof bowl. Remove the thyme from the cream mixture, return the pan to a low heat and bring to a simmer. Pour the hot infused milk over the chocolate, whisking all the time until the chocolate has melted, then add the egg mixture to the chocolate and whisk together.

3 Divide the mixture into the glasses and put them in the prepared baking dish, then pour enough warm water into the dish to come halfway up the sides of the glasses to create a bain marie. Bake the glasses for 10–12 minutes, or until just trembling. If necessary, return to the oven and cook for a further 5–10 minutes. Remove from the oven and transfer the glasses to a wire rack to cool completely. Cover with cling film, then chill in the fridge for 2–3 hours. Serve the chocolate pots with biscotti, *pain de gênes* or warm madeleines.

Crushed Strawberries and Tarragon Crème Fraîche

This recipe is so French and holds great childhood memories for me. I must have picked strawberries in my garden hundreds of times, and every time with the same enthusiasm. I was always the first to answer when Mum said, 'Who wants to go to pick some strawberries?' And I was often the last to come back as I was too busy eating them! We'd enjoy a big bowl with a slice of toasted brioche spread with lovely fresh farm butter – so good! But here is a new way to serve them with crème fraîche and freshly chopped tarragon.

SERVES 4
PREPARATION TIME 20 minutes, plus 20 minutes macerating

800g/1lb 12oz/5⅓ cups strawberries, hulled and roughly chopped
115g/4oz/½ cup caster sugar
juice of 1 small lemon
250g/9oz/1 cup crème fraîche
1 tbsp chopped tarragon leaves
300g/10½oz fresh brioche loaf, thickly sliced

1 Mix the strawberries with the sugar and lemon juice in a bowl, cover and leave to macerate in the fridge for 15–20 minutes.

2 Preheat the grill. Remove the strawberries from the fridge, add the crème fraîche and mix together, lightly crushing the fruit with the back of a fork. Add the tarragon and stir once more.

3 Toast the bread and serve with the tarragon cream strawberries.

Orange, Cardamom and Thyme Salad

I love to make this refreshing salad with blood oranges when they are in season. Oranges combine so well with so many desserts, especially chocolate, as the soft, sweet acidity cuts through that rich texture. Try this with my Chocolate, Chilli and Lemongrass Tart (see page 208). The hint of thyme adds an elegant and unexpected touch that will surprise your guests.

SERVES 4
PREPARATION TIME 15 minutes, plus 30 minutes macerating and 30 minutes cooling

2 small blood oranges or ordinary oranges
2 cardamom pods, lightly crushed
2 tbsp caster sugar
½ tsp freshly picked thyme leaves

1 Finely pare the orange zest, then peel and segment the oranges over a bowl to catch the juices. Put the cardamom into the juice and leave for 30 minutes. Pat the orange segments dry on a clean tea towel.

2 Put the zest in a saucepan, cover with cold water and bring to the boil over a medium heat. Remove from the heat, drain, refresh under cold water, drain, then repeat the process. Return the zest to the pan, add the sugar and 3 tablespoons of water and stir to dissolve. Bring to the boil and cook for 5 minutes until the zest is transparent, then leave to cool.

3 Strain the flavoured juice into a small pan over a medium heat and cook for a few minutes until reduced by half and syrupy. Stir in the zest and syrup, then leave to cool. Toss with the orange segments in a bowl, then add the thyme leaves to serve.

Caramelized Pear and **Rosemary Cake**

I love the flavour of just-ripe autumn pears, roasted in a red wine syrup with flaked almonds, in a *tatin*, with chocolate and vanilla ice cream or simply on their own when they're juicy. But you will never enjoy them more than when they are caramelized, then folded into a cake mix with a hint of scented rosemary. Of course, you could replace that with spices but somehow that did not feel right. I wanted some freshness to spread through the cake while it was cooking so I added the rosemary only after the pears were caramelized and cooling to allow the scent to infuse the cake.

SERVES 6–8
PREPARATION TIME 25 minutes
COOKING TIME 30 minutes

FOR THE PEARS
100g/3½oz/scant ½ cup caster sugar
50g/1¾oz unsalted butter
2 pears at room temperature, peeled, halved, cored and roughly chopped
leaves from 1 rosemary sprig, finely chopped

FOR THE CAKE
100g/3½oz unsalted butter, plus extra for greasing
a little flour, for dusting
60g/2¼oz/½ cup icing sugar
3 eggs
110g/3¾oz/scant 1 cup plain flour
1 tsp baking powder

1 Preheat the oven to 160°C/315°F/gas 2½ and butter and flour a 1kg/2lb 4oz loaf tin or use a silicone mould. To cook the pears, put a large frying pan over a low heat, add the sugar and cook gently for a few minutes until it turns to a light golden caramel. Add the butter and when foaming, add the pears. (Once more, it is essential that the pears are at room temperature, otherwise the caramel will block – it will form lumps of hardened caramel and then it's a matter of starting again!) Cook the pears for about 10 minutes until they are soft and caramelized. Remove from the heat, add the rosemary and toss to combine, then lay the pears on a clean tea towel to cool and dry out slightly – you want the tea towel to absorb any juices.

2 To make the cake, the butter mixture needs to be really light in colour and in texture so whisk the icing sugar and butter, using an electric whisk, until almost white in colour and very, very light and fluffy. Only then, add the eggs, one at a time, beating well between each addition. Sift the flour and baking powder together into a bowl, then sift two-thirds into the mixture. Add the pears to the reserved flour and toss to coat thoroughly, then fold the dusted pears gently into the cake mix.

3 Spoon the mixture into the prepared tin and bake for 25 minutes until a skewer inserted into the centre comes out clean. If not, return the cake to the oven for a further 5 minutes and check again.

4 Transfer the cake to a wire rack and leave to cool for as long as you can wait, then cut a slice and serve with a cup of tea. And if I were you, I'd sneak a slice quickly before everyone else smells it and wants some too.

Chocolate Marble Cake with Citrus Fruit Glaze

When I was younger, I always wondered how the pattern on a marble cake was created! It looked so pretty when it was sliced, and the chocolate aroma used to pervade the room. As always, quality ingredients are crucial, so do make sure the cocoa powder is of great quality, as the success of the final result will depend on it. You may need a little practice to perfect the technique of folding and swirling the mixture, but the chocolate aroma will make it all worthwhile. Don't forget to drizzle over the citrus syrup while the cake is still warm so the liquid gold can gently find its way down this beautiful cake.

SERVES 6–8
PREPARATION TIME 25 minutes, plus 5 minutes cooling
COOKING TIME 30 minutes

FOR THE MARBLE CAKE
175g/6oz/1⅓ cups strong plain flour, plus extra for dusting
½ tsp baking powder
4 eggs
200g/7oz/heaped ¾ cup caster sugar
a pinch of salt
6 tbsp double cream
60g/2¼oz unsalted butter, melted, plus extra for greasing
2 tbsp good-quality dark cocoa powder

FOR THE CITRUS SYRUP
juice of 1 orange
juice of 1 pink grapefruit
juice of 1 lime
2 tbsp caster sugar

1 Preheat the oven to 160°C/315°F/gas 2½ and butter and flour a 1kg/2lb 4oz loaf tin or use a silicone cake mould.

2 Sift the flour and baking powder into a bowl. Put the eggs, sugar and salt in another large bowl and whisk, using an electric whisk, for a good 8–10 minutes until really light, thick and foaming. Fold in the cream, then add the sifted flour and baking powder and fold gently together. Finally fold in the melted butter. Remove one-third of the mixture into a small bowl. Sift the cocoa powder into the remaining mixture and mix gently until all the cocoa is combined.

3 Put half the cocoa mixture into the bottom of the prepared cake tin, add the reserved plain cake mix, then finish with the rest of the cocoa mixture. Put the handle end of a spatula into the mixture at the left-hand side of the tin at a 45 degree angle. Using a folding action, gently pull the handle round the edges of the mixture, then down through the centre, making three 'folds' while moving from left to right down the length of the cake tin. This will give you a great marbled effect.

4 Bake for 25–30 minutes until a skewer inserted into the centre comes out clean. If the cake is not quite ready, then slide it back into the oven and bake for a further 5 minutes, then check again.

5 Meanwhile, put all the syrup ingredients in a small saucepan over a low heat and heat gently until the sugar has dissolved, then turn the heat up to medium and cook until there is about 2 tablespoons of syrup, which is thick enough to coat the back of a spoon. Remove from the heat and leave to one side.

6 Remove the cake from the oven and put the tin on a wire rack to cool for 5 minutes. Turn the cake out of the tin and drizzle the citrus syrup over the top. Leave to cool a little before slicing and serving.

Kitchen Terminology

I hope you find this short glossary useful when you are using the recipes. Many of the terms may be familiar, others less so, and there are some that you may take for granted but not really know the precise details.

Bain marie: Literally a water bath, the food is cooked very gently, on the stove or in the oven, in a dish surrounded by hot water in a larger pan.

Bake blind: To cook a pastry case without the filling, lined with baking paper and covered with baking beans to keep it flat, for about 10 minutes, then without the paper and beans for a further few minutes to finish.

Beignet: A fritter.

Blanch: Briefly immersing food in a pan of boiling water to barely cook it, before lifting out the food and submerging it briefly in iced water to stop further cooking.

Bouillon: A broth or stock made with meat and vegetables.

Boulangère: A dish made of layers of sliced vegetables, usually potatoes, and meat.

Bouquet garni: A small bunch of mixed herbs – usually made up of a bay leaf, thyme, parsley and celery leaves – used to flavour a soup, stew or sauce.

Braise: To roast or brown a piece of meat, poultry or vegetable in fat, then add a small amount of liquid and simmer gently in a covered pot.

Bruise: To gently crush an ingredient, such as a lemongrass stalk, to release the flavour.

Caramel: A rich golden brown syrup made by heating sugar and water together.

Cartouche: A circle of baking paper with a small hole in the centre used to cover foods while they cook.

Ceviche: Raw fish marinated in citrus juice in order to 'cook' the fish without heat.

Clarify: Gently melt butter so that the solids separate from the liquid and can be discarded.

Confit: The French word for 'preserved', this most usually refers to pork, goose, duck, chicken or turkey, cooked in its own fat and stored, covered in fat, in a pot, but it can also refer to foods preserved in syrup.

Coulis: A thick sauce of purée made from fruit or vegetables.

Cure: To preserve food, usually by salting, smoking or drying.

Deglaze: Adding liquid to a pan in which meat or vegetables have been cooked and stirring to dissolve the caramelized brown bits on the bottom of the pan to incorporate them into the liquid, and then boiling to reduce the liquid.

Dehydrate: Dry out a food in order to preserve it and intensify the flavours.

Emulsify: Combine two ingredients, like oil and water, that don't usually mix by gradually whisking them together.

En cocotte: Eggs individually baked in cream or butter in small ramekin dishes.

En papillote: Food cooked in a parcel made of baking paper or kitchen foil.

Farci: The French word for 'stuffed', often referring to stuffed vegetables.

Flambé: To pour a measure of alcohol, often brandy, over hot food in a pan and briefly set it alight to burn off the alcohol.

Fold in: To combine two mixtures very gently, using a large metal spoon in a figure-of-eight movement, in order to knock out as little air as possible.

Fricassée: A dish of small pieces of meat, often chicken, served in a thick white sauce.

Gratin: A dish with a topping, often including cheese and breadcrumbs, browned under a hot grill.

Julienne: Cutting vegetables or fruit zest into thin sticks, 2 x 30mm/$\frac{1}{16}$ x 1$\frac{1}{4}$in, using a knife or a mandolin.

Macerate: To soak and soften before cooking or serving.

Marinate: To soak in a spiced liquid to impart flavour before cooking.

Mandolin: A manual slicer with different blades so that you can use it to slice very thinly, grate or cut into strips.

Pithivier: A round double-crust pie made with puff pastry.

Poach: To cook food gently in a very hot but not bubbling liquid, keeping it just below a simmer.

Ragoût: A stew made from meat, poultry, game, fish or vegetables cooked with herbs and spices.

Reduce: To boil in an uncovered pan to evaporate some of the liquid and, by doing so, to reduce the quantity of liquid and thereby strengthen the flavours of a finished stock or sauce.

Refresh: To quickly immerse cooked food in iced or very cold water to stop the cooking process and set the colour.

Rémoulade: A mayonnaise-based sauce seasoned with various ingredients, sometimes including chilli, capers or paprika.

Rillettes: Cooked, shredded meat preserved in fat.

Sabayon: A light, frothy sauce made by whisking egg yolks with liquid in a bowl set over a pan of simmering water.

Sauté: Cooking in a little fat in a shallow pan over a medium to high heat to brown or cook ingredients, keeping the food moving around the pan.

Sous-vide: To cook food in a vacuum pack, either by boiling or steaming.

Steam: To cook food in the heat from the steam from boiling water.

Tian: A dish made of alternate layers of various sliced vegetables and other ingredients, such as seafood, flavoured with herbs and seasoning.

Velouté: One of the basic sauces in classic French cuisine, a rich sauce made from chicken, fish or veal stock thickened with a roux, a blend of butter and flour.

Index

Author Acknowledgements

I would like to thank the following people:

My entire family, for their support, friendship, patience and love.

The team at HHB, especially Heather Holden-Brown, for believing in me, for your valuable support and for setting up this second book.

My publishers, Duncan, and to Grace – you are a star. And the rest of the gang at DBP – you are brilliant.

Janet Brinkworth, for working so hard to help me put the book together.

The management and my team at The Vineyard for allowing me the time I needed to work on the book and to do the photoshoot. In particular, Anthony Millon, my pastry chef, for giving me lots of tips on my dessert ideas to help make them happen. And to Greig Young for your help in The Vineyard kitchen when I was testing recipes.

My supplier, Peter, at Aubrey Allen, for helping me with the gorgeous produce – thank you very much.

Also Wendy Hobson and Nicola Graimes for editing the recipes and trying to keep me on time (or not!) and for your everlasting patience.

Manisha, Yuki and Aya – you are all very talented in what you do. It is always a privilege to work with you and I could not have done this book without you. You are the team!

And finally, Heston Blumenthal – your foreword is a joy to read, and thank you for being my friend. It is always appreciated.